Life Lessons from Two Worlds

My Jamaican-American Journey

Eric G.W. Jones

A heartfelt story of identity, resilience, and the hard-won wisdom of an immigrant life.

Life Lessons from Two Worlds

For permission requests, contact the author at
ericjones@ericgwjones.com.

Published by Eric G.W. Jones
www.ericgwjones.com

This is a memoir. Events and conversations are reconstructed to the best of the author's recollection. Some names, identifying details, sequences, and chronologies have been changed or omitted to protect the privacy of individuals.

ISBN: 979-8-9957389-0-9 (Hardcover)
ISBN: 979-8-9957389-1-6 (Paperback)
ISBN: 979-8-9957389-2-3 (eBook)

Cover design by BookCoverHub.com
Cover photos by Cesar Jimenez

A Note on Spelling
While this memoir is written in American English, you may occasionally encounter British spellings. These occur when a word is part of an official name, such as a Jamaican organization, school, or government title. When Jamaican Patois is used, translations are provided in block quotes or footnotes.

To my mother,
Kerean Harper Jones,
My inspiration and role model.

(This page intentionally left blank.)

The degree of a challenge is directly related to one's capacity to overcome it. The universe, in its infinite wisdom, molds challenges to match one's capability.

–Eric G.W. Jones

(This page intentionally left blank.)

Contents

Acknowledgements

Writing this memoir was a mission full of excitement, deep introspection, catharsis, and overwhelming gratitude. As I retraced my Jamaican-American journey, I felt profound appreciation for every person along my path. Thanks to each of you who helped shape my resilience and creativity. Without you, my story would not have been possible.

To my mother, Kerean Harper Jones, I felt your ever-present spirit despite your physical absence, a buoyant force as I put thoughts to script. Thank you for nurturing me to become the man I am today.

To my Aunt Vanny and older siblings, Mavis, Judy, and Dave, your recollections of facts to which I was not privy—by virtue of my age or long absence from Jamaica—were invaluable.

My brother Gerry, thank you for the old family photographs you provided from your archives. They are like beacons of light illuminating the narrative of my roots.

I am very thankful to my cousin Ingrid, whom I fortuitously met while researching my maternal family tree. Your assistance enabled me to map my ancestors in rich detail and obtain a photo of my grandfather in his prime. Thank you for connecting me with aunts, an uncle, and introducing me to cousins I never knew.

To my wife and soulmate, Jackie, thank you for your unwavering belief in my dream of becoming an author and your ardent support at every step along the way. Your encouragement, your patient listening while I read aloud, your careful reading of drafts, and your insightful feedback have been priceless.

And finally, to you, the reader, I'm deeply grateful that you have chosen to walk this journey with me—no man stands alone. We move in unison, consciously or subconsciously, down the road of this wondrous thing we call life.

(This page intentionally left blank.)

Preface

Your Guide for the Journey

My journey started humbly in Jamaica before emigrating to the United States as a young adult—a winding path full of challenges, unexpected turns, resilience, survival, and deep transformation, ultimately leading to joy. This is an immigrant's story of survival, hope, and growth, woven across two cultures.

The seeds of this memoir were planted in 1997, with rough notes scribbled down in stolen moments, but they lay dormant for decades. When I retired in early 2025, those dormant seeds finally germinated. What began as a personal act of reflection and healing soon evolved into something greater: a calling to give voice to a lived experience shaped by two worlds. I felt compelled to share my most personal struggles, losses, triumphs, and lessons learned—believing that others might recognize echoes of their own journeys within them.

My story is but one thread in the vast fabric of the immigrant experience, not only within the Jamaican diaspora but also, more broadly, for all who now call America home. We share so much: leaving home to pursue opportunity, balancing two cultures, and raising children who must navigate dual worlds. This book pays tribute to that journey and to those who live it.

In these pages, I celebrate the wisdom of my Jamaican roots through rich storytelling, cultural references, and the vibrant rhythm of our beloved language—Jamaican Patois, or Patwa, in the local spelling. Proverbs and idioms—passed down as nuggets of wisdom—are woven throughout, providing grounding and uplift amid uncertainty. They remind me of who I am and where I come from: a small nation mighty in spirit.

Life Lessons from Two Worlds is a personal memoir set amid cultural landscapes. Part I: Foundations explores my ancestry, early years in Jamaica, the people and places that shaped me, and the key trials that influenced my sense of self. Part II: Finding My Way traces my educational journey, young adulthood, my navigation of love and faith, and the pivotal crossing that defined my bicultural identity: my immigration to the United States.

Part III: Trials and Transformation explores the emotional toll of societal inequalities, the joys and challenges of fatherhood, the private struggles of marriage, and the strength needed to forge a new path when the old one stalls, all while pursuing one's personal vision. Finally, Part IV: Renewal and Arrival focuses on healing, restoration, the power of love, rediscovering happiness, reflections on career and legacy, and the journey ahead.

At the end of each of the twenty-three chapters, I've distilled a few hard-won life lessons—truths drawn from my own journey. I hope they reveal the shared nature of human struggles while quietly encouraging us all to rise above them. These are also compiled in a compendium, after the last chapter, for easy reflection.

Wherever research lent depth and texture to my story, I've tucked those sources into endnotes near the end of the book. This keeps the narrative flowing without interruption, while inviting anyone who wishes to explore further—whether driven by curiosity or scholarly interest—to follow the trail and begin their own journey of discovery.

I hope these pages will inform, entertain, and—above all—inspire. Everyone has a story worth telling, rich with wisdom forged from life's challenges and triumphs. If mine encourages you to reflect on your own path and look ahead to what awaits beyond your horizon, then this journey has already borne fruit.

Let the story begin. Faawud and trod wid mi!

PART I

FOUNDATIONS

(This page intentionally left blank.)

CHAPTER 1

Where My Story Begins

Ancestral roots, family, place, and identity

My journey began on December 25, 1967, when I was born to my mother, Kerean Harper Jones, and father, Eric Washington Jones. I entered the world at the Hargreaves Memorial Hospital in Mandeville, Manchester Parish, Jamaica. As a "Christmas baby," my mother received warm congratulations from the hospital staff.

My father wanted me to bear his name with the suffix "Jr.," but my mother felt an extra distinction was needed. She added "George" as a second middle name, making me Eric George Washington Jones. Sharing my full name often draws smiles or chuckles.

As a child, when I first realized that I bore the full name of the first U.S. president as my middle name, I questioned my mother's motive. She initially explained that she named me without regard to its implications. Still, she later advised that I consider it a tribute to George Washington Carver (1864–1943), the renowned African American scientist and inventor. In hindsight, my name, nominally tied to the United States from birth, inadvertently foreshadowed my life's bicultural journey.

As the youngest of six siblings from my parents' marriage, I'm known as my mother's "wash belly."[*] My five older siblings, listed by nickname from oldest to youngest, are Judy, Jill, Gerry, Tex, and Olive.

---

[*] "Wash belly" is a colloquial Jamaican term for the last-born child in a family. The term is a literal expression: the youngest child metaphorically "washes the mother's belly" (or womb) of childbirth, signifying the end of her childbearing. The wash belly is typically stereotyped as being indulged or "spoiled."

Why the nicknames? In Jamaica, nicknames are a cherished tradition. For some siblings, nicknames arose when a parent's preferred name didn't make it onto their birth certificate—it became their home moniker. My first nickname was simply "Junior," but, not surprisingly, more came later, which I'll share in later chapters. For most of our lives, my siblings and I called our parents Mama and Dada. Friends and neighbors knew them as Laura and Buck, my father's self-ascribed nickname.

At the time of my birth, I also had four half-sisters and two half-brothers who did not reside in our home. The eldest, Mavis, is my mother's first child, born several years before she met my father. The remaining five are my father's children: Dave, Carl, Pat, Terry, and Sandy, listed from oldest to youngest.

Genealogy

Jamaica's official motto, "Out of Many, One People," which appears on the country's coat of arms, reflects a recognition and celebration of the nation's multiethnic heritage. It symbolizes that Jamaican identity transcends racial background, prioritizing national unity above individual origins.

Christopher Columbus landed in Jamaica on May 4, 1494, during his second voyage, and claimed the island for Spain. He found it inhabited by the Taíno people (or Arawaks), who arrived from South America around 1,000 AD and called it "Xaymaca," meaning "land of wood and water." The name was later adopted by the Spanish as Jamaica. By the British conquest in 1655, the Taínos had been almost wiped out by Spanish disease, violence, and forced labor.[1]

The Taínos were replaced by enslaved Africans, first brought in by Spanish settlers starting in 1513. Over the centuries since the British conquest, various ethnic groups arrived: thousands of white British immigrants early on; an estimated 927,000 Africans, forcibly brought until the abolition of the British slave trade in 1807; about 4,000 French refugees from Saint-Domingue (Haiti) in the late eighteenth century; then, after emancipation (1838), indentured Germans (around 1,200), Indians (approximately 37,000 from 1845–1921), and Chinese (about 1,300 from 1854–1886); and later, Syrian and Lebanese merchants. Jamaica remained a British colony until it gained independence in 1962.[2]

Jamaicans—whether mono-ethnic or multi-ethnic, African, East Indian, white, Chinese, or any combination—almost always identify first as simply Jamaican, without prefixes, unlike the common practice in the United States. My family lived this tradition: we honored our roots, but Jamaican identity always came first.

I recognized my multi-ethnic heritage early through the physical traits of my family and relatives, but my active exploration began in 2018. Before 2012, genetic testing for determining one's ethnic origins was neither easily accessible nor affordable.

Before sharing the findings from my 2018 AncestryDNA results, I will summarize family tree details gathered from relatives and online sources. While archival records support some of this information, there are gaps and possible inaccuracies.[3]

My Paternal Family Tree

I traced my paternal lineage back four generations to 1799. The most notable gaps were my grandmother's ancestry and, on my grandfather's side, his mother's ancestry.

I was only able to trace one of my great-great-grandfathers: William Jones (1799–1894), born in Jamaica of European roots. He later moved to England, married Mary Brunton in 1836, and had five children with her. In 1847, after returning to Jamaica, he married my great-great-grandmother Rebecca Walch and fathered my great-grandfather, William Henry Jones (1847–1918). By 1851—or perhaps earlier—he was back in England, where he had five more children with Mary. He lived to the impressive age of ninety-five, passing away in Ulverston, Lancashire, in 1894. Archival records list his occupation as carpenter, a modest trade that quietly reassured me he was not an enslaver during his time in Jamaica.

My great-grandfather, William, fathered ten children. He had three children with Phoebe Cohen before marrying my great-grandmother, Ann Elizabeth Powell (1848–1935), in 1886. With her, he had six children. His tenth child was born in 1908 from a later marriage to Isabel Powell. His ten children, born between 1874 and 1909 and listed from oldest to youngest, were: Easton, George, David, William, Charles, James (my grandfather), Jane, an unnamed female, Ruth, and Ena.

An aunt recalled being told that he abandoned his wife, Ann, and their children, went to England, and never returned. However, most online family trees show his later marriage to Isabel in Jamaica and his death in Christiana, Manchester, in 1918. An archival birth certificate for one of his children lists his profession as a planter, while another christening record lists him as a butcher.

My grandfather, James Albert Jones, was born in Berkshire, Manchester, in 1884, and died in 1968 at the age of eighty-four. He married my grandmother, Olive Lea Dwyer, in 1918. I was told that she was multi-ethnic but believed to be of mostly African ancestry; however, no records of her ancestors were found. She died in 1933 at the age of thirty-nine, shortly after giving birth to her eighth child, who also died. From oldest to youngest, my grandparents' seven children, born between 1915 and 1930, were: Clarence, the twins Rudolph and Mildred, Pearl, James, Eric (my father, 1925–2013), and Louise. It is believed that James died as a baby or toddler.

After my grandmother passed away, my grandfather married Rosalie Adelaide Bell in 1934. They had six children between 1935 and 1944, two of whom are still alive. Listed from oldest to youngest, their names are Mabel, Sylvia, David, Betty, Vanny, and Bertie. My Uncle David and Aunt Betty died young, at twenty and ten years old respectively, due to diabetes.

My step-grandmother's willingness to marry a man twenty-three years her senior is noteworthy. She became a mother to his six children, aged four to sixteen, and later had six more of her own.

Curious, I asked an aunt, "Did Gang-Gang (as we affectionately called her) ever talk about why she married him?"

She said that Gang-Gang viewed my grandfather as a father figure, not just for the children but also for her—and that was part of his appeal.

My grandfather's occupation was primarily livestock farming. He started building his wealth by buying and selling goats, pigs, and, later, cows for slaughter. He invested much of his income in land, buying property in his home district of New Hall and in Knockpatrick, about six miles away. At his peak, he is estimated to have owned between fifty and seventy acres of land. Aside from roughly ten acres surrounding his family residence, he progressively subdivided, sold, or gifted the remainder of the land until his passing.

The land was primarily used to raise numerous dairy cattle, from which milk was harvested and sold daily to a condensery that processed it into canned sweetened condensed milk. He also had horses for herding cattle and pulling his enclosed four-seater horse-drawn carriage to town and church.

He was an exemplary father to his children, a strict disciplinarian, and a God-fearing, philanthropic man. He leased land on very affordable terms to less fortunate farmers in the district. He helped his neighbors and counseled those who sought his wisdom. Whenever his neighbors needed urgent transport to town, he facilitated it with his carriage.

He was a deacon at the Richmond Church of Christ, where he delivered inspiring sermons once a month. His legacy and influence on the district of New Hall were commemorated in 2020, when a street was named “Jones Close” in his honor by the local government.

I never knew my grandfather, who died when I was only ten months old, nor any of my grandaunts or granduncles. However, throughout my childhood, I was closely acquainted with and fond of my many aunts and uncles, except Rudolph and Louise, who both immigrated to the United States, and Bertie, who immigrated to England.

My Maternal Family Tree

Like my paternal family tree, my maternal lineage could be traced back four generations, to the mid-1800s. The most significant gap was the lack of information about my grandmother’s ancestry. On my grandfather’s side, the lineage was nearly complete across the four generations except for one unidentified great-great-grandmother.

I identified two great-great-grandfathers of Indian ancestry who both emigrated from India to Jamaica under indentured-labor contracts. One was Bassie Dalley, assumed to be his adopted English name. The adoption of a British surname, often at the urging of plantation managers, was commonly done to facilitate easier assimilation into local society and to signal that the associated Indian caste status had lost social value.

It is believed his original Indian name was Basalat or Basant Ali. This conclusion was reached based on archival information, name research, accounting for British colonial misspellings or anglicizations, and his Muslim roots, as evidenced by a *dua* (a personal invocation to God) he passed down orally.

Bassie Dalley's story of how he ended up in Jamaica has been passed down through four generations and is recounted here as I heard it from a cousin. He lived in Fatehpur, Uttar Pradesh. On his way home from work one day, he was caught in a monsoon. To save himself from drowning or being carried away by the floodwaters, he held on to a mango tree and recited a Muslim *dua* for protection.

His *dua* is still being recited today by some of my relatives, but a recorded recitation could not be fully translated into English using artificial intelligence (AI). However, the opening phrase, "Bismillah-ir-Rahman-ir-Rahim," was unmistakably Arabic, meaning "In the Name of Allah, the Most Gracious, the Most Merciful." The language that followed was identified as belonging to the Bhojpuri/Hindi language group but had been phonetically altered over generations, making it too difficult to translate accurately.

When the floodwaters receded, he made his way home. However, instead of being greeted by his wife with elation at his survival, she asked only for the money he had earned. Convinced of her total disregard for his well-being, he decided to leave her and his three sons for greener pastures. He signed an indentured-labor contract and boarded a ship in Calcutta destined for Jamaica.

Most Indians during that era became indentured laborers due to extreme poverty, loss of land, family breakdown, or deception by recruiters. Caste status did not protect Indians from the devastating economic and social collapse in those regions of India during the late nineteenth and early twentieth centuries.[4]

The grueling voyage lasted almost four months. Throughout the journey, he was stricken with fear and repeatedly whispered the same *dua* that had saved him when he clung to the mango tree. The *dua* not only rendered him safe passage but blessed him with the chance meeting of a young lady. She later became his second wife and my great-great-grandmother, adopting the British name Sarah Dalley. She died in 1905. Her maiden name, believed to be Surjudi, based on an archival record, is likely a colonial anglicization of an Indian Muslim name, such as Siraj-ud-Din, common among North Indian Muslims.

Upon arriving in Jamaica, they worked on a plantation in Gales Valley, Trelawny, got married, and started having children. He allegedly named his three sons exactly as the three he had left behind in India. On the plantation, he worked his way up to become the overseer, otherwise known as the "Busha." At the completion of his five-year contract, he decided to stay in Jamaica and never returned to India.

From oldest to youngest, the seven children from their union, born between 1867 and 1886, were: Isabella (my great-grandmother, 1867–1912), Rebecca, Manoah (Munoo), Samuel (Sabbie), Wadji, Jamie, and Jane.

My great-grandmother, Isabella Dalley, married my great-grandfather, Richard Hines, a shopkeeper, in 1888. He died in 1912. From oldest to youngest, the nine children from their union, born between 1889 and 1904, were: Jemima, David, an unnamed female, Maybell, Ethel, Eliza, Samuel (my grandfather), Adina, and Rebecca.

The only record found of Richard's family lineage was his father's (my other great-great-grandfather) name, handwritten on his marriage certificate. In my research, I found that it was customary for Indian indentured laborers to identify themselves on official colonial records by only one name. Though difficult to decipher confidently, I determined, with the assistance of AI, that it was "Guha."[5]

I found that Guha is a surname commonly associated with the Hindu Bengali Kayastha caste, originating in Bengal. He probably became an indentured laborer for similar economic reasons as my other great-great-grandfather, Bassie. Based on the aforementioned marriage certificate, it appears he kept his Indian name but gave his son the British surname Hines.[6]

My grandfather, Samuel Augustus Hines (also known as Cubby), was born in 1901 and passed away in 1977 at the age of seventy-six, when I was nine years old. His first child, born before his first marriage, was my mother, Kerean Harper Hines (1928–2010). She did not know her father's parents, who were both deceased at the time of her birth.

My grandfather, Samuel, married his first cousin, Lillian Andora Dalley, in 1927. She was a daughter of his uncle, Manoah Dalley. That marriage produced no children, and she died during childbirth sometime before 1934.

In 1934, my grandfather remarried another of his first cousins, Isabella Dalley, who shared his mother's name. She was a daughter of his uncle, Samuel Dalley. From their union, they had two boys and two girls between 1937 and 1943, named Aston, Callie, Deta, and Livingston. They later divorced, and she remarried, but my grandfather remained single for the rest of his life. My mother told me that he married his first cousins to keep wealth, primarily land, in the family.[7]

Years after my mother's stepmother, Isabella, became a widow, my mother visited her occasionally. As a child, she took me on some of those visits to Isabella's home in Falmouth, Trelawny, while on our way to my grandfather's home in Wakefield.

From her early teens, my mother had limited contact and interaction with her four half-siblings. The only time I met three of these aunts and uncles in person was at my grandfather's funeral in 1977, when they were all residing in the United States and Canada. Thanks to a cousin I discovered during my genealogical research, I have recently been in touch with two of these surviving aunts and an uncle.

My grandfather's primary occupation was tailoring, but he also owned and operated a village grocery shop. Both businesses faced the main road and were connected to his residence in the rear. However, by the time I got to know him, he had closed the businesses and retired. He was a deeply religious Christian and dutifully attended a nearby Seventh-day Adventist church. You could often hear him humming or singing the hymn "Beautiful Star, Shine On" many times throughout the day.

My grandmother was Florence Keane (1900–1940). Her parents were believed to be descendants of enslaved Africans. They reportedly died before my mother's birth, and I could find no records of their identities. My mother was her first child and the only one born from a short-lived relationship with my grandfather.

She later bore a son, Clarence, and a daughter, Joyce, to different fathers. Coincidentally, like my paternal grandmother, she died around the age of forty, shortly after giving birth to her fourth child, who also died soon after. She lived her life mostly as a single parent, and her occupation primarily involved domestic work.

Throughout my childhood, I was acquainted with my Aunt Joyce, who occasionally visited our family home. However, I did not meet my Uncle Clarence until my late-teen years.

While I feel enormous satisfaction at having traced so much of both my paternal and maternal family trees, I am equally saddened by the lack of information about the African side of my ancestry. I spent endless hours searching genealogical websites and speaking with older relatives, but came up mostly empty. This void may be attributed, in part, to the unfortunate coincidence that both grandmothers—who carried most, if not all, of my African lineage—died prematurely at around the age of thirty-nine or forty. Their premature deaths likely occurred before they could establish or pass down an oral history of their roots or be photographed for posterity.[8]

Results of My Genetic Testing

Given my preceding family trees, the results of my genetic testing were not surprising. Grouped by continent, they were as follows: Africa 46 percent, Asia 28 percent, Europe 24 percent, and Oceania (Polynesia) 2 percent. Six ethnic groups accounted for 75 percent of my DNA; in descending order, they were South Asia (India) 26 percent, Ivory Coast/Ghana 23 percent, Cameroon/Congo 11 percent, Western Europe 9 percent, European Ashkenazi Jew 6 percent, and Ireland/Scotland/Wales 4 percent. The remaining 25 percent of my DNA comprised eleven other countries or ethnic groups spread across Africa, Asia, and Europe.[*]

Discovering the Ashkenazi Jewish component of my lineage ignited my curiosity. Upon further research, I learned that Ashkenazi Jewish immigrants began arriving in Jamaica during the eighteenth century. By the 1880s, Jamaica's Jewish population had peaked at

---

[*] Genetic composition data based on analysis conducted by AncestryDNA (April 2018). Note: The author exercised his right to privacy by requesting and receiving confirmation that the raw genetic data and test results were deleted from the company's archives.

around 2,500, including both Ashkenazi and Sephardic Jews who had settled during the Spanish era and early British rule.[9]

I deduced that the Jewish element in my lineage most likely came from my paternal great-great-grandmother, Rebecca Walch, based on her Jewish surname. Her genetic contribution—halved over four successive generations—aligns almost perfectly with my 6 percent Ashkenazi Jewish DNA.

Historically, the parish of St. Elizabeth in Jamaica was home to large numbers of European immigrants, including Jews. A large percentage of birth and death records from my paternal family tree show that my ancestors and relatives resided primarily in Christiana, Berkshire, Watson Hill, Newport, and Chudleigh, all of which were part of the parish of St. Elizabeth until 1814, when a portion was taken to form Manchester.[10]

The journey of tracing my ancestral lineage—confirmed by DNA evidence—has been both humbling and illuminating. The vast, multi-continental, and multi-ethnic reach of my familial roots has deepened my appreciation for our shared humanity—transcending race, color, and creed.

LIFE LESSONS

1. A family tree should not be an unbending dictate for one's belief system, principles, and actions, but as the roots of a tree meander deep into the ground in search of nourishment, so too can we find strength from the spirit and knowledge rooted in our ancestors.

2. The human race is a quilt where patches of ethnicity are sewn together to make the whole, each contributing to its beauty, form, and function.

3. The stupidity of human division, by race, color, or caste, is inevitably exposed by the shared weight of inescapable catastrophes.

My paternal grandfather, James Jones, around the 1960s.

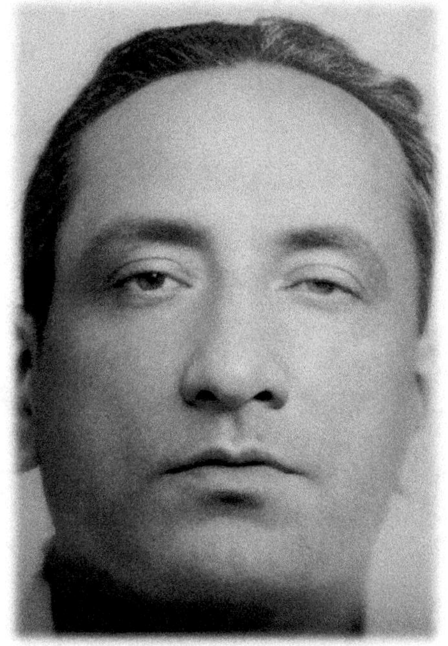

My maternal grandfather, Samuel Augustus Hines, around the 1930s.

My mother and father, Kerean and Eric Jones, Sr., around the late 1950s to early 1960s.

Me, around 1977.

My siblings and I, left to right in the rear: Judy, Pat, Jill, Olive, Gerry, and me, with Tex in front, around 1972.

My eldest sister, Mavis (1977), and brother, Dave (1988).

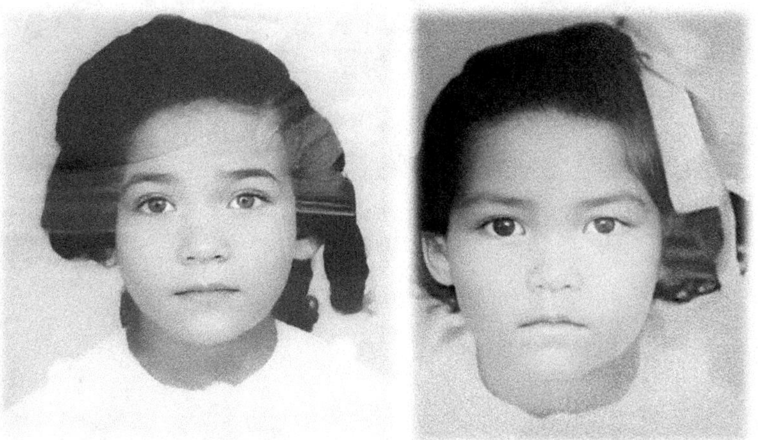

My sisters, Terry (left) and Sandy, 1968.

This street in New Hall was named in honor of my grandfather in 2020.

CHAPTER 2

Jamaica and the United States in 1967

The socio-political, economic, and cultural landscape of my childhood era

I came into the world in 1967 in a Jamaica still young and newly sovereign—only five years after independence, which followed centuries under British colonial rule that ended in 1962. While my country was in the early stages of forging a national identity, the United States was gripped by the Vietnam War, the Civil Rights Movement, a rising counterculture, and mounting economic pressures.

Jamaica's relationship with the United States during this period was marked by deep economic ties and a generally pro-American foreign policy shaped by Cold War realities. Dependence on U.S. trade and investment—especially in bauxite mining and tourism—reinforced this alignment, as did Jamaica's support for the U.S. trade embargo against Cuba, its closest neighbor.[11]

These geopolitical currents, though usually not resonant in a child's daily life, formed part of the broader environment of my youth and helped shape my developing sense of self and the world.

The Socio-Political Landscape in Jamaica

Since the introduction of universal adult suffrage (the right to vote in elections) in 1944, Jamaica has maintained a dominant two-party political system controlled by the People's National Party (PNP) and the Jamaica Labour Party (JLP). Both parties contested their first election in 1944. In February 1967, Donald Sangster led the JLP to victory but died shortly after, and Hugh Lawson Shearer became Prime Minister, serving until 1972.

This era was marked by sharpening political rivalries, socio-economic grievances, and increasing violence, exacerbated by issues like the bulldozing of squatter communities, particularly in urban areas, and deep-seated class and color hierarchies that persisted from the colonial era.[12]

In foreign relations, Jamaica was establishing its place on the international stage. It had joined the International Monetary Fund (IMF) and World Bank and was navigating Cold War politics. While maintaining ties with the United States and the United Kingdom, it also began to engage with the Non-Aligned Movement, a bloc of countries seeking independence from both the American and Soviet spheres and supporting anti-apartheid efforts.

The social and political currents of the time fueled the resurgence of the People's National Party (PNP) under Michael Manley, culminating in a decisive victory in the 1972 election. His democratic-socialist vision—promising social justice and economic empowerment—struck a deep chord with much of Jamaica's working class and poor. That victory marked the beginning of a transformative era in our country's politics and economy.[13]

As a child, I wasn't shielded from the political conversations swirling around our home and neighborhood—talk of upliftment and equality for the masses. In 1973, word spread that free education would finally be open to everyone, regardless of class. My mother celebrated the Minimum Wage Act of 1975, which promised a livable wage for workers. I watched her joy at the Equal Pay Act that same year—equal wages for equal work, a real step toward women's rights. Out driving with my father through the countryside, I spotted the "Project Land Lease" signs, part of the push to give poor farmers their own land. I saw low-cost housing being built for working-class families through the National Housing Trust. And I remember my mother helping with the government food distribution program for those in need.

I memorized the lyrics, sang, and danced to politically charged reggae songs like *Better Must Come* by Delroy Wilson, *No Joshua No* by Max Romeo, and *I Man Born Ya*, by Pluto Shervington—the rhythms filling our home with excitement. However, not everything was bright. Almost daily, as elections approached, the radio brought news of political violence—shootings, injuries, deaths, arson—mostly in the capital, Kingston. Thankfully, our quiet rural district of New Hall and its surrounding areas were spared from such turmoil.

The Socio-Political Landscape in the United States

In the United States, the escalating Vietnam War was consuming vast financial resources, mounting human casualties, and deeply dividing the U.S. public. Anti-war protests became larger and more frequent.

Although the U.S. Civil Rights Movement had achieved landmark legislative victories (the Civil Rights Act of 1964 and the Voting Rights Act of 1965), it faced new challenges. The focus shifted toward economic inequality, de facto segregation in the North, and the rise of the Black Power movement, which emphasized self-determination and racial pride.

The summer of 1967, often referred to as the "long, hot summer," witnessed over 150 race riots and urban uprisings across the country, underscoring the deep frustration and anger within Black communities over poverty, police brutality, and systemic discrimination. This placed President Lyndon B. Johnson's ambitious "Great Society" programs, aimed at eradicating poverty and racial injustice, under increasing challenges. The immense cost of the Vietnam War diverted crucial funding and attention, and political opposition to some programs grew.

The Democratic Party was fractured, particularly over Vietnam and civil rights. Republicans, though in the minority, gained ground by arguing for prioritizing "law and order" over addressing the root causes of social unrest through social justice initiatives.[14]

The Civil Rights Movement's impact, particularly its success in achieving legislative and judicial victories against discrimination, resonated with Jamaicans. This shared struggle for economic equality and self-determination likely contributed to the political environment in Jamaica leading up to the 1972 elections.

Jamaica's Economic Environment

Following independence in 1962, Jamaica's economy received some support from the Colonial Development and Welfare Act, first passed by the British Parliament in 1940. This act provided grants and loans for economic and social development projects in the British colonies. The economy grew in sectors like tourism, bauxite mining, and light manufacturing. The first post-independence Five-Year Plan (1963–1968) prioritized economic development, targeting a 5.6 percent annual growth rate in GDP. It included significant public investment in agriculture, expansion of educational and social services, export growth, and an industrial development policy.

The plan achieved around 5.2 percent economic growth, which funded increased spending on healthcare, housing, and education, boosting primary school enrollment.

Despite economic growth, job creation couldn't keep up with the expanding workforce, leading to high unemployment. Immigration to the United Kingdom, the United States, and Canada helped alleviate this and provided crucial remittances for the economy.[15]

In retrospect, I was a direct beneficiary of these public investments and, later, of Manley's economic empowerment policies. The emphasis on education, with free education starting in 1973, enhanced the public school system from infant/basic through high school, granting me greater educational access and establishing a solid foundation for future achievement.

The United States Economic Environment

While Jamaica developed post-colonially, the United States faced economic strains from Vietnam War spending and strong domestic demand, which led to inflation. To combat this, monetary policy tightened, and interest rates rose.

Unemployment was low overall but persistent among minorities and unskilled workers. Despite general prosperity, over thirty million Americans lived in poverty, highlighting disparities between affluent suburbs and struggling urban areas.

Despite these challenges, Jamaicans still viewed the United States as a land of opportunity. From the late 1960s to the early 1970s, driven by the 1965 U.S. Immigration and Nationality Act, which eased immigration restrictions, many immigrated to the United States in growing numbers. Upon arrival, Jamaicans found varied employment and living conditions, often in cities like New York and Miami, but also faced discrimination and socioeconomic disparities.[16]

The allure of the United States wasn't lost on my family. I grew up hearing stories of its grandeur and endless opportunities, fueling desires of emigration.

Jamaica's Cultural Environment

In the late 1960s, Jamaica sought to define its cultural identity, distinct from its colonial past. This was evident in the embrace of indigenous expressions through language (Jamaican Patois, or Patwa), music, and art, reflecting the young nation's aspirations and anxieties.

A pivotal shift in Jamaican music arrived in 1967. Ska, which had dominated the early 1960s, evolved into rocksteady—a slower-tempo, bass-heavy sound often carrying romantic or socially conscious lyrics. Artists like Alton Ellis (the "Godfather of Rocksteady"), The Paragons, The Techniques, and Hopeton Lewis helped define this new era.

Rocksteady's reign was short-lived. By 1968, it had evolved into reggae, which quickly took over Jamaica's music scene with its deeper basslines and even slower, more deliberate tempo. Before long, reggae became the unmistakable soundtrack of the island's political struggles and socioeconomic realities.

Several reggae artists of that era began to reach the world stage, including the United States. Among the most iconic were Bob Marley and the Wailers, Peter Tosh, Toots and the Maytals, Lee "Scratch" Perry, Jimmy Cliff, and Burning Spear. During my childhood, reggae stirred my imagination and filled me with excitement—it became an integral part of my life, a theme I'll return to in a later chapter.

The Rastafarian movement, which emerged in the 1930s, gained significant influence during my childhood, reshaping the island's music, language, and social consciousness. Its calls for Black pride, repatriation, and justice resonated with the masses, yet the establishment often maligned it.

As a child, I often heard, mostly from classmates, that Rastafarians (also known as Rastas) were dangerous "Blackheart Men"—the boogeymen of frightful folklore. Despite these warnings, I don't recall any Rastas living in my immediate neighborhood. It wasn't until my teens that I began interacting with Rastas; far from the maligning of those early myths, I found every encounter to be positive, enlightening, and deeply uplifting.

Jamaica was also finding its own literary voice in those years. Writers and poets explored themes of identity, colonialism, and the promise of new nationhood. Such poets included the celebrated Louise Bennett-Coverley (1919–2006), affectionately known as Miss Lou, whose bubbly recitations—always in Patois—evoked national pride amid laughter. Her poems were often memorized and animatedly recited by my sisters at home, and by classmates during school performances.

The visual arts scene was equally vibrant, blending local traditions with bold, emerging modern styles. In 1972, Jamaica's first major feature film, *The Harder They Come*, starring Jimmy Cliff, premiered in Kingston and soon reached audiences in the United States and numerous countries worldwide.

A burgeoning theatre movement was taking shape as well, with plays like Trevor Rhone's *Smile Orange* capturing Jamaican life and humor; it was later adapted into a film that debuted in New York City in 1976. I still remember going with my brother, Tex, to the movie theater in Mandeville to see that film, feeling enormous pride as I heard Jamaican Patois—resounding and unapologetic—pouring through the theater's sound system.[17]

The United States Cultural Environment

A significant counterculture movement marked the United States' cultural landscape during this era, incorporating experimentation, individuality, and alternative lifestyles. This was reflected in music, art, and fashion, with rock and roll becoming more diverse and Hollywood cinema embracing more challenging themes.

The Vietnam War and the Civil Rights Movement energized the counterculture's opposition to the established order. Political protests and demonstrations became a way for young people to express their views. The movement brought awareness to environmental issues, embraced recreational drug use, communal living, and political protests, and challenged traditional gender roles and sexuality, with a focus on peace and love. Afros, long hair, unconventional clothing, and a rejection of traditional dress became popular, reflecting an embrace of individuality.

Rock and roll evolved into various subgenres, while folk music gained popularity, giving rise to iconic musicians such as the Beatles (from Britain), Jimi Hendrix, and Bob Dylan, who influenced generations of singer-songwriters.[18]

Summary

Jamaica and the United States were at significantly different stages of economic and political development during this era. Yet, despite this disparity, they were both experiencing comparable socio-political and cultural evolution.

Both nations grappled with social injustice, inequality, and civil rights. This fueled the rise of Rastafari and the democratic-socialist movement in Jamaica, as well as the counterculture and Civil Rights Movement in the United States. All of this was set against the backdrop of a vibrant music scene, with the emergence of new musical genres, such as the heart-pounding beats of reggae in Jamaica, and new subgenres of rock, folk, and soul in the United States.

These intertwined global and local forces created the precise cultural, economic, and political environment into which I was born, establishing the intellectual and philosophical foundation for the rest of my journey.

LIFE LESSONS

1. No geographic and man-made political boundaries will ever separate us, as we are forever bonded by the shared pulse of human desire and experience.

(This page intentionally left blank.)

CHAPTER 3

Word, Sound and Power

The language that defines a people

The Origins of Jamaican Patois

The first language I learned to speak at home was Jamaican Patois—or Patwa, as we affectionately call it. Patwa is considered a creole language, having its own grammar, vocabulary, and pronunciation. It evolved during the seventeenth and eighteenth centuries through a combination of linguistic influences, including primarily English and West African languages, with traces of other European languages such as Spanish, French, and Portuguese.[19]

Patwa's lexicon and the dominant accents with which it is spoken are arguably the most powerful drivers of Jamaican culture and the bond that binds us together—yes, even above the food, music, and athletics for which Jamaicans are internationally known. It is the first identifiable trait of a Jamaican. Its foundations of defiance and cultural expression are deeply embedded in everyday life, the dominant reggae music genre, theater, and literature.

Rastafarians' Influence

The Rastafarian movement, previously referenced in Chapter 2 and which I'll cover more fully later, has played a profound role in expanding the expressive range of Jamaican Patwa. Since emerging in the 1930s, its expressions have been heard, adopted, and emulated by the broader Jamaican society.

As a conscious rejection of negative syllables and connotations associated with certain English words—and to highlight positivity—they purposefully developed a linguistic register known as Iyaric (or Dread Talk). For example: "understand" was replaced by "overstand"; "oppress" became "downpress," making an "oppressor" a "downpressor"; one should not "dedicate" but "livicate," and "icentrate" instead of "concentrate."[20]

Perhaps the most powerful phrase they coined was "InI (I and I)," which replaces "me," "you," or "we," emphasizing oneness with Jah and all humanity. They also created new words or changed the meaning of old ones: "Babylon" means a system of oppression; "irie" means positive vibes, one love, happiness, peace, and everything is alright; "Zion" refers to Africa as the promised land; and "livity" signifies righteous, natural living.

Rastafarian believers have also been among the main purveyors of reggae music since its creation in the late 1960s. Consequently, famous artists such as Bob Marley, Peter Tosh, and Burning Spear, among others, incorporated and popularized these expressions in their songs, spreading them throughout the global diaspora.

What began as Rastafarians' mystical act of linguistic reclamation and independence helped make Patwa even more dynamic and capable of carrying deep cultural and philosophical meaning.

The Language of My Childhood

Although the official language of the island is Jamaican Standard English, it was rarely spoken at home or by neighbors, relatives, and friends. The main sources of my childhood exposure to English were books, school, church, and radio. During my childhood, I do not remember ever encountering Patwa in written form. Instead, all written communication was in English, which facilitated my accelerated learning of the language.

While both of my parents spoke Patwa by default, my father could more easily switch to English when necessary, but for my mother, it was more difficult. My mother's Patwa fluency and accent were profound. A typical weekday morning instruction from my mother in Patwa while trying to get me ready for school went something like this:

> *Junior, git up an guh kleen up yuhself. Mek sure yuh wash yuh face, brush yuh teet, comb yuh ier an shine yuh shoes. Yuh kaki skool uniform deh pan di bed. Wen yuh dun put ahn yuh clothes cum fi yuh breakfast.*

Translation:

> *Junior, get up and go clean yourself. Make sure to wash your face, brush your teeth, comb your hair, and shine your shoes. Your khaki school uniform is laid out on the bed. When you're done putting on your clothes, come for your breakfast.*

As a child, I observed that in some social and other family circles, there was a distinct stigma attached to one's inability to master English. Some children were prohibited from speaking Patwa at home in front of their parents, as it was believed that speaking Patwa would delay their ability to speak and write "proper" English, making them appear "lower class." I considered myself blessed to have had no such restrictions, but quickly grew to understand that there was a time and place for both Patwa and English.

As I grew into late adolescence, I began to see Patwa gaining increasing respect and recognition. Today, it is more widely acknowledged as a distinct language and is internationally celebrated, thanks in part to the global popularity and influence of Jamaican reggae music. There has also been a growing number of studies and published works by linguists that affirm Patwa's distinct structure and grammar.[21]

Every word of Patwa, when spoken, seems to unfold like the lyrics of an unwritten song, expressing emotions through its cadence, accompanying facial expressions, and occasional hand gestures. Simply put, Patwa is the language of vibes.

In telling my story, I will employ Patwa, when appropriate, to share Jamaican proverbs, memories of impactful dialogues, and expressions of sadness, joy, fear, and astonishment—with translations. When referring to the language itself in an English context, I will generally write "Patois."

LIFE LESSONS

1. Honor your heritage without apology. What feels ordinary to you today may one day be treasured by humanity.

CHAPTER 4

The Village That Raised Me

Circumstances, people, and places of my childhood

Life in the Countryside

My childhood family home, until age ten, was in the district of New Hall, approximately five miles from the town of Mandeville. The district's landscape features rolling hills adorned with wild vegetation, fruit trees, and cultivated farmland—all nourished by abundant rainfall.

The district's average elevation, almost equal to Mandeville's, is around 1,900 feet above sea level. Throughout my childhood in the 1970s, the region experienced a mild tropical climate with average temperatures ranging from around 70°F (21°C) to 80°F (27°C). However, occasional dips in temperature from late December through February necessitated wearing sweaters or jackets. I recall temperatures dropping to a low of 50°F (10°C) during one cold spell. The high altitude and pleasant climate of Mandeville and its surrounding areas earned it the title "Cool, Cool Mandeville."

Our house was situated on the slope of a hill at the end of a long driveway that stretched about an eighth of a mile from the main road. Close to the house was a substantial metal gate. The house's elevation provided a panoramic view of the countryside and our distant neighbors, the closest being about an eight of a mile away.

We had a few grazing cows and goats, and coops of chickens, pigeons, and rabbits. In addition to dogs, a parrot, and the occasional cat, the family—or more aptly, my father—owned a rare pet—a crocodile. This exotic pet was kept in a secure, four-foot-tall-walled enclosure complete with a plunge pool and a sun-drenched concrete basking and feeding area.

Our house wasn't connected to the grid, not because of any environmental or philosophical preferences, but because my parents chose to build on off-grid land that my grandfather gifted to my father and three of his siblings in adjoining five-acre parcels.

The house was constructed of cinder blocks, galvanized roofing, and glass louvered windows, with a painted forest-green exterior. The flooring was finished with a mix of tile, hardwood, and red-stained and polished concrete. It was also replete with the requisite electrical infrastructure in anticipation of the district's electrification.*

It had three bedrooms, a living room, a dining room, a kitchen, a bathroom, and a single-car garage. There was also an adjoining workshop where my father practiced his trade as a self-employed dental technician and unlicensed dentist. The walls were sparsely decorated with a few framed pieces of art and photos, including one of U.S. President John F. Kennedy—prominently displayed in the dining room.

In the large backyard, there were three primary structures. The first included a room for the occasional helper hired to assist with household chores, an adjoining barn where the goats were herded at night, and a large chicken coop for laying hens and those raised for meat. The second structure was an outdoor kitchen, primarily used for traditional cooking fueled by charcoal or dry wood. The third was an outhouse with a pit latrine and an adjoining bathing enclosure, used in the early years before the indoor bathroom was completed.

Growing up off-grid meant having to find innovative solutions to cope with the lack of amenities such as electric lighting, refrigeration, washing machines, entertainment, a public water supply, a telephone, cooking fuel, and public transportation.

Lighting was provided by traditional kerosene lamps with those famous "home sweet home" lampshades. When more luminous lighting

---

* The electrical grid terminated about half a mile from the end of our driveway, and despite numerous petitions by my parents to the utility company, the grid was not extended throughout the district until shortly after we moved away when I was age ten.

was needed for homework, studying, or hosting parties, the grander Tilley lamps were lit.*

To avoid the need for extensive refrigeration, perishable food products were purchased in small batches as needed, prepared, and consumed mostly the same day. For example, for a meal of chicken, one or two live ones would be taken from our coop or bought from a neighbor, then slaughtered, cleaned, and cooked the same day. Similarly, milk was provided fresh each morning by milking our cows or occasionally received as a gift from a neighbor who had excess.

Limited refrigeration came from large blocks of ice bought from a vendor in Mandeville, stored in our big icebox with the perishables, from which we chipped pieces to cool drinks.

Clothes were washed by hand in large metal tubs and hung on wire lines to dry in the abundant sunshine. At first, this chore was done by a helper whenever one was present in the home, but later the kind and gentle Miss Mertie, who lived in the district, was hired to provide this service one day per week. She would arrive very early in the morning, allowing her ample time to wash, wait for the clothes to dry, and then iron.

At first, the ironing was performed with solid metal flat irons that were heated in a rotating fashion on a charcoal stove, but were later replaced by a charcoal-powered steam iron, which was more efficient. My sisters would also help with these chores on the weekends whenever the quantity of clothes exceeded what Miss Mertie could handle.

Our principal electronic entertainment source was a small compact system that included an AM radio and a vinyl record turntable, powered by eight "D"-size batteries. We were often amazed by the longevity of these batteries, despite listening to the radio for hours each day and playing 45 RPM vinyl records on the turntable weekly. We religiously gathered around the radio every evening about 6 p.m. to be entertained by the popular radio novel (or soap opera) *Dulcimina,* which was performed in Jamaican Patois.[22]

Not having electricity also meant we didn't have a television, but we were often invited by a family friend, affectionately known as Mass Ceril, to watch one at his home, located at the end of the electrical

---

* A Tilley lamp is fueled by kerosene. It works by using a hand pump to pressurize the kerosene and create a vapor, which then burns on a mantle, creating a very bright, warm light.

grid about half a mile away. Television broadcasts in Jamaica during my childhood consisted of a single black-and-white channel that signed on at 6 p.m. on weekdays and signed off around 1 a.m. each morning.

My mother ensured that we never abused Mass Ceril's kindness and accepted invitations only for the most popular broadcasts. This was where I first saw the television miniseries based on the book *Roots*, written by the renowned African American author Alex Haley. *Roots* was my first introduction to the history of slavery, its atrocities, and lasting scars, which I'll explore more deeply as my story later unfolds.[23]

Despite having no connection to a public water supply, we were never short of water—thanks to the region's abundant rainfall. Gutters channeled the runoff from our roof into a large in-ground concrete tank—I'd guess it was about fourteen feet long, fourteen feet wide, and twelve feet deep.

A mechanical hand pump on the tank's exterior filled large metal drums perched on a tall wooden tower; we called them "air tanks." Gravity moved the water from those drums down to the faucets and toilet in the bathroom. The chore of pumping to fill the drums was rotated among my siblings. I joined in when I grew tall and strong enough to operate the pump.

New Hall lacked a communication infrastructure. Using a telephone meant traveling to the nearest district with a working public booth or all the way to Mandeville. So, without any urgent need to speak to someone in a distant town or abroad, most communication happened face-to-face or by mail. Mail was not delivered to the district, so a three-mile walk was required to both send and receive mail at the nearest post office.

The telegraph was still in use, and occasionally a bicycle-riding telegram courier would pedal up to our gate with an urgent message for my parents.

The kitchen stove was fueled by a tall, fifty-pound gas cylinder, secured on a concrete pad in the garage, alongside a spare to ensure an uninterrupted supply. Replacement tanks were ordered when necessary and delivered by a supplier from Mandeville. On occasion, when replenishment was untimely, cooking was done in the outdoor kitchen using charcoal or wood for fuel.

Outside Kingston, there was no government-run bus system. The public railway linked only a few towns to the two main cities—Kingston and Montego Bay—but it never met the everyday need for local travel. Privately operated buses and taxis filled the gap, running routes where passenger demand—and profits—were highest.

Most taxis operated on a ride-share basis, picking up and dropping off passengers along their route, cramming as many people into the car as possible. It wasn't uncommon to see seven or more passengers squeezed into a standard sedan. New Hall, with its low population density, had only a couple of reliable taxi operators, which often meant long waits or a mile-long walk to the busier neighboring district of Richmond. While we were fortunate that my father had a car—one of the very few in the district—we still depended on taxis when he was away or otherwise occupied.

Grocery shopping for the week happened on Saturdays in Mandeville, but supplies sometimes ran low before the weekend. When that happened, I was usually the eager volunteer—happy to make the quick walk to the nearby over-the-counter shops. They sold baked and canned goods—bully beef (corned beef), mackerel, sardines—along with basic staples scooped from large vats. A big scale hung above each counter, where shopkeepers weighed out small orders of rice, flour, sugar, salt, pickled mackerel, pigs' tails, and salted beef.

One of the three shops I frequented, in the neighboring district of Richmond, had electric refrigeration and sold frozen chicken backs—a popular, low-cost staple in Jamaica.

These shops also served as centers for congregating and socializing. The shop in Richmond had an attached rum bar with a jukebox—usually blaring the latest reggae hits. Along the way, it was not uncommon to encounter a couple of drunk men who had overindulged at the bar, either staggering home or lying on the side of the road.

My Family Life

Despite the challenges of living in New Hall, I was generally a happy child, and my fondest memories remain indelible. Growing up as the youngest among my five siblings engendered mostly love and protection from them. However, because of my mother's extra nurturing, I was perceived as her favorite child, which occasionally elicited envy.

It is a common belief in Jamaica, as may be the case in other cultures, that the wash belly (last-born child) often receives preferential treatment from their parents. My earliest recollection of this was the surprise gift of a tricycle from my parents at around age three or four, and being told by my siblings that they never received one.

To my mother, I was her baby to protect, love, and nurture. I often got first dibs on a basket of mangoes, and she'd come home from work with little treats—candy or peppered shrimp—just for me.

My father, at least until I was age five or six, showered me with hugs and took me almost everywhere he went when I wasn't in school. I remember those long drives to neighboring parishes, where he provided dental care to rural, underserved communities and proudly introduced me to his friends and clients. On some of those trips, though, I also witnessed his philandering—something I'll describe more fully later.

I was around age five when I first began meeting my other five siblings, who were born from my father's relationships outside his marriage. My first meeting was with sisters Terry and Sandy; their mother had emigrated, leaving them in the care of their grandparents in Clarendon. My father occasionally brought them to our house for short visits, or he would stop by their home when I went with him on road trips. They eventually left before or during their early teens to join their mother in the United States.

Next was sister Pat, whom I met when she was around age eleven. Pat's mother had immigrated to England, leaving her in the care of family, who, in my father's opinion, were not providing her with optimal care. At my father's request, my kind-hearted mother consented to welcome Pat into our family, raising her with the same love as she showed to her biological children.

Then came my brother Dave. I met him when he was around age twelve. His mother, like Pat's, had also immigrated to England, leaving him in his grandmother's care.

One Saturday afternoon, my father drove up, called us outside, and—to our surprise—said, "Dis ah Dave; im ah unuh bredda."*

It didn't take long for us to excitedly welcome him into our family. He was warm, likable, and full of good humor. My mother, upon

* Translation: "This is Dave, he is your brother."

meeting him—perhaps that same day or soon after—was just as charmed. Before long, Dave was spending occasional weekends and summer holidays with us.

Carl was the fifth to be introduced to us, which my father did in a very similar, surprising way. At that time, Carl was around age seventeen and had lived most of his life with his mother in Canada. After this introduction, I saw Carl only a few times.

By the time I was around age eight or nine, three of my older siblings—Judy, Jill, and Gerry—had already left home to chart their own paths. My eldest sister Mavis's four daughters came to live with us temporarily. The oldest was a year and nine months my senior, while the others were younger by a few months to a couple of years. I enthusiastically welcomed my nieces as playmates. No longer would I have to walk to and from school alone or be at home lonely, awaiting my older family members' return.

Unforgettable Individuals

Outside the home, my life in the district was enriched by having a nearby step-grandmother, Gang-Gang, who lived in the Jones's ancestral family home with my Aunts Mabel and Sylvie, and cousins Chris and Tyrone. Also nearby were the homes of Uncle Clarence and Aunt Mildred. Our closest neighbor was the soft-spoken, kind, and joyful Miss Prim, whose family home was built on land bought from my father. All our neighbors were friendly and seemed to hold our family in high esteem.

I hold fond memories of religiously visiting Gang-Gang every Sunday and occasionally dropping by unannounced to see Uncle Clarence, Aunt Mildred, and neighbors to chat or raid their fruit trees. Gang-Gang was the embodiment of a loving, gentle, and joyful grandmother, effervescently welcoming us with treats at the ready—bread-and-butter or jam sandwiches, and the "stinking toe" fruit were staples.*

---

* The "stinking toe" (also known as jatobá or *Hymenaea courbaril*) is an edible fruit with a strong, foot-like odor emitted by its brown, toe-shaped pod. The pulp inside is sweet and floury and is consumed directly or with honey.

I recall the many adventures with my cousins, hunting birds with slingshots across acres of family-owned, forested land, though I was never successful at shooting one. These were some of the experiences that filled the day-to-day empty spaces inherent in my rural, off-grid upbringing.

There were also a few eccentric characters who roamed the neighborhood streets. Each of them had a profound impact on the neighborhood's children and me, mostly due to the gripping fear—justified or not—that they agitated within our psyche. I particularly recall three such individuals, each with their own peculiarities, whom I most feared whenever I had to walk the streets alone.

There was an old man, Ben, who was considered the oldest person in New Hall. Many adults recalled him appearing almost physically the same as when they were children. Some neighbors believed, based on the stories he told, that his parents had lived some of their lives as slaves prior to emancipation in 1838.

Disheveled and armed with a broken, rusty machete, Ben roamed the streets of multiple neighboring districts daily, walking for miles. He begged or was benevolently offered food and money by residents and shopkeepers. Because he was often teased and mocked by rowdy youngsters, he thought all children were worthy of his wrath. He almost invariably grunted threatening utterances while wielding his broken machete whenever children passed him in the street.

Next, there was Spaddy, an old white man reportedly of Irish or Scottish ancestry. Although not as frequently seen as Ben, nor armed with a machete, he similarly roamed the streets and was the brunt of provocation by the same set of troublemakers. They would shout at him, "Spaddy, spit spidee," then run away as he attempted to chase them. My most frightful encounter with him occurred when I was around age eight.

I was walking home after visiting one of my older sisters, who by then was married and living over a mile away in the neighboring district of Richmond. Normally, I would be alert, looking far ahead, with occasional glances behind, and ducking into any safe niche if I saw any of these three arch-nemeses approaching. But on this fateful day, as I got closer to home, I let my guard down—singing and not looking ahead.

At the most opportune moment, I heard an inner voice say, "Look up." As I raised my head, I was mortified by the sight of Spaddy no more than about twelve feet in front of me. He must have noticed my horrified demeanor and decided to add insult to injury by thrusting his hands forward, stomping his feet, and shouting some incoherent words, which signaled my imminent apprehension.

Fortunately, between him and me was an entrance to a shortcut that led across an open field to our property, so I made my escape. I don't believe I ever ran as fast as I did that day, jumping a fence at the border of our property and eventually reaching our backyard, totally out of breath and exhausted, with my heart beating harder than ever before.

The third, and most threatening, was a woman named Nellie, who had been clinically diagnosed as mentally ill. The story told by neighbors was that, as a baby, she was accidentally dropped and suffered brain damage from the fall. She was often seen walking the streets, invariably twirling a twig she had extracted from the nearest bush at the start of her journey. She was usually peaceful whenever forced to take her medication by relatives with whom she lived.

Unfortunately, there were many times when she left her house unmedicated, and the result was scandalous at minimum and life-threatening at worst. Her insanity often drove her to remove all her clothes. With her private parts exposed, she would bend over, point her rear end at passersby, curse incessantly using all the taboo words in the Jamaican Patois lexicon, and throw any rock she could find within reach.

Typically, whenever Nellie was unmedicated and ranting, one could hear her in the distance and make plans to avoid an encounter. However, while walking to school one morning, I saw Nellie calmly approaching in the distance, customarily twirling her twig, so I cautiously plowed ahead.

As she got nearer, unexpectedly, she started to curse, picked up a discarded "D"-size battery from the side of the road, and threw it at me with tremendous force. Fortunately, I was able to move out of the path of this oncoming missile, and an adult, not very far behind, loudly reprimanded her to "Stop it!" She ran off.

Rounding out the list of eccentric characters were Shorty, Shirley, and Blossom, who lived on the side of a distant hill, separated from our property by a shallow ravine and the main road. Their claim to fame stemmed not from the fear they stoked in children's hearts but from the unwelcome entertainment they provided with an almost unbroken cadence.

Shorty was a motorbike repair mechanic who loved Jamaican white rum and frequently overindulged, presumably in celebration after collecting payments from his clientele. Two or three nights per week, he would start singing at the top of his voice at the most inopportune times—with the sound echoing across the ravine. To his credit, he stuck to the melodies, typically from a church hymn, but uttered nonsensical words of his own making. I can still remember his infamous "stenous stenous stenous tay ya…" an ode to the hymn "What a Friend We Have in Jesus."

Shirley and Blossom hated each other with a passion. Their mutual loathing stemmed from sharing the same man, with whom they both had children. A few times per week, their animosity boiled over, punctuating the air with echoes of every Jamaican curse word and combination imaginable.

Sometimes the cursing paused midway—long enough for them to catch their breath and plan the next creative round of attack—then resumed like clockwork with even greater intensity. If one wanted advanced lessons in using Jamaican "bad wud" (bad words), this was the place to be.

Unfortunately for both of them, their fights were for naught. The man went on to marry another woman in the neighboring district.

The Celebratory Times

I excitedly anticipated the arrival of every Christmas season. Most of the pocket money I received throughout the year was saved for the Grand Market celebration on Christmas Eve in the town of Mandeville.* The anticipation in the district was marked by government-hired day laborers working each day arduously to remove overgrown shrubbery from the sides of the main road.

---

* Grand Market (or Gran' Market) is an annual tradition in Jamaica that takes place on Christmas Eve in all the major towns. It's a day filled with shopping, socializing, and entertainment, lasting into the early morning of Christmas Day.

At home, our lawn was cut, overgrown trees were pruned, the house was painted, windows were washed, and new curtains were installed. One or two goats were bought or selected from our small herd for slaughter on Christmas morning—for mouth-watering curried goat and mannish water (goat soup) dishes. Huge bottles of dried fruits that had been soaking in red wine and rum for months served as the key ingredient for baking Jamaican black (fruit) cakes. Copious quantities of sorrel drink, infused with ginger and pimento, sweetened with brown sugar, and steeped with rum for preservation and pleasure, were brewed and bottled. *

Starting around three weeks before my birthday each year, I went about the district excitedly inviting everyone I saw to my birthday party, which was routinely held on Christmas Day. My parents, particularly my mother, ensured there was an abundance of food, soda, and liquor for all. Of course, on such occasions, those bright Tilley lamps provided lighting.

Our family friend, Mass Hugh, who lived half a mile away, provided entertainment with his high-wattage soundsystem. It was powered by a dozen or more "D"-size batteries with backup supplies to keep the party swinging late into the night. He brought boxes of the latest and best ska, rocksteady, and reggae vinyl records, which he spun on his professional turntables.

At an opportune moment during my birthday celebrations, I had the honor of cutting my icing-covered birthday cake with one of my female playmates, whom I considered my girlfriend at the time. Except for my mother's separate gifts, each gift I received was for both my birthday and Christmas. Even the greeting cards often read, "Happy Birthday at Christmas," or similar. I grew to realize that being born at Christmas had a significant disadvantage: 50 percent fewer gifts than everyone else.

My second-most anticipated season was the two-week Easter break from school—Jamaica's version of spring break in the United States. A key difference is that in Jamaica, both Good Friday and the Monday after are public holidays. Apart from the obligatory trip to

---

* Sorrel drink's main ingredient is the sepals of the sorrel plant (*Hibiscus sabdariffa*), the part of the flower that supports the petals. It is a popular drink that's made and consumed mainly during the Christmas season.

church over the weekend, the real joys were eating "bun and cheese" and making and flying kites.

A Jamaican Easter bun is a sweet, dense bread packed with dried fruits and spices, sliced and served with cheddar cheese, creating a mouthwatering combination. Throughout the Easter weekend, I craved "bun and cheese" for breakfast, lunch, and dinner, and my mother did her best to ensure an ample supply for all—including any visitors who dropped by.

My enthusiastic involvement in kite-flying during Easter—like most Jamaican children at the time—began early. Back then, kites were all locally made. Early on, I either received one as a gift or bought one using my pocket money. Later, I learned how to construct my own, using the midribs of dry coconut-tree leaflets for framing and then binding the structure with thread to provide shape and tension. Multicolored crepe paper was then cut and pasted onto the panels framed by the midribs and binding threads. Old clothes or sheets were cut into long strips and tied end-to-end, which I attached to the lower end of the kite frame to provide stability during flight.

The final step was getting a kite line for control and steering, preferably a 250- to 500-yard spool of strong sewing thread. My mother, being a dressmaker, had an ample supply, which she willingly provided. Then off I went, running to an open field with the neighborhood boys and hoisting my kite into the trade winds.

As each summer approached, my eagerness grew for Jamaica's Independence Day celebrations, held on the first Monday in August.* The Festival Song Competition was the highlight that sparked my interest in childhood. Shortlisted songwriters and performers had their original compositions recorded and played in heavy rotation on radio stations starting in early July. The excitement built until a live final performance with the winner announced around Independence Day. I memorized the lyrics to all my favorites and sang them nonstop around the house and in the neighborhood.

---

* In 1997, the government fixed the date as August 6 to honor the actual anniversary of independence.

Duppy (ghost) and Anansi Stories

There was no shortage of folklore and personal accounts of encounters with duppies from the older relatives and neighbors. I shuddered at the fright of hearing these tales, but was somehow intrigued and always wanted to hear more. My siblings and I often asked Uncle Clarence to recount his many experiences crossing paths with duppies, which he would repeat verbatim each time.

I recall specifically one of his accounts involving a man who was fitted with a wooden leg, whose duppy, following his demise, walked the streets at night. My uncle said that on multiple occasions, when he was returning home late at night, he heard the distinct sound of the wooden leg against the road surface just a few feet behind him. Whenever he stopped, the sound would stop, only to resume when he continued walking.

My mother also recounted two or three of her personal experiences, the details of which I've forgotten. However, one year, while visiting our neighbor, Miss Prim, a few days before Christmas, she expressed fear about noises she had heard on the main road around 2 or 3 a.m.

She asked, "Miss Laura, yuh ier di wul heap a nize pon di road couple nites dis week, early inna di mawning, lakka ah wul heap ah cow an chain an whip ah crack?"

My mother's response was immediate: "Den yuh nuh kno sey ah Rolling Calf Duppy? Deh cum roun ah Chrissmusstime, a common sinting dat."[*,24]

My father told the story of being awakened one night by the loud noise of a grunting pig in front of the house. Upon opening the front door to investigate—armed with his handgun—he saw a humongous boar approaching the house with large, fiery eyes and its entire body covered in flames. He fired a round into the beast, but it kept coming; then, after a second and a third shot, it burst into a huge fireball and rapidly rolled up and over the hill from where it came.

---

[*] Translation: "Miss Laura, did you hear the great noise on the road a couple of nights this week, early in the morning, like a large herd of cows with chains and a whip cracking?" Mother's response: "Don't you know that is the Rolling Calf Duppy? They come around at Christmastime; that is a common thing."

Then there were the abundant Anansi stories and folklore, with origins tracing back to Ghana, Africa. This oral tradition was brought to Jamaica by enslaved people. The chameleon-like Anansi took many forms but was usually depicted as a spider with human characteristics. The humorous stories I heard depicted Anansi as the ultimate trickster—cunning, intelligent, and capable of outsmarting anyone. His chicanery at times could be selfish, harmful, or beneficial, revealing his ambivalent moral character.[25]

The heart of most Anansi stories was simple: learn to be resourceful and clever, but always mind the consequences of your actions. The versions I heard as a child were often long and winding—many now faded from memory—so I won't try to retell one here. I invite you, though, to seek them out online; plenty are still alive and waiting to be discovered.

Shadows in the Sunlit Room

Amid the happy, unforgettable moments, the sun often dimmed beneath life's gathering storm clouds. I had my share of childhood struggles—some I'll share here, others later. Unlike my first affectionate nickname, Junior, my earliest sting came from the second one: "Big Head," a label ungraciously pinned on me around age three or four by a relative.

In Jamaica, nicknaming goes far beyond affection or harmless fun. Almost every Jamaican ends up with one—or several—bestowed by family, friends, classmates, coworkers, or even rivals. The practice is richly layered: it can express creativity, humor, and deep respect, but also cruelty, honesty, historical weight, and social standing.

Unfortunately, nicknames—especially the undesirable ones—often stick for life. They might stem from physical features, mannerisms, or a single embarrassing moment. Once given, a nickname becomes almost inseparable from the person, and trying to fight it usually only makes it more entrenched. Over time, even Jamaica itself has earned affectionate nicknames that stir national pride: Jamdown, Jamrock, and Yaad.

As a young child, I lacked the emotional resilience to withstand perceived insults. I remember protesting and often bursting into tears whenever someone called me "Big Head," but it rarely made a difference. Luckily, the nickname faded over time—I like to think it was because my body eventually caught up with the size of my head.

Adding to my torment, whenever I cried from anger or hurt, my body would shake, and my breath would shorten—physical signs of distress I couldn't control. During those episodes, I was always confused by the repeated demand to "calm yu tempa!" (calm your temper)—as if I could simply switch it off. The symptoms only eased after the episode had run its course. My parents did their best to shield me from whatever triggered these outbursts, often with sharp reprimands to my siblings. But this only served to entrench their belief that I was the spoiled "wash belly."

Another of my childhood struggles was my high susceptibility to viruses. I often caught colds and flus, as well as more serious illnesses like mumps, measles, dengue fever, and whooping cough. Because of my fragile health, my parents forbade me from walking barefoot—a habit my siblings and neighborhood children took for granted. One day, I broke that rule and paid the price. I stepped on a piece of broken glass, which cut a one-and-a-half-inch gash on the bottom of my right foot. The scar is still visible today. As the Jamaican saying goes, "Haad iez pickney nyam rockstone."*

At around age eight, a constant pain developed in my right shoulder—usually dull but sometimes intense. At first, my mother turned to trusted Jamaican home remedies: topical herbs and Tiger Balm (a pain ointment). They provided no relief. My father then brought me to a doctor in Mandeville, who misdiagnosed my condition and gave an overly optimistic prognosis. The pain worsened, eventually spreading to my left shoulder. That's when my mother insisted on a second opinion from a more respected doctor.

A blood test confirmed I had rheumatic fever—an inflammatory disorder that can follow a streptococcal infection and, if untreated, can damage the joints, heart, skin, and brain. I was put on a monthly regimen of penicillin injections in the buttocks that lasted eighteen months, with blood tests every six months to monitor progress. I dreaded those shots so much that each trip with my mother to the doctor's office filled me

---

* Translation: "Stubborn children will eat rocks," meaning a child, or anyone, who refuses to follow instructions or advice will face the consequences.

with terror. The soreness from the shots lasted for days, forcing constant adjustments whenever I sat or lay down.

Thankfully, I survived the ordeal with no identified long-term impacts from the disease. As the old Jamaican saying goes, "Wah nuh kill yuh, fatten yuh."*

LIFE LESSONS

1. Hardships in childhood quietly and unconsciously plant the seeds of lifelong resilience and ingenuity.

2. The extended family is often a child's earliest classroom, teaching the quiet arts of connection, belonging, and interdependence.

3. Folklore and fables carry morals in one hand, heritage in the other, and in the space between, they quietly unlock a child's imagination and creativity.

---

* Translation: "What doesn't kill you will make you fatter," meaning when you endure and survive tough situations, you will emerge stronger.

A panoramic view of a part of New Hall, 2010

(This page intentionally left blank.)

CHAPTER 5

The Dawn of My Adolescence

Transition, adaptability, and maturation

A couple of months after I started high school in 1978, at age ten, I experienced my first major, life-altering event. I remember it vividly. It happened one evening, shortly after my two siblings, Tex and Olive, who were still living at home, and my four nieces, and I had returned from school. My father, driven by his demons, threatened the entire family with annihilation—to kill us all and burn the house down.

The threat felt imminent, so we all ran to the shelter of our kind, welcoming neighbor, Miss Prim. There, we waited anxiously for my mother to return from work. As soon as her taxi pulled up, we rushed out, practically dragging her toward Miss Prim's house.

In frantic voices, we pleaded, "Mama, wi haffi lef; wi doan waah fi liv deh. Wi fraid, pliiiz, wi a beg yuh, fine ah house fi rent suh wi cyaah move rite aweh."

In disbelief, she exclaimed, "Lawd a massi!"*

By the time we calmed down enough to explain to her what had transpired, we saw our father driving away. Knowing his routine, we felt convinced that he wouldn't return home that night, and most likely not for a few days. We thanked Miss Prim and headed back to our house, hearts still pounding.

We barely slept that night, all in a heightened state of anxiety. My mother did her best to console us, promising to skip work the next day and spend the time searching for a house to rent.

---

* Translation: "Mother, we have to leave; we don't want to live there. We are afraid, please, we are begging you, find a house for rent so we can move immediately." Mother's response: "Lord, have mercy!"

As was her custom, she delivered on her promise, finding a house in the district of Hillside, located about five miles away. We spent the following day packing, with a moving truck arriving the next morning. The speed with which our move occurred seemed almost inexplicable, and Miss Prim relayed to us my father's expressed astonishment upon his return to find the house empty.

My New Environment

The district of Hillside had a landscape similar to New Hall's—rolling hills with lush green vegetation—but was more populated and developed. The entire district, its environs, and our new home were connected to the electrical grid. This allowed us to enjoy the modern conveniences of electricity. Suddenly, we had electric lights, and soon a refrigerator, an electric iron, a television, and an audio system. We never got a home telephone, but a public phone stood just half a mile away. Ride-share taxis were more plentiful and reliable, offering a quick two-mile trip to Mandeville.

The house sat on about a quarter acre of land, much smaller than our multiple acres at New Hall. We had neighbors on both sides, each less than a hundred feet distant. The house was significantly smaller in square footage but had three bedrooms, a living room, a combined dining room and kitchen, a bathroom, and a veranda, with a pink-painted exterior. The backyard was devoid of any structures, though my mother later hired some local help to build a chicken coop.

Clothes continued to be hand-washed by a local washerwoman, when one could be found, and line-dried. As in New Hall, we were not connected to a public water supply, and rainwater was similarly caught, stored, pumped to "air tanks," and gravity-fed to the faucets and toilet. A thirty-pound cylinder of cooking gas fueled our stove.

Our driveway, previously around an eighth of a mile long, was now much shorter—roughly a hundred feet. In less than five minutes, we could walk to the primary road and district square, which hosted three over-the-counter grocery shops and rum bars, one with a jukebox. Gone was the relative tranquility we experienced in New Hall.

Like New Hall, Hillside had its share of eccentric characters, a couple of whom are worth mentioning. First and most annoying was our landlord. He frequently got drunk and showed up unannounced—

knocking on the front door at the most inopportune times while muttering incoherent platitudes. My mother, on multiple occasions, had to give him a good talking-to during his sober moments.

Next was Precious, who seemed to suffer from mental issues. She would, at any hour of the day, wander through the ungated driveway entrance. Unannounced, she would open and enter through the front door—if left unlocked—or walk into the backyard. Consequently, her unwelcomed intrusions terrified us all.

Upon reprimanding her for trespassing with phrases like "Gyal, ah wah yu ah duh yah? Cum outta yah an doan cum bac," she would snap back with "Eh bekaaz mi luv yuh mek mi a luk fi yuh, ah wha mek yuh ah run mi wheh soh?"* It usually took a few more shrieking admonishments and the collective effort of more than one of us to get her to leave.

This, my second home and neighborhood of Hillside, turned out to be my last in Manchester before leaving for university in Kingston, seven years later, at age seventeen.

The End of our Full House

Within a year after moving to Hillside, my four nieces left to join their parents in the United States. Soon after, my sister Olive finished high school and departed. That left only my mother, my brother, Tex (then attending West Indies College), and me at home.

Soon after, my mother began traveling abroad to procure goods for her small store in Mandeville—mostly to the Cayman Islands and the United States, though she once traveled to Haiti. For weeks, and sometimes months at a time, Tex and I were the only ones left in the house.

A few years later, my brother Dave, discharged from the Jamaica Defence Force after a lingering injury, came to live with us.

---

* Translation: "Girl, what are you doing here? Get out and don't come back," she snapped back with "It's because I love you why I'm looking for you, so why are you chasing me away?"

Adapting to New Life Challenges

In the absence of a permanent father figure, my mother endeavored to fill that role as best she could. However, her need to work extended hours to pay for the added expenses of rent and utilities, and her frequent extended overseas trips, compelled me to become increasingly self-sufficient.

My self-sufficiency meant navigating high school's academic and physical demands, household chores, the pull of adolescent temptations, friendships, growing attraction to girls, and the quiet dream of a future career—all at once, in the early dawn of my adolescence.

Academics

My academic focus—a subject I'll revisit in later chapters—was far from optimal during my high school years. My mother's primary concern was ensuring the material requirements for my education were met; as long as parent-teacher meetings yielded no behavioral complaints or failing grades, she was content. Academic excellence, by default, was left to my own devices. Lacking formal academic guidance at home, I relied on whatever natural ability I had. Apparently, I possessed enough of it to coast through most subjects, and for the rest, I did just enough to pass. This misguided efficiency left a wide and tempting opening to explore non-academic lures.

Having a television for the first time at age ten became a major distraction. I voraciously consumed as much TV as I could, from the time broadcast commenced at 6 p.m. each weekday until it signed off around 1 a.m. This meant rushed homework completion and little time for in-depth study.

At that time in Jamaica, except for the few wealthy enough to have the late-1970s and early-1980s-era ten- to sixteen-foot satellite dishes, viewing television was limited to the one available public channel—the state-owned Jamaica Broadcasting Corporation (JBC). Until 1981, JBC's broadcasts were only in black and white. Despite the introduction of color broadcasts in 1981, we had to make do with the single black-and-white TV we were lucky to have—rotating the antenna daily to improve reception.

The realization that my peers lived under far greater parental scrutiny than I did came abruptly one day during a conversation with classmates. As I began narrating the latest happenings on a popular TV drama, one classmate looked at me and said with apparent disdain.

"Suh, yuh watch TV pon skool days wen yuh pose fi ah study?" he asked. Then exclaimed, "Mi parents wud ah neva low dat!"*

Unfortunately, I processed this revelation with the flawed logic of youth. I looked at him as a deprived soul and marveled at how lucky I was to have unfettered access to the television.

Another major distraction came at around age eleven or twelve, when my mother brought me a bicycle from the Cayman Islands. My excitement was palpable. I rushed home from school every day, quickly changed clothes, and off I went riding—rarely returning home before dusk. Owning a bike also quickly facilitated friendships with other like-minded boys, further magnifying my level of inattentiveness to schoolwork.

I usually felt the cumulative impact of all that wasted time as exam season approached, forcing me to cram months of missed study into compressed pockets of time. As the saying goes, "Wah gaan wrang eena di mawning cyaah cum gud eena di eveling."† Yet, by some recurring miracle, I always managed to pull it off, albeit not always with the highest marks I believed I was capable of achieving. This cycle repeated itself throughout most, if not all, of my high school years.

Physical Education

It was in high school that I first encountered structured, compulsory physical education (PE), and I quickly realized that contact sports were not my forte. Football (soccer) in particular provided an early and gruesome lesson. During one of my first PE sessions, I watched as two students collided mid-tackle; one sustained a broken arm. The sight of that dangling arm served as a permanent warning to avoid midfield collisions at all costs.

---

* Translation: "So, you watch TV on school days when you are supposed to be studying? My parents would never allow that."

† Translation: "What went wrong in the morning cannot become good in the evening," meaning bad decisions cannot be easily undone.

To my chagrin, as a totally unskilled player forced to participate, I was relegated to defense. This role demanded exactly what I feared most: tackling oncoming players. With the image of that broken arm still fresh in my mind, I developed a signature maneuver. As an opponent approached, I would invariably step out of his path and then give chase in a spirited but entirely feigned attempt to stop him. My coach and classmates saw through my "strategy" almost immediately—an assessment that, to my immense gratitude, kept me on the bench for most of the season.

Second, there was cricket. This was a sport I truly loved—at least the version I played with family and friends in my neighborhood. We used dense sponge balls or lawn tennis balls and bats carefully hewn from the sturdy stalks of coconut tree leaves. However, during my first PE cricket class, my excitement quickly evaporated. To my disappointment, the coach brought out official cricket balls: rock-hard, leather-bound, and unforgiving. My "safe" version of the game had suddenly become a serious, and potentially painful, endeavor.

After being hit by this apparent cannonball for the first time, I quickly added cricket to the list of contact sports that required my strategic evasion. This wasn't too difficult a task; whenever I faced a fast bowler, I would politely step out of the way of the incoming delivery. This well-timed evasive action meant that I was bowled out almost instantly—a result that suited me perfectly. As the saying goes, "Cowad man kip soun' bone."[*]

Third was track and field (athletics)—a sport woven into the very fabric of Jamaican culture and a source of immense national pride, buoyed by the international success of our athletes. Our high schools are the legendary nurturing grounds for world-class sprinting talent, and I thought, finally, here was my opportunity. As a non-contact sport, it seemed the perfect stage to redeem myself from the strategic avoidance tactics I practiced in football and cricket. However, reality set in just as quickly as the starter's pistol. I lacked even a hint of sprinting ability, finishing dead last in the 100-, 200-, and 400-meter trials.[26]

Determined not to give up, I decided long-distance running was my best bet and resolved to start training on my own. For weeks, I got

---

[*] Translation: "A cowardly man keeps sound bones," meaning that being a coward will keep you safe from injury.

up every morning at 5 a.m. and ran a three-mile route, getting back home in time to shower, eat breakfast, and head off to school.

All seemed to be going well until one frightful morning. On the last leg of my route, about half a mile from home, the pre-dawn silence was broken by the rapid patter of feet gaining on me from behind. Convinced I was being chased, I summoned as much sprinting ability as I could muster. I bolted home as fast as I could and watched from the safety of my yard, heart pounding, to see who was in pursuit. When the figure failed to pass by my gate, I was certain I had been a deliberate target. That morning marked the unceremonious end of my dream of becoming a long-distance champion.

Finally, a teacher, with access to a private lawn tennis club in Mandeville, secured permission to use the facility for student instruction. As a non-contact sport, it suited me perfectly, and I signed up immediately. However, not owning a tennis racket meant I was at the mercy of classmates who were kind enough to share theirs. Since buying me a tennis racket was far from my mother's financial priorities, my eager participation eventually waned under the weight of my empty hands. Yet, that brief exposure ignited a lifelong passion. I eventually returned to the court as a young adult, and I continue to play to this day.

The Awakening of Desire

Long before I understood what desire really meant, my father planted its first seeds through remarks about girls and women that I later recognized were deeply inappropriate. The rest of that story will come later.

My attraction to girls began early. In infant/basic school, I befriended identical twins, Yvette and Bevette, and proudly announced to everyone that they were my girlfriends. I deliberately sat between them at our three-seater wooden desk and played only with them during breaks. After infant school, my circle shifted to two other girl playmates. Each Christmas, we took turns cutting my birthday cake—one year, one girl, the next the other. They gave me my first innocent kisses, and I continued to claim one of them as "my girlfriend" right up until I was twelve.

At age thirteen, through my neighborhood circle of friends, I met a more mature seventeen-year-old girl who attended a vocational secondary school. She needed math tutoring, which provided the perfect pretext to visit me frequently. Since we were typically the only ones home, two hormone-charged teenagers were left entirely to their own devices—a risky situation. Thankfully, no life-altering consequences transpired, and we escaped the forebodings of the Jamaican adage, "Wha sweet nanny goat a go run im belly."*

As my mother's overseas stays grew longer, so did my freedom and independence. By age fifteen, with new girlfriends in the picture, I spent far more time caught up in youthful romances—again at the expense of my academic focus. My nighttime escapades became more frequent. From my teenage banter with male classmates, I realized few, if any, were engaged in similar time-consuming relationships. Still, I did the minimum necessary to maintain decent grades: attending classes punctually, completing critical assignments, and imploring any girlfriend I had to allow me time alone in the weeks before and during exams.

I was never interested in marijuana or cigarettes. To this day, I have never smoked weed, despite the stereotype that clings to Jamaicans. I recall one night returning home from a club, my clothes reeking with the stench of secondhand cigarette smoke. As my mother opened the front door, her voice echoed with betrayal and desperation:

"Lawd Gad, Junior! Nuh tel mi sey yu staat smoke cigarette—tel mi sey ah nuh chuu!"†

I vehemently explained that the smell was only on my clothes. Finally, to prove it, I put my mouth over her nose and exhaled. Only then was she convinced.

I started dabbling in alcohol at age fourteen, and by fifteen I was occasionally getting drunk—thankfully only on weekends or holidays. At age eighteen, one day, I pushed my limits too far by drinking almost a quart of a newly released coconut rum in just a few hours. The aftermath was brutal—extreme nausea, violent vomiting, and a crushing

---

* Translation: "What is sweet to a nanny goat may cause it to have belly runs (diarrhea)," which means indulging in something pleasurable can have negative consequences.

† Translation: "Lord God Junior! Don't tell me that you started smoking cigarettes; tell me that it's not true."

hangover that lasted the entire next day. That was the last drink I took for twenty-one years. The reason I eventually broke my abstinence comes later in my journey.

Early Glimpses of a Career Path

Unlike most little boys I knew in childhood, I was never intrigued by or interested in pursuing a career as a police officer, firefighter, tradesman, or soldier. The first time I was asked, "A wey yuh waan bi wen yu grow up?" my response was "docta," meaning a medical doctor.

When I was asked why, my response was, "Bikaaz mi waah fi help people."* This ambition was later buoyed by my experience of being diagnosed and treated for rheumatic fever.

At around age fourteen, I developed two incisor cavities that needed filling, a task that my father, the unlicensed dentist, claimed he could perform but lacked the equipment to do so. Before this, all my dental care, which involved two molar extractions, was performed by my father. For the first time, I sought the services of a licensed dentist and discovered that there was only one in Mandeville.[27]

Realizing the dire need for more dentists in Mandeville and across the island, I decided to shift my career ambitions to dentistry. In retrospect, it may also have been subconsciously driven by a desire to achieve something my father had hoped for but never attained. This would remain a career ambition until about two years after emigrating to the United States, a change that I'll explain in a later chapter.

My Adolescent Sunset

I approached age eighteen with much trepidation, seemingly unprepared for the responsibilities of adulthood. On the morning of my eighteenth birthday, I felt no desire to celebrate; instead, I was overwhelmed by a contemplative daze. It was an impactful realization that, by all standards, I was now an adult, fully responsible for my decisions and well-being. I understood, though my mother never stated it, that she no longer had a legal or obligatory responsibility for my care. In that

---

* Translation: Query: "What do you want to be when you grow up?" Response: "Doctor." Query: "Why?" Response: "Because I want to help people."

moment, I had a choice: either continue to hide behind the protective shield of adolescence or man up to the responsibilities of adulthood. I ultimately and thankfully chose the latter.

LIFE LESSONS

1. A child or adolescent without adequate supervision will invariably explore adult vices; only a stroke of luck will save them from life-changing consequences.

CHAPTER 6

When a Father Falls Short

Misguidance, absence, and the power of unspoken lessons

His Appearance and Personality

My father, Eric Washington Jones, also known as Buck, was forty-two years old when I was born, and my earliest memory of him dates back to when I was about age three. He stood at five feet eleven inches, was of medium build, and had a light complexion. He kept a clean-shaven face with a well-groomed mustache and sported short, soft, wavy hair with early pattern balding. His arms, legs, and chest were densely furred, giving him the appearance of a remarkably hairy man.

He had a commanding presence in both mannerisms and appearance, drawing attention to himself in any setting. He was confident and bold, with a larger-than-life personality, and could exude an effusive charm or wrathful anger. As part of his charm offensive, he made up fantastical, humorous, and hyperbolic stories that he would repeat almost verbatim to all acquaintances with a truthful conviction. He invariably delivered his stories with a high degree of animation, varying the volume of his voice, making hand gestures, and slapping, poking, or touching the listener to ensure they remained engaged.

The Patois lexicon is cursed or blessed, depending on one's point of view, with many taboo words—four of which carry the greatest impact—that under the "Bad Word Law," one could be arrested for using them in public. [28]

Each curse word is usually accompanied by the suffix "claat" and mixed and matched to creatively supersede an adversary during a verbal altercation. They are also used simply for hyperbole, or to express surprise or sadness, by varying the tone of delivery. These word combinations—rassclaat, bumboclaat, bloodclaat, and pu…claat—were included by my father in almost all his conversations or storytelling. He seemingly never subscribed to the adage "Taak an tayse yuh tong."*

One of his incredulous stories—clearly created to entertain but maybe also to convince himself his misdeeds would carry no consequences—was that he once visited hell, only to be kicked out by Satan and told never to come back. From what I can recall, it went something like this:

> *Wen mi reach ah hell mi mek ah deal wid Satan fi opn ah ice factri an share di profit wid im, but mi trik im suh mi cudda mek mo monih dan im. Wen im fine out im tel mi fi get mi rassclaat outa hell an doan cum bak.*

Translation:

> *When I reached hell, I made a deal with Satan to open an ice factory and share the profits with him. However, I tricked him so that I would receive a bigger share of the profits. When he found out, he told me to get my "rassclaat" out of hell and never to come back.*

With strangers, he tended to be amiable, cordial, and respectful, regardless of one's social status. In the district, he was respected mostly because he was considered a dentist and feared mainly because he carried a licensed firearm, which he gratuitously displayed or otherwise made known.

He was an avid, perhaps even rabid, cricket fan—never missing radio broadcasts of minute-by-minute commentary during matches. He consumed it all—regional inter-island and international matches between the West Indies and other teams. He was vociferous in his excitement when Jamaica or the West Indies team was leading and castigating when they lost. He memorized a wealth of historical cricket

---

* Translation: "Talk and taste your tongue" advises caution and restraint in speech, meaning one should think before speaking or weigh one's words carefully to avoid trouble or offense.

statistics, knew every rule of the sport, and could discuss cricket for hours with fellow fans.

He was not a Christian despite his upbringing in the religion, as I don't recall him ever attending church, hearing him pray, or seeing him read the Bible. On the contrary, he believed in the power of Obeah, a transcendental and supernatural practice originating in West African traditions.

Obeah is not a formal, organized religion, and its practitioners, called Obeah men or women, operate independently. They are believed to be able to heal, protect, and guide, though some may use their powers for malicious ends. He occasionally visited these practitioners and sometimes returned with forebodings and various herbs, oils, and other paraphernalia, which we all found objectionable.[29]

Smoking and overindulging in alcohol were not among his vices, at least not as far back as I can remember. I never saw him intoxicated or drunk, or smoking marijuana, and he ceased smoking the occasional cigarette before I was age five. Instead, his vices were pursuing women and guns. These indulgences will be elucidated later in this chapter.

His Early Life and Career

My father's mother died in 1933 when he was only eight years old. I don't recall him speaking about her demise or its impact, but I imagine that this must have been a very traumatic experience. However, within a year, his father remarried, and so he had the care of a stepmother until he departed his childhood home in his late teens.

As far back as I can recall, he always showed my step-grandmother, Gang-Gang, much respect and empathy, which led me to believe she treated him well. However, an aunt recalled that when their father died—leaving cattle as part of Gang-Gang's and the unemancipated children's inheritance—my father orchestrated the sale of most of the cattle and kept the money for himself.

His father, a strict Christian, insisted on discipline and complete obedience, but by all accounts, he was very much a rebel. From an early age, he was taught the trade of his father's cattle-rearing business, and by his teens, he was herding cattle and supervising hired help. Some of his contemporaries related that he was a bully, beating up the neighborhood boys and paying hired help less than their full day's wages.

He attended an all-age school located in a neighboring district until age fifteen. Thereafter, he set his sights on learning the skilled trade of a dental technician. He later found work and mentorship with a qualified, licensed British dentist in Mandeville, where he worked for several years. Reportedly, that was the only licensed dentist practicing in the town at the time. At some point during my late childhood or early adolescence, he shared his reason for leaving, some of which I took with a healthy dose of skepticism.

He said that the dentist became very fond of him and supremely confident in his abilities, leaving him at times on his own to perform all dental procedures, including fillings, extractions, taking impressions for, and fabricating dentures. The dentist was even planning to send him to England for formal studies to become a licensed dentist.

The dentist's wife was also fond of him, but in lustful ways. During the dentist's absences, her advances led to shenanigans. The dentist grew suspicious and began issuing threats—brandishing his gun and vowing to kill anyone who "messed with" his wife. Even so, she continued her incessant overtures. Fearing for his life, my father fled his job, losing the opportunity to study abroad.

Following his departure, he decided he had learned enough to set out on his own as an unlicensed dentist, which was not uncommon or strictly prohibited in that era. Instead of a fixed office, he chose the path of a traveling dentist, performing extractions and fabricating dentures. He eventually bought a used Ford Anglia—an affordable small car—and plied his trade primarily in the rural areas of three adjoining parishes: Manchester, Trelawny, and Clarendon. He later upgraded his car to a new Morris Oxford.

He encountered no obstacles purchasing dental equipment and supplies—Novocain, surgical needles, and the rest—from pharmacies and suppliers. They all called him "Dentist Jones." In retrospect, I assume he built many of those relationships while he worked for the licensed dentist.

Meeting My Mother and Starting a Family

Shortly after moving from Falmouth to Mandeville—with a family she worked for—my mother developed some cavities and began treatment at the dental office where my father worked. The fillings required multiple visits, and during that time, my father used his charm and good looks to woo and seduce her. He soon started visiting her at the home where she worked, a habit that eventually resulted in her losing her job.

Their relationship blossomed, and they eventually got married in 1952. Following their marriage, they rented their first home in Georges Valley and later commenced construction of their own home in New Hall. They moved into their partially completed home around a year later.

To bring in extra income, he hired help to farm the land—planting yams, sweet potatoes, bananas, sugar cane, and chocho (chayote), along with an expansive orange grove. Over time, various fruit trees were added in abundance: tangerine, grapefruit, coconut, sweetsop, avocado, guava, star apple, custard apple, Otaheite (rose) apple, mandarin, and soursop (guanabana).

At the time of their marriage, my mother's first child, Mavis, born from a premarital relationship, was living with her grandparents in Trelawny. On one of the early visits with my mother, he took seven-year-old Mavis, promising to return her in a couple of weeks. However, his true intentions were for her to remain with them permanently, which she did until age seventeen, when she departed to start life on her own.

While attempting to have more children, my mother was diagnosed with a gynecological issue that required minor surgery. It was successful, and they were blessed with their first child three years after their marriage. This was followed by four more children, each only one or two years apart. I came unexpectedly five years after their fifth child, my sister Olive.

His Increasing Absences

As far back as I can remember, my father was periodically absent at night and on weekends. These absences couldn't be explained by his trade as a traveling dentist. The territories he worked in were all within a short driving distance from home—about an hour at most. By the time

I was four or five, these mysterious absences became increasingly predictable.

He was typically absent on Sundays, departing on Saturday evenings, allegedly to deliver dentures he had fabricated during the day to his clients. He would return early on Monday mornings, just before we left for school and my mother for work. We would all pile into his car—my mother defiantly sitting in the backseat. Her decision, which eventually became permanent, followed a sharp verbal altercation he had triggered one morning. He would then make the rounds, dropping us at our respective schools and my mother at her dressmaker shop in town.

Normally, he slept at home on Monday and Tuesday nights, after working in his home-based dental workshop and attending to local clients who came for his services. He would again transport us on Tuesday and Wednesday mornings, but by the time we returned home on Wednesday evenings, he was invariably gone. Following his midweek departure, we would not see him again until Saturday morning. Only then would he reappear to drive my older sisters and mother into town for grocery shopping—with me in tow as his silent sidekick.

While they shopped, he would take me with him to the barber for our grooming. The only haircut he ordered for me was a crew cut, which he loved, but I disliked. Then he would make his rounds to pharmacies to stock up on needed dental supplies. Since most pharmacies at the time sold children's books, I would usually pick a book or two from their collection, which he would buy willingly.

Since my mother worked at her business on Saturdays, my sisters would arrange a meeting time and place with my father to bring home the groceries. When he returned home, he would spend the rest of the day in his workshop before leaving for the evening—restarting his weekly cycle of part-time fatherhood.

His Financial Shortcomings

My mother recounted many stories of my father's lack of financial acuity. Shortly after their marriage, they opened a joint savings account, in which she ended up making most of the deposits from her earnings. This was money secured for major, jointly agreed-upon expenditures and investments: home building, livestock purchases, planting cash crops, or unforeseen emergencies.

On one occasion, when the need for emergency funds arose, she went to the bank and discovered that he had previously withdrawn all the money. He was unapologetic and provided no account as to its use. Since she knew that "Ebry day deb'l help teef; one day God wi help watchman," she immediately opened and from then on maintained a separate account.*

On other occasions, she would return home to find that he had sold some or all of the cows and goats, or produce from the farm—providing no account for how the money was used. Over the years, he also subdivided and sold lots of the land he was gifted—again with mostly unknown or unwise use of the proceeds. Then there were his concocted or real hard-luck stories, playing upon my mother's empathy to lend him money, which was never repaid.

By all measures, he earned a significant income. His dentures were famous for their perfect fit and durability, ensuring he rarely lacked work. Besides local clients, he had a steady flow of referred Jamaican expatriates who traveled from the United States, Canada, and the United Kingdom to get their dentures made—attracted by his reputation and the reportedly higher costs of dentures abroad.

Whenever he was home, he spent almost every waking moment in his workshop fabricating dentures. As a child, I often saw his wallet bulging with cash, yet painfully little of it went toward our well-being or the upkeep of the home.

Every Monday morning, he would dispense lunch money to my siblings and me—just enough to carry us through Wednesday. Since he was invariably absent on Thursdays and Fridays, the responsibility of bridging the shortfall fell solely to my mother. His Saturday grocery contributions followed a similar pattern of insufficiency, covering less than half of our weekly needs. He often supplemented this with farm produce that clients gifted him, but the true weight of our upbringing remained on my mother's shoulders. All other expenses—clothing, school uniforms, textbooks, shoes, and miscellaneous fees—were provided from my mother's labor.

---

* Translation: "Every day the devil helps the thief; one day God will help the watchman," which is a promise of eventual divine intervention and the need to persevere regardless of injustice.

While my older siblings remember a marginally greater level of support in their early years, my own upbringing was more austere. My father bought me clothes only once in my life—an event so rare that an image of the pair of jeans and a yellow-and-white floral polyester shirt remains permanently in my memory. I was roughly six years old when he made the purchase at a cousin's store in the town of Christiana. It was, quite clearly, an opportunistic reward for tagging along on his dental rounds that day—a fleeting act that was never repeated.

At age nine, I needed to register for extra lessons in preparation for the Common Entrance Examination (CEE)—required for entry to high school. A one-time registration fee of JA$5 was required. Following our childhood norm, I turned to my mother. As she reached into her purse, she paused, struck by the realization that my father, who was home, could surely spare such a measly sum. Closing her purse with an air of fatigue, she said:

"Son, yuh fada cyaah at leas gi yu di fighv dolla; guh aks im fah."

Thinking her logic sound, I ran to him with the request, only to be met with a blunt, demoralizing dismissal: "No, mi nuh hab non fi gi yu."*

There was no explanation or promise that he would provide it another day; his body language and tone of voice portrayed a total lack of interest or concern. Crying, I returned to my mother, who offered consolation as she reached into her purse again for the $5.

On the day of the exams, I was naively content. Knowing my father was home and aware of our need for transport, I believed—without even asking—that he would drive my older niece and me to the venue. As we were eagerly getting dressed, we heard the start of the car's engine in the garage; in a flash, he was gone.

Left in a frantic scramble to reach a venue some five miles away, we turned to my ever-resourceful mother. She urged us to run to my sister Jill's house, half a mile distant, in a desperate hope of catching my brother-in-law, Tony, before he left for work. We arrived just as he was starting his engine. He whisked us away on the back of his motorbike,

---

* Translation: Mother: "Son, your father can at least give you the five dollars; go ask him for it." Father: "No, I do not have any to give you."

weaving through the morning air to deliver us to the examination center in the nick of time.

Months later, the results were published. I was the only successful candidate from grade five and had been awarded a slot at my preferred high school. That morning, a classmate rushed to tell me that my father was waiting at the school gate. When I reached him, I was met with celebratory hugs and kisses. He was emphatic, radiating pride in my achievement, and he promised then and there to buy me the bicycle I had long desired. For me, that promise brought even more joy than the exam results themselves; I ran back to my friends, heart racing, to share the news of my impending reward.

As days of waiting stretched into weeks, my impatience finally gave way to courage. I asked him when I would receive the promised bicycle, only to be met with a dismissive voice that echoed the cruel adage, "A promise is a comfort to a fool." He responded with a rhetorical sting:

"A wich bicycle yaah taak bout?"

Once again, my only sanctuary was the warm embrace of my mother. In a gentle but resolute voice, she promised, "Yu doan need tuh aks im again. Mi nuh kno wen mi ah guh fine di money, buh mia guh mek sure yu git ah bicycle wan day."*

When we moved to Hillside in late 1978, Tex, Olive, and I were still minor children entitled to paternal financial support. Unsurprisingly, my father provided none, withdrawing even the paltry, inconsistent contributions he had made while we lived in New Hall. As a result, my mother was forced to bear the full weight of our survival, answering for 100 percent of our financial needs with her quiet, dedicated resolve.

Occasionally, my mother would say, "Yuh shud guh visit yu fada an aks im fi at leas gi yu a pocket money."† I went very infrequently and with much reluctance, each time receiving around $20. I recall one

* Translation: Father (rhetorical): "Which bicycle are you talking about?" Mother: "You don't need to ask him again. I don't know when I will find the money, but I will make sure you get a bicycle one day."

† Translation: "You should go visit your father and ask him for at least some pocket money."

morning, during my first year of high school, he appeared on campus out of the blue and handed me $40—the most I ever received.

At around age fifteen, I had my last truly painful encounter asking him for money. My sister Mavis was visiting from the United States and brought a friend to have her dentures fabricated. I went with them on the day the dentures were fitted, and he received the large balance owed.

In a light, hopeful voice, I asked, "Dada, gi mi ah money nuh?"

In response, he reached into his pocket, pulled out a knife, brandished the blade, pointed it at me, and said, "Cum fah nuh."*

The combination of his verbal challenge and knife threat froze me in fear and humiliation. I turned and walked away without getting a dime.

His Treacherous Path of Infidelity

In my teen and adult years, my mother confided in me the many hardships and deep emotional pain she endured because of my father's persistent philandering. Her first hint of betrayal came shortly after the birth of their second child.

After expressing her eagerness to resume pursuit of her dream of becoming a dressmaker, my father facilitated this by introducing her to an established dressmaker—a woman he said had been highly recommended by friends. After the classes started, my mother grew suspicious of their overly "friendly" rapport. When word reached her that he had been seen in public with the woman displaying questionable behavior, she confronted him, and an explosive argument followed. That was the beginning of his long, treacherous path of infidelity, which continued with numerous women throughout their marriage.

Of the many indiscretions I was told, some occurring before I was born, I remember a few with startling clarity. On one occasion, my mother visited her father in Trelawny, leaving my siblings in the care of a live-in helper. She came back a day earlier than expected and found him in the house with another woman. When she erupted in justified

---

* Translation: Me: "Dada, why not give me some money?" Father: "Come for it then." The combination of the verbal challenge and the brandishing of the knife created a deeply frightening and humiliating scenario.

anger, my father didn't apologize; instead, he took an aggressive stance, shielding the woman while threatening my mother. Knowing he was armed and fearing for her life, she ran out of the house and hid in the outhouse, where she spent most of the night in a cold, terrified vigil.

On another occasion, he informed her one Saturday evening that he was headed to Mandeville to watch a movie—pointedly excluding her from the outing. She became suspicious and decided to find her own way to the movie theater and observe him. Her suspicions were confirmed—she found him sitting arm in arm with another woman. When she confronted them, the woman was visibly shaken and said my father had told her his wife was deceased. Upon discovering the depth of his deceit, the woman was apologetic—and reportedly so unsettled by his continued pursuit—that she eventually fled to the United States to escape him.

Beyond his external affairs, there were the recurring incidents of my father enticing or pressuring our household domestic helpers into clandestine trysts. He often personally recruited these women under the guise of relieving my mother of her heavy domestic burden, particularly while she was away at work. Time and again, however, she would uncover the improprieties. These discoveries inevitably led to the helpers being summarily fired—leaving my mother not only betrayed but also once again alone in managing the household chores.

My own observations of his infidelity began around age five, when he would take me along on his rounds as he provided dental services. It was at this same age that my mother, having reached her breaking point, devised a strategy to drive him from their shared bedroom. Leveraging my status as her "baby," she insisted that I sleep between them rather than with my siblings. This arrangement sparked a series of heated arguments until, frustrated and defeated, my father eventually retreated to my brothers' room. This move marked the definitive end of their physical intimacy, though they continued to share the same house as strangers until we departed for Hillside when I was ten. My parents were formally divorced several years later.

My mother once recalled throwing him a birthday party. In a room packed with his family and friends, he stood and made the following wish: "I wish to have children like snakes in the grass with nothing to cover their ass." To my knowledge, he bore eleven children from his various extramarital liaisons, bringing the total of his biological offspring to seventeen—though rumors persist that the actual number is far greater. While his birthday wish was dismissed as a tasteless joke at the time, in retrospect, it appears to be a dark prophecy of the neglect he would go on to sow. You be the judge.

What He Taught Me

Up to around age five or six, I spent a lot of time with my father in his home workshop, and he often took me on his long road trips to provide dental services to rural communities. Like a sponge, I soaked up everything he taught me. But most of his lessons—in words and in conduct—were deeply inappropriate for a child. Thankfully, my mother always stepped in at just the right moment to redirect me.

The big four Jamaican "bad words" were part of almost every conversation or story my father told, and it didn't take long for me to start imitating him. Sadly, he found my foul language amusing and even encouraged it.

When I complained about a sibling's mistreatment, he'd say, "Guh tel dem bout dem rassclaat."[*]

Most people laughed in disbelief at hearing such words from a young child's mouth, so I thought—wrongly—that they were charmed.

At around age four, when my mother believed I was capable of reason, she sat me down and explained that it was wrong for me to follow my father's example and speak these "bad words."

She said, "Wen yuh chat bad wud an people lahf, dem a tink ah di same time sey yuh a wah bad likkle pickney who no hav manners; dat nuh good, Junior."[†]

The message was clear, and my refusal to curse with or without my father's encouragement became obvious thereafter.

When I tagged along on his road trips, he invariably stopped at the homes of two women, where his intent was clearly not to provide dental services. Instead, he openly pursued them in my presence. On one occasion, he even had me stay overnight with him at one of these

---

[*] Translation: "Go tell them about their 'rassclaat' [curse word]."

[†] Translation: "When you speak bad words, and people laugh, they are thinking at the same time that you are a bad little child who has no manners; that is not good, Junior."

residences. As it turned out, these were not mere stopovers, but properties he rented and maintained—a profound financial betrayal that came at the direct expense of his own marital household.

When I returned home the following day, my mother was understandably livid. Out of concern for my well-being, she questioned me, and I provided a candid account of where I had been and who had been present. In her characteristically loving and compassionate way, she explained that my father's actions were a profound betrayal of his role—a moral failure that was no example for a child to follow. I heeded her guidance instantly. From that day forward, I resisted his invitations to join him on his routes, or I made it abundantly clear that I would only go if I were returned home to Mama by nightfall.

Another unnerving part of those long road trips was his visits to an Obeah man, which I witnessed at least twice. I still remember the red flag tied to a tall pole in the center of the compound—apparently to mark the place. On the way, he'd buy a bottle of Jamaican white rum and present it to the practitioner on arrival. During their consultation, the Obeah man would intermittently sprinkle rum across the floor. I can't recall what they discussed, but when I told my mother afterward, she was furious. She confronted my father and demanded that he never take me there again.

While his earlier lessons were deeply inappropriate for a child, they were ultimately overshadowed by those learned from his love of guns. My father proudly adopted the self-ascribed nickname "Buck," an ode to his gunslinging ways and his passion for Western movies. He took it from the lead character Buck in the 1972 film *Buck and the Preacher*, played by the legendary Sidney Poitier. He even bought and often played the 45 RPM movie-tribute record "Buck and the Preacher" by the renowned artist I-Roy on our battery-powered turntable—the reggae rhythm filling the house as he grooved to the beat.

He owned two guns: an unlicensed shotgun for bird hunting and a licensed handgun. Up until about age six, on the rare Sundays he was home, he'd go bird shooting. He never ventured far—just to the middle of our long driveway—with the shotgun and my older brothers in tow. From there, he'd lie in wait for the popular Jamaican Baldpate (also known as White-Crowned Pigeon) as they made their habitual dawn commute. After a few shotgun blasts, my brothers would run to retrieve any fallen birds. The successful kills were brought home and handed to my mother or sisters to clean and cook, contributing to our Sunday breakfast.

Of his two firearms, his licensed handgun—a Browning 9mm semi-automatic pistol—was the more fearsome one. It was an extension of himself: always with him during the day, tucked beneath his pillow at night. At least once a week, he would sit in the dining room for nearly an hour, carefully cleaning it with oils and small tools. He even showed me, on occasion, how to load it and work the safety.

Occasionally, when I complained or cried to him about mistreatment by a sibling, he would pull out his gun in jest and say, "Here, guh shoot dem."* He never allowed me to take possession of the gun, and I never tried.

In my childhood innocence, my tears would turn to laughter—I understood that this was his twisted way of downplaying my complaint and making me forget about it.

On the rare occasions my father forgot the gun under his pillow before leaving home, he would come back in a frenzy—no matter how far he had driven. One morning, around age six, I found it there and decided to take it out to scare my siblings in the backyard.

I remember carefully avoiding the trigger as I approached them quietly, then yelled, "Stick it up!" They calmly took it from me and gave me a strong reprimand.

Clearly not understanding the danger, I kept insisting, "Mi know weh mi did ah duh; mi neva put mi finga pon di trigga."†

My father soon returned, heard what had transpired and my explanation, but treated the matter with far less seriousness than the situation deserved.

That evening, when my mother came home, she spoke to me calmly but firmly: "Junior, it nuh rite fi pickney touch or hold gun. Dem

---

* Translation: "Here, go shoot them."

† Translation: "I know what I was doing; I never put my finger on the trigger."

danga-rous an cyaah kill yuh and odda people. Pramise mi dat yuh wil avide an stay wey fram gun wen yuh si dem."*

I heeded her advice.

A few months later, a family friend was visiting and offered to take pictures. As I posed with my sister Olive, my father walked over, pulled out his gun, and said, "Pose wid dis."

I refused at first, but he insisted.

The family friend, visibly frightened at the thought of photographing a six-year-old pointing a gun in his face, quickly handed the camera to my father.

Increasingly, my father would fire his gun at random targets in the backyard—for example, a breadfruit hanging from its tree. Each loud shot sent shudders through my body and fear racing down my spine.

Eventually, my increasing understanding of the danger and my justified fear of guns reached its peak. One day, unexpectedly, with my mother away, my father announced—perhaps tired of shooting at lifeless targets—that he was going to put three of our oldest dogs to sleep.

He calmly walked over to the first one, Jakes, and shot him in the side in cold blood. The dog squealed in pain, bolted, leaped the back fence, and was never seen again. He then went after Rex, whose fate was the same, though Rex ran and hid for a moment, only to be found and shot again before escaping to his assured death.

The third and oldest dog, Rover, whom he believed was too old to run, was leashed and led to a wooded area, where he was shot. In that moment, a dark cloud seemed to settle over our home, and I vowed right then that I would never own a gun for the rest of my life.

Finding greater solace and wisdom in my mother's guidance, I increasingly avoided being alone with my father. I no longer ran down the driveway to open the gate when he arrived or hopped into his car for the short trip to the garage. I also stopped accepting his invitations to join him on road trips.

---

* Translation: "Junior, it's not right for children to touch or hold a gun. They are dangerous and can kill you and others. Promise me that you will avoid and stay away from guns when you see them."

He eventually came to grips with the fact that my mother's counsel carried more weight. When I declined his offers, he'd respond with a cynical "Galang ah yuh Gad."*

I assumed that casting aspersions, claiming I worshipped my mother, was his way of belittling my loyalty to her advice and my affinity for her virtues.

Avoidance eventually turned into deep resentment. I began to see him as a father of broken promises—big and small: the $5 CEE fee he didn't pay, the morning he drove away on the day of my most important exam, and the promised bicycle he never bought. That deep resentment reached its peak with the circumstances that forced us to leave our home in New Hall. As we left that life behind, I found myself quietly celebrating his absence.

Much to my surprise, my mother—with her forgiving heart and her belief that I should continue to acknowledge my father—encouraged me, and sometimes even insisted, that I visit him occasionally. Yes, she hoped he would give me some pocket money on those visits, but the amounts were always small, never anything close to the child support she could have legally demanded.

I eventually gave in and visited him roughly every two to three months. However, most of these trips were really just a pretext for my friends and me to ride our bicycles on a nine- or ten-mile round trip. That ended after I was shaken awake by a nightmare. In it, perhaps triggered by buried trauma, my father pulled out his gun and started shooting at us as we pedaled up the driveway toward his house. My heart pounding, I stayed awake the rest of the night. The next day, I told my mother about the dream and said I wouldn't go back. She understood, apologized for pushing me to visit, and never raised the issue again.

The overwhelmingly negative examples set by my father could have easily led me down a morally bankrupt path. Thankfully, my mother's constant vigilance and gentle interventions, combined with my own developing sense of right and wrong, kept that darkness at bay. In retrospect, these negative examples of fatherhood served as unspoken lessons—they taught me what I should never emulate or become.

Although he failed as a positive role model in almost every way, there was one valuable lesson he taught me around age five that I have

---

* Translation: "Go along to your God."

never forgotten. It happened during a conversation he was having with an older neighborhood boy, who was probably looking for paid work. The boy was disheveled—clothes soiled and ragged—and I must have been put off by his appearance. From behind my father's legs, I reached around and kicked him.

What followed my awful, disrespectful behavior was the one and only real ass-whipping I ever got from my father. It was a harsh but lasting lesson in respecting others, no matter how they looked or their station in life.

In retrospect, despite his many glaring shortcomings, there were glimpses of a good nature beneath the surface. Sadly, he never fully manifested or magnified those qualities in his broader life.

His Life and Redemption After Our Departure

Shortly after we left the New Hall family home in 1978, my father moved one of his women into the house. He reportedly told a neighbor that my mother did him a big favor by moving out—saving him the monthly rent he'd been paying to house this woman. My mother, though legally entitled to at least 50 percent of the marital assets in a divorce and child support for her three minor children, chose not to pursue any.

The woman, more than thirty years his junior, bore him four children, with the youngest born in the mid-1980s. Unlike my mother, who always worked to fill the gaps left by his financial shortcomings, she relied on him entirely. As he aged and could no longer work as he once did, his financial situation deteriorated sharply.

To supplement his income and afford major purchases, such as a car, he continued to subdivide and sell parcels of the land. He also gifted a small piece to one of my older sisters. Over time, less than a third of an acre remained—the plot with the house. In his final years, with nothing left to sell, he depended entirely on the kindness of my eldest brother, Gerry, who stepped in to provide financial support.

In the early 1980s, the government revoked firearm licenses across Jamaica, requiring owners to surrender their weapons. To get a new one, he had to reapply, provide a stronger justification, and pass a thorough background check. During the investigation, a detective from the Mandeville Police Station interviewed my mother about the circumstances of their separation. His application was ultimately denied. I never learned whether he ever owned a gun again—legally or otherwise.

He also, in the early 1980s, suffered a stroke that left him partially paralyzed on one side. In this instance, his self-confidence and toughness served him well. He followed a strict, mostly self-directed regimen of physical therapy and regained full mobility within a few months.

In the mid-1980s, my father filed for divorce from my mother—at the reported insistence of the woman he was living with. She had become increasingly anxious that, after his death, she might not have any legal claim to his house and land. My mother signed the papers without hesitation and made no claim to the 50 percent share of the marital property that was rightfully hers.

After I stopped my bimonthly visits around 1981, I saw and spoke to my father only a handful of times before and after I immigrated to the United States—right up until his death in 2013. The last time I saw him, for perhaps less than an hour, was while visiting my mother about a month before she passed away in December 2010.

The day following my return to Jamaica for my mother's funeral, I was told by one of my cousins that he said, "Now dem Gad dead, a wey dem a guh duh?"[*] It was a cynical jab at the virtuous role my mother played in our lives, echoing similar remarks I'd heard as a child.

In my moment of sorrow, this served as a painful reminder of his cold, inhumane nature.

Upon his passing, I felt no remorse and chose not to attend his funeral. Going would have been inconsistent with my true feelings.

In conversations with my siblings, Dave and Judy, while documenting my journey, they revealed details of his attempts—hopefully successful—at seeking redemption in his final years.

Dave told me he had many talks with him before our mother's passing, urging him to acknowledge the wrongs he had done and apologize to her. Dave, being steeped in his Christian faith, warned him

---

[*] Translation: "Now their God is dead, what are they going to do?" This cynical and jealous statement echoed his earlier "Galang ah yuh Gad" statement during my childhood and a final, bitter resentment toward me and my siblings' affinity toward our mother.

that, without his apology, repentance, and giving his life to God, he would lose his pathway to heaven.

Judy told me that about a week before my mother passed, my father slowly ambled up her driveway, supported by his walking stick, as if on an undeterred mission. Upon entering the living room where my mother was seated, he said, "Laura, a yuh mi cum fi taak tuh."*

My mother, who would usually disappear to her quarters whenever he visited, remained seated and listened attentively.

Over the course of what became an hour-long conversation, he apologized repeatedly. With her forgiving heart, she responded simply, "Nuh worry, mi fagive yuh."†

After my mother's death, a pastor from the nearby Richmond Seventh-day Adventist Church visited him regularly. He eventually embraced the Christian faith and was baptized. In his last years, digestive issues became his greatest burden. Dave, who was at his hospital bedside hours before he passed, recalled his final words as cries of pain from the stomach agony he endured.

He died at age eighty-seven on December 15, 2013, and was buried in the family plot at his ancestral home, beside the graves of his parents and siblings.

In moments of introspection, I still wonder why I have not yet been able to forgive him when my mother—who suffered far more—found it in her heart to do so. I have come to accept that I still have growing to do, and I hope to reach that place of forgiveness before my own life ends.

LIFE LESSONS

1. For a child to thrive amid pervasive maladies, at least one parent must guide wisely and well.

2. A child learns from both spoken words and unverbalized actions.

---

* Translation: "Laura, it is you I have come to talk to."

† Translation: "Don't worry, I forgive you." This exchange represents the final reconciliation between my parents and the ultimate act of grace from my mother.

3. A parent's absence makes a child's heart grow harder, not fonder.

4. Poor life choices and bad financial decisions are symbiotically linked; avoid one, and the other will almost always improve.

5. A promise is like money—if it cannot be traded for something of value, it's worthless.

6. A gun in a home is a dark current running beneath every ordinary day, with fear, accident, and tragedy waiting for its moment.

7. A gun's core purpose is to wound or kill, human or animal; it makes no distinction.

8. To say a gun is for protection from another gun is a gun-perpetuating tragedy.

9. To forgive is not to forget, lest you become a repeat victim of bad memory.

10. If divine redemption is an ever-present promise to spare one the consequences of their deliberate, harmful actions, then what is their deterrent?

11. Turn every negative childhood experience into wisdom: unspoken lessons of what never to emulate or become.

My father, Eric Jones, Sr., around the late 1950s

My father, Eric Jones, Sr., and I, around late 1973.
Photo taken at my childhood home.

CHAPTER 7

The Mother Who Fathered Me

Tenderness rooted in pillars of strength

Her Appearance and Personality

My mother, Kerean Harper Jones, also known as Laura, gave birth to me at age thirty-nine, one month before her fortieth birthday. My earliest memory of her, like that of my father, dates back to when I was about age three. She stood gracefully at five feet two and a half inches, with a medium build and long, wavy black hair. She had a dark complexion with a soft countenance, and her eyes portrayed warmth and wisdom. She exuded both external and profound internal beauty. Her name, Kerean, frequently elicited surprise, as it was generally perceived to belong to a more contemporary generation rather than her own.

She had a warm and inviting aura, and everyone felt welcome, important, and respected in her presence. Her humility and comportment in words and deeds demonstrated a profound love for humanity, especially the less fortunate. She saw herself as no better than anyone. Her warm greetings and queries to family, friends, neighbors, and strangers started with equal meaning and fervor in her beloved Patwa: "Suh, how yuh duh?"*

She was a deeply spiritual Christian woman, a member of the Church of Christ denomination, and never wavered in her faith. Her love of God defined her principles and was a source of strength and resilience throughout her life. She punctuated every expressed desire she heard with a reminder that such could only be achieved if it was the will of

---

* Translation: "So how are you doing?"

God. She endeavored to start and end each day by reading her Bible, praying, and singing praises to God.

She was more than just our family matriarch; she dedicated much of her life and influence to uplifting individuals and her community. Her door, both figuratively and literally, was always open to anyone who needed a meal, clothes, or just some conversation. She knew that "Evri fish inna sea nuh shaak,"* and gave everyone the opportunity to demonstrate the sincerity of their intentions without prejudice. She was always frank and direct—never afraid to say what was on her mind.

She was intellectually curious, a keen reader with a hunger and thirst for knowledge. She even sought a greater understanding of evolving technology. I recall her asking questions about the internet and how it worked when she was around age seventy-five. My siblings and I listened astutely to her ideas and opinions and regularly sought her guidance.

Besides her love for God, children, family, and community, she was also passionate about her kitchen gardens and flowers. Our verandas were always filled with potted plants, resplendent from her care, and nothing seemed to upset her more than our failure—in her absence—to water them sufficiently.

Her Early Years

Over the years, my mother shared many details about her early life with my siblings and me. She was raised by her single mother until she was eight years old, but due to financial hardships, she was placed in her father's custody shortly after he remarried. She was later pulled out of school—after completing only third grade—to help with the household chores of her father's growing family.

Her stepmother failed to give her the care she needed as a young child and instead treated her very poorly. She recounted one incident where her stepmother cut off her long, flowing hair and expressed that

---

* Translation: "Not every fish in the sea is a shark," meaning that not everyone's story should be treated with suspicion of malintent or deception; instead, give everyone a fair chance.

"Mi hope seh ih grow bak jus lakka nehgah ier"[*]—a clear indication of racial prejudice toward her mixed-race ethnicity by her Indian stepmother.

Fed up with the ongoing mistreatment and deprivation of an education, she eventually ran away to her mother's home in the town of Falmouth. Her stepmother arrived a few days later and demanded that my mother be returned to her, but her mother refused.

Because her mother was still struggling financially, she eventually sent her to stay with an aunt who promised to teach her dressmaking. Instead, with five children to care for, the aunt mostly made her do household chores—only giving her minimal instruction in dressmaking.

At age fourteen, she was forcibly abused by her aunt's husband and threatened into silence. Ironically, he was a pastor at a local church and held in high esteem by the community. She later gave birth to a sickly child who died shortly after. How I first learned about this traumatic event in her life, I'll share later in the pages ahead.

After her aunt discovered her husband's atrocities, she was forced to leave the home. By then, her mother had passed away, and she was left to support herself, so she sought and found domestic work. At age eighteen, she met my oldest sister's father and gave birth to Mavis a year later. Their relationship ended when he immigrated to England during the Windrush era.[30] Mavis was left in the care of her paternal grandparents while my mother continued working mainly as a live-in domestic helper.

During one of these jobs, her employers—who led the Falmouth Anglican Church—were reassigned to Mandeville. To keep her position, my mother moved with their family. She later recalled learning most of her culinary skills during that time. As described in the previous chapter, her need for dental treatment in Mandeville led to a chance introduction to my father. Drawn in by his charm and seduction, they eventually married and had six children.

---

[*] Translation: "I hope that it grows back similar to Negroid hair." This was a hateful expression of racial prejudice aimed at her half-Black ancestry.

A Career Marked by Entrepreneurship

Formally educated only through third grade and raised in deep financial hardship, my mother never realized her dream of becoming a nurse. Yet, driven by her survival instincts and later by the need to provide for her children, she became a true "jack of all trades." In the Jamaican saying, she knew how to "Tun ar han an mek fashion."* In her teens and early twenties, she worked as a domestic helper, but her natural entrepreneurial spirit led her to learn dressmaking and start her own small business.

After she became more confident in her dressmaking abilities, she bought her first Singer pedal sewing machine. Working from home, she made women's clothing and girls' school uniforms for residents in New Hall and the neighboring districts. This lasted about ten years.

In 1969, as my father's financial support dwindled, my mother needed a larger clientele to increase her income. She searched for, found, and rented commercial space for her first official dressmaking shop in Mandeville. Her reputation for quality work quickly spread, attracting more customers. The heavy workload—especially prior to the start of a school year—often meant a six-day workweek and late-night work from home. Eventually, she moved to a larger, more spacious location in a different part of town.

She never rested solely on the laurels of her thriving dressmaking business. At the same time, she tended her kitchen gardens—yams, sweet potatoes, callaloo, strawberries, and more. For a while, with help from my siblings, she also farmed bok choy and sold it wholesale to market vendors. Additionally, she raised a few goats and cows, sometimes selling them for a profit. The cows also occasionally provided fresh milk for the household.

Despite the heavy demands of motherhood and managing her growing dressmaking business, my mother still found time for philanthropy and activism. She was eventually recruited by the People's National Party (PNP) as an area leader and grassroots organizer for New Hall. In recognition of her ongoing contributions, around 1976 or 1977,

---

* Translation: "Turn her hand and make fashion" (or "Turn her hand and make something happen"), meaning finding a way to make a living through one's resourcefulness and ingenuity despite limited means.

she was offered tenancy of one of five newly built, government-owned store spaces in a prime location in the center of town, at an affordable monthly rent.

The new store spaces were earmarked mostly for retailers of Jamaican souvenirs and craft merchandise—an underserved niche market in the town. After obtaining permission to use a part of the space for her dressmaking business, she quickly accepted the offer and launched the "Jones Art and Craft Shoppe." She became highly skilled and efficient at sourcing goods from local and regional artisans, often traveling to Kingston to buy merchandise not available nearby.

She later traveled internationally—mainly to the Cayman Islands and the United States—to source non-craft goods and diversify her shop's inventory to increase profits. She also completed a floral arrangement course, creating bouquets for sale or fulfilling custom orders. She ran the business successfully for about nine years until emigrating permanently to the United States in 1985. Before leaving, she handed it over to my sister Jill.

Upon arriving in Brooklyn, New York, at age fifty-seven, my mother assessed her options and chose to become a Home Health Aide (HHA). In the 1980s, this required completing a Department of Health-approved training program: fifty-nine hours of classroom instruction, sixteen hours of supervised practical experience, and passing a competency evaluation. She met all the requirements successfully and worked as an HHA for about eight years until retiring and returning to Jamaica in 1993.[31]

Although her dream of becoming a registered nurse never came to pass, her caring spirit lived on through two of my sisters, who both chose nursing as their profession. This brought her immense joy—she proudly lived that dream vicariously through them.

Her Financial Acuity and Self-Sacrifice

Unlike my father, my mother was the model of financial self-discipline. From the account given in the previous chapter, she realized that keeping joint bank accounts and making joint investments with my father could jeopardize her ability to care for her children. With the earnings from her entrepreneurial endeavors, she ensured that her children's needs were met. We were clothed, fed, schooled, and given the comforts of home to the best of her ability.

She saved diligently for major expenses and emergencies—setting aside whatever she could, always guided by the Jamaican adages "Wan wan coco full basket," and "Evri mickle mek ah muckle."*

She also routinely ran a "partner" (or "pardner") as the banker, or joined those organized by trusted friends. This tradition is basically an informal rotating savings and credit association—still widely practiced in Jamaica and elsewhere under different names. Participants contribute a fixed amount weekly, bi-weekly, or monthly for a set period, with each person receiving the full pool once per cycle. My mother always timed her payout to cover major expenses, such as back-to-school needs at the start of the year.

Although she loved fashion—especially through her dressmaking craft—she never adorned herself with expensive clothes or jewelry, nor did she indulge in the fruits of her labor. Instead, she dressed modestly yet gracefully, always putting her children's needs—and often their wants—ahead of her own.

She occasionally took us on bus rides to the beach, paid for ad hoc school outings, gave us extra pocket money during holidays, gifted us on birthdays and Christmas, and carefully considered the merits of any wants we expressed.

I fondly remember telling my mother in 1979 how much we wanted to experience our first train ride—she cheerfully made it happen. With two siblings and four nieces in tow, she took us to Kendal, Manchester, where we boarded the train for a one-day round trip to Montego Bay. About fifty miles and three hours later, we arrived, ate, explored a little of the city, and then hurried back for the return journey. At age twelve, she gifted me my first airplane ride and a two-week stay with friends she had made in the Cayman Islands.

Beyond assuming my father's neglected financial duties, my mother routinely stepped in to make good on his broken promises, such as the bicycle I mentioned earlier. She was a woman of her word—never shirking her responsibilities, whether they were rightfully hers or

---

* Translation: "One by one, the coco [a root vegetable] fills the basket," and "Every little bit makes a lot." These two popular Jamaican proverbs counsel that putting away or saving a little at a time can add up to something larger and more significant in the end.

imposed on her due to circumstances, and she never sought another man to fill the gaps left by my father's shortcomings.

In 1985, when I was accepted to attend the University of the West Indies (UWI), my mother couldn't afford the substantial costs, but she was undeterred. She assured me, "Where there is a will, there is a way," and set out to find a solution. Ultimately, she decided I would need a student loan to supplement her support, and she made sure every requirement for the application and approval was met.

Perhaps her greatest sacrifice was emigrating to the United States at age fifty-seven. She received her green card through a successful petition from my oldest sister, Mavis. Permanent residency was never about her own ambitions; for her, it meant being able to provide me with greater financial support at UWI and to file green card petitions for two other siblings and me. She believed we would have far better educational, employment, and economic opportunities in America—and that her personal sacrifice was necessary to make it possible.

Emigrating meant abandoning her thriving business and entrepreneurial freedom, saying farewell to her beloved Jamaica, adjusting to cold winters, starting a new career, and learning how to navigate New York City's public transportation—all while managing hypertension and type 2 diabetes. Yet, at an age when most people turn toward retirement, my mother made perhaps her greatest sacrifice—for us.

My mother's selflessness and lifelong sacrifices for us have borne their just rewards. None of us has brought her dishonor; all have achieved success in our own ways. Four of us completed college, two earned master's degrees, and two rose to executive positions—vice president and president—in large U.S. organizations. Following in her footsteps, four of us have launched, operated, or continue to run at least seven entrepreneurial ventures throughout our careers.

Managing Infidelity

Approximately five years into their marriage, my mother first learned of my father's infidelity. As detailed in the preceding chapter, his betrayals grew increasingly frequent, brazen, and unapologetic. After about fifteen years of enduring this emotional suffering, she reached her limit in 1972 and ended all physical intimacy with him. By then, he already had five known children outside their marriage, with no sign of stopping.

On many occasions, I asked her which of his traits—which I found mostly undesirable—could have attracted her to him. Her consistent answer was that the father I came to know was not the man she married. She described him in those early years as a good man—a dedicated husband and father focused on building their life together. With a glow in her eyes, she often added that he was handsome and charming, and that he literally swept her off her feet.

In my rejoinders, I usually asked, "Suh wah mek yu put up wid im cheating an alla di sufferation fi suh lang?"

Her responses, rooted in her selfless dedication to her children, always started off with "Mi neva wah mi pickney dem fi grow up widout fadda," and in her empathic way often added, "Ah nuh alla di time im did bad." She invariably ended her explanations with "Den, Junior, eff mi did lef im, mi wud ah neva hab yu, suh mi glad mi wiet til afta yu baan."[*]

After that, I usually had no comeback, and my interrogation would abruptly end.

Over time, I have grown to understand and empathize with her perspective. Beyond her explanations is the realization that she lived in a different time, a more male-dominated era when this level of infidelity was not uncommon and—sadly—often tolerated.

Her Philanthropy and Activism

One of my earliest memories of my mother's compassion for others—beyond our immediate home—was for her ailing father, who was sixty-seven years old at the time of my birth. Although he hadn't stood firmly against the abuse she suffered as a child at the hands of his former wife, that fact played no part in her commitment to his care.

---

[*] Translation: Me: "So what made you put up with his cheating and all the suffering for so long?" Mother (Primary reason): "I never wanted my children to grow up without a father." Mother (Empathy): "It wasn't all the time that he was bad." Mother (Ultimate justification): "Then, Junior, if I had left him, I would have never had you, so I'm glad I waited until after you were born."

At least every two months, she would make the arduous, roughly three-hour journey by country bus*—through winding roads and precipitous hills—to his home in Wakefield, Trelawny. She occasionally brought me and sometimes another sibling along for the two- to four-day stays.

She was the only one of his children who regularly visited, kept up with his doctor's appointments, and ensured he had sufficient necessities. A couple of years before his death, likely in gratitude for her dedication to his care, he started the process of gifting her about a quarter of an acre of land. The land was surveyed, and the subdivision plan received approval. However, after he passed away, her stepmother reinserted herself into the estate's affairs. She told my mother that if he truly intended to give her the land, he would have completed the transfer before his death.

The fact is, she cared for her father unconditionally, without expecting anything in return, and chose to walk away empty-handed. At the time, I was upset with her for so easily relinquishing what was rightfully hers, to which she responded, "Son, mi lef dem dey sinting inna Gad han; mi nuh gwine fight dem fi nutten."†

Back in our home district of New Hall, my mother was renowned for her philanthropic spirit. Her kindness was not a mere occasional gesture but a cornerstone of her reputation. Old man Ben, whom I described in Chapter 4, was just one of many fortunate individuals who benefited from her quiet, persistent generosity.

Frequently on Sunday mornings, and religiously during the Christmas and Easter holidays, Ben would amble up the driveway—his trademark rusted machete in hand—to be treated to a hearty breakfast. Upon seeing him approaching, I would animatedly notify my mother, "Mama, Ben a cum!" We were never allowed to tease or otherwise show

---

* A typical country bus in the 1970s wasn't sleek or air-conditioned; it was usually old, with hard bench seating, prioritized capacity over comfort, and had loud, fumy diesel engines and hissing air brakes. It was usually packed to capacity, and on top, you would find loads of baskets and sacks of various farm produce, and even live animals.

† Translation: "Son, I leave all those things in the hands of God; I will not fight with them for anything."

Ben any disrespect, but out of fear of his machete, I usually kept my distance.

He would sit in the open garage and wait for my mother to bring him the appetizing fare. As he ate, she would begin her interrogation to determine the state of his well-being: "Suh ow everyting? Yu aright? Yu ah git enuff fi eat?"* Ben would usually respond in his muttering, muted style, which only my mother seemed to understand.

Especially on holidays, if his clothing was tattered and dirty or he appeared in need of a bath—or both—she would escort him after he finished eating to the backyard bathhouse. There, she would encourage him to remove his clothing and bathe—under her direction—from a large metal tub filled with warm water. His worn and tattered garments would be replaced with clean clothing selected by my mother from my father's or older brothers' wardrobes. He always departed well-fed, clean, properly attired, and noticeably revitalized.

Her recruitment by the People's National Party (PNP), mentioned earlier, as an area leader for New Hall and its environs marked a significant step in her activism. In this role, she regularly received telegraphed invitations and attended the PNP's local and regional meetings and events, as well as its annual national conference held in Kingston.

Her political involvement and alignment with the PNP were not instigated by political ambitions. Instead, she was driven by democratic socialist ideals—political and economic democracy, solidarity among all members of society, and, above all, reducing inequality and uplifting the poor through social welfare.

In her assigned district, she led government food distribution to the poor and helped to secure seasonal street-cleaning work for unemployed individuals. Following storms, she ensured the government's financial and material assistance was fairly allocated to poor individuals who had suffered severe damage to their homes.

She was a trusted confidante of Winston Jones (no known familial relationship), who was the Member of Parliament (MP) for various constituencies in Manchester Parish from 1955 to 1980. I met him on many occasions during my childhood and recall him even

* Translation: "So, how is everything? Are you alright? Are you getting enough to eat?"

knowing me by name. She also occasionally brought me with her to the PNP's local office and political events. On one occasion, I received a handshake from Prime Minister Michael Manley. Winston Jones lost his seat in 1980 during the landslide electoral victory of the Jamaica Labour Party (JLP).[32]

As her political activities subsided following our move to Hillside and the PNP's loss in the 1980 election, it allowed more space for her philanthropy. She quickly spotted individuals in need of help as they wandered along the street past our house. As she did in New Hall, she extended to them whatever assistance she could offer.

There was one apparently destitute and mentally afflicted lady to whom she paid particular attention. At the first opportunity, she invited the lady to the house and sat with her in the backyard shade, assessing her situation.

She offered the lady some water and instructed me to fetch it for her. Thinking that perhaps a disposable cup was more suited for the occasion, given her condition, I decided to use one.

As I approached the lady with the disposable cup of water, my mother got outraged: "Ah since wen yu gi guests wata outta plastic cup? Mi nuh teach yu betta dan dat? Guh back inna di house an bring di wata inna wan addi good drinking glass."*

This, among others, was a lesson in equality, respect, and humility that I would never forget. It was not only a reprimand, but a reminder that charity must come from the heart.

Also, for a while after we moved to Hillside, my mother saw me off each morning as I left for school before she went to work. Unbeknownst to me, she watched from the front veranda as I routinely passed a group of young men sitting on a wall, engaged in idle conversation. Perceiving their behavior was unproductive, I deliberately avoided interacting with them as I walked by.

My mother, after observing my behavior for a few days, asked, "Junior, a wey mek yu waak paas dem dey yung man dey evri day an

---

* Translation: "Since when do you serve guests water from plastic cups? Didn't I teach you better than that? Go back in the house and bring the water in one of the good drinking glasses."

nuh sey good mawning? Yu tink yu betta dan dem? Mi nah tel yu fi tap an igle wid dem, but yu fi show dem respeck an sey good mawning."*

I heeded her advice the next morning, and their warm reaction taught me that respect triggers reciprocity. Through their subsequent actions, these same young men became my defenders whenever they perceived that I was threatened by others.

My mother's good deeds were not limited to the neighborhood districts in which we lived, as she brought the same charitable zeal to Mandeville—every day she went to work. She would intercept the needy or mentally afflicted whenever she saw them passing by her shop and offer them food, clothing, money, or whatever they appeared to need. Some would routinely come for their rations, and in my mother's absence, whoever was left in charge of the shop was also expected to attend to their needs. Mostly, they accepted her charity with excitement, but there were a few rare refusals; these only served to strengthen her resolve.

I recall one woman who was regularly stationed in a gazebo in the center of a small park located behind my mother's shop. My mother brought her food regularly. On one occasion, she decided to bring a bag of clothes, which she had selectively packed at home.

I was at the shop with my mother the following day as she anxiously awaited the woman's arrival, assigning me the job of lookout. As soon as I spotted her, I exclaimed, "Mama, she dey ya!" and off she went, gift in hand.

A few moments later, she returned with the bag. "Mama, ah wah hap'm?" I asked.

Dejectedly, she responded, "Shi sey shi nuh want ih."†

However, this did not dampen my mother's continued charity toward the woman.

She often encouraged and, whenever possible, involved me directly in her charitable efforts. On one occasion, she saw a teenager

---

* Translation: "Junior, why do you walk past those young men every day without saying good morning? Do you think you are better than them? I'm not telling you to stop and idle with them, but you should show them respect by saying good morning."

† Translation: Me: "Mama, she's here." Then, "Mama, what happened?" Mother: "She said she doesn't want it."

lying on the sidewalk in dirty, tattered clothes, emitting a bad odor due to poor hygiene. I recognized him because he had dropped out of my high school due to mental illness and was now aimlessly wandering the streets of the town.

Without hesitation, she reached into her purse, pulled out some money, handed it to me, and commanded, "Guh geem dis."

I hesitated but heeded the command and stepped toward him, and from a distance held the money outstretched. With a headshake, he rejected the offer.

As I turned back toward my mother, she asked rhetorically, "Yu kno wey mek im sey no? Ah kaaz yu neva a dweet fram yu haart. Ah hope yu learn yuh lessen."[*]

My Mother, My Pillar of Strength and Role Model

My mother's approach to parenting was diametrically opposed to my father's macho, egocentric style, which amounted to an abdication of his truly important fatherly responsibilities. Where he faltered, my mother stepped in and became the mother who fathered me, demonstrating the true traits of both a phenomenal mother and father.

She knew that children often mimicked their parents' behavior and took counsel from the adages "Chip nuh fly fur fram di blak," and "Sheep cyaan mek goat."[†] Consequently, her conduct exemplified the positive role model that we needed. Despite her many stressful challenges, she never resorted to harmful vices; instead, her only refuge was her Christian faith.

In her fatherly role, she filled the gaps in financial and material support, provided a secure emotional base, taught me discipline, showed me how to navigate challenges, and guided me toward becoming a responsible man of integrity and purpose. Whenever I was being misguided by my father, she intervened and redirected me. Through my

---

[*] Translation: Mother's initial: "Go give him this." Mother's follow-up: "Do you know why he said no? It's because you never did it from your heart. I hope you've learned your lesson."

[†] Translation: "A chip does not fall far from the block," and "A sheep cannot make a goat." Both adages underscore the indelible influence of parental behavior on a child.

observation and admiration of her many attributes, I developed a profound respect for women—a trait lacking in my father.

As a mother, she was the embodiment of a loving, nurturing, emotionally supportive, and protective parent, with an impeccable work ethic both at home and in her business. She strived to create a safe environment that fostered my emotional, social, moral, and intellectual development and celebrated my successes, both big and small.

As a child with health challenges, as detailed in Chapter 4, my mother was vigilant in ensuring that I received the necessary medical care, whether taking me to a doctor or administering proven home remedies.

Through her respect and empathy for the less fortunate or afflicted, she taught me to have compassion and humility. Through her independence and ability to overcome extreme personal challenges, I learned to be self-reliant, resilient, and to make difficult decisions when necessary. Ultimately, she equipped me with the tools necessary to become a confident, capable, caring, and well-adjusted adult.

By sharing her most painful personal experience, she taught me one of her most enduring lessons: how to overcome trauma with unwavering resilience.

One day, when I was about fourteen years old, she said to me, "Junior, mi hab sinting fi tel yu wey yu neva ier yet; ih nuh easy, but mi feel compel fi mek yu kno."[*]

I could sense the seriousness in what she was about to reveal by the sadness that overtook her countenance.

As she started to recount the incident of being forcibly abused at age fourteen, my heart sank. How could this possibly happen to the most decent, honest, empathetic, and kind-hearted person I had ever known? I sank into a chair and sat there in silence for a few minutes as my eyes filled with tears, feeling powerless to face the reality of what I had just heard.

Eventually, as I regained some composure, I exclaimed, "Mama, oh Gad, mi really sarry seh yu guh tru dis yah sufferation; wat a wicked man!"

---

[*] Translation: "Junior, I have something to tell you that you haven't heard yet; it's not easy, but I feel compelled to let you know."

Following a few more expressions of outrage, my mood must have turned to self-pity, as I asked her the rhetorical question, "Mama, a weh mek yuh gi mi dis yah burden now fi bear?"*

The answer was evident: she wanted me to learn, through her experience, that with resilience and steadfast resolve, I too could overcome great challenges that the passage of time would undoubtedly bring.

My mother laid the foundation for who I am. She was my pillar of strength, guiding light, beacon of hope, and the unwavering role model whose virtues I will forever strive to emulate. All that is good and valuable within me is a testament to her influence.

Her U.S. Residency, Returning Home, and Final Years

Overall, my mother found living in the United States challenging and had limited enjoyment, primarily because she arrived at a late middle age of fifty-seven. She had to adapt to life as an employee after decades of self-employment, endure cold winters, adjust to Brooklyn's busy urban atmosphere, learn to use the subway, and cope with the confines of apartment living.

Despite these challenges, she plowed on as a home health aide and successfully filed a petition for my permanent U.S. residency. Luckily, my university tuition and expenses were mostly covered by an academic scholarship in my last two years. However, she assisted me financially whenever I needed it until I completed UWI in 1989. From my first arrival in the United States in 1987, she accommodated me the best she could in her small, humble one-bedroom apartment, from where I commenced my American journey.

In 1993, after about eight years of living and working in Brooklyn—and accomplishing her dream of securing permanent residency for two siblings and me—she retired and returned to her beloved Jamaica. For the first few years of her retirement, she chose to live on her own, albeit at times with a grandchild or two for company.

---

* Translation: My exclamation: "Mama, oh God, I am really sorry that you went through this suffering—what a wicked man!" Rhetorical question: "Mama, why did you give me this burden to bear now?"

For several years, at our insistence, she returned to the United States every summer, splitting her stay among her children. I recall her eventually putting an end to these trips by saying, "Mi nah cum back. Mi nuh hab di stamina nuh more fi fly up an dung."*

Eventually, when her health declined and she could no longer manage on her own, she moved in with our sister Judy, a registered nurse at Mandeville Hospital, who lovingly cared for her.

A few months before her eightieth birthday in 2008, my siblings and I discussed and agreed to mark this significant milestone of our family matriarch with a grand celebration in Jamaica. Although she gave her entire life to her children, family, friends, and community, she never asked for anything in return. Therefore, this was just a small demonstration of our immense gratitude for her profound impact on all our lives.

We rented an event center in Mandeville, and almost all her children, grandchildren, great-grandchildren, relatives, and close friends attended. She was moved to tears by the appreciation and gratitude of numerous attendees, who expressed how she had positively impacted their lives.

A couple of years later, in November 2010, she was admitted to Mandeville Hospital with symptoms of a failing heart. The severity of her condition and dire prognosis prompted most of her entire clan—children, grandchildren, and great-grandchildren—to rush to Jamaica to see her alive for possibly the last time.

As some of us gathered around her attending physician, he delivered a shocking revelation. He said that her condition was not uncommon for a patient with hypertension and for one who had smoked for many years. I was flabbergasted as a flood of thoughts and questions rushed through my mind. My mother—the woman I revered above all others, my role model, the smartest person I had ever known—how could she have harbored such a secret?

The uncomfortable truth was that, despite her innumerable virtues, she was human and capable of making consequential mistakes. In her twenties, before her last six children were born, she had succumbed to the vicissitudes of cigarette smoking and continued the

---

* Translation: "I'm not coming back. I don't have the stamina anymore for flying back and forth."

habit for several years. Her strong reaction when she wrongly suspected me of smoking at age fourteen, coupled with never telling me she smoked herself, made it clear she didn't want her children to pick up the habit—a vice we all avoided.

Within a few days of her initial hospitalization, her vital signs improved, and she was discharged. I left Jamaica hopeful that she had weathered the storm and, with medication and care, would be around for at least a few more years.

Just a couple of weeks later, on December 13, 2010, while at work in my office in New York, I received the sad, unexpected news of my mother's death. The official cause of her death was congestive heart failure. My sister Judy later informed me—unbeknownst to most of us at the time—that her hospital discharge was not for anticipated improved health but to spend her final days comfortably at home.

Upon receiving the news, I broke down in uncontrollable tears, hit by the stark realization that I no longer had someone to call Mama. I gradually pulled myself out of the depths of despair, spurred by the realization that her indelible footprints would live on in my heart, mind, and soul forever.

At the time of her death, she was eighty-two years old and had mothered seven biological and two adopted children, twenty-seven grandchildren, and twenty-nine great-grandchildren, all of whom were privileged to have received her guidance, counsel, and wisdom.

The night before my mother's funeral, in a tent erected in the long driveway leading to my sister Judy's house, a Jamaican Afrocentric-style wake was held in her honor. The ceremony was attended by well-wishers from the neighborhood and beyond, who played goatskin drums, sang, chanted, danced, and partook of Jamaican white rum.

For almost all of her adult life, my mother was a member of the Church of Christ. This was a somewhat conservative denomination that relied mainly on the New Testament for faith and practice and did not embrace or incorporate Afrocentric religious practices. Therefore, I do not recall her ever attending a wake like the one being held in her honor.

Amid the reverberating drums and the bellowing chants, an electrical outage occurred. Real or imagined, I felt her presence in that moment, as if she was saying, "I do not approve." A few minutes later, electrical power returned, and I reckoned that, true to her benevolent self, she understood the intent of her well-wishers was good, regardless of their mode of expression.

I wrote my mother's eulogy before leaving New York and delivered it at her funeral on December 20, 2010. As I entered the church and looked at her body in the casket, the lingering sadness of her loss lifted, eclipsed by a feeling of enlightenment. In that moment, I realized her physical body was empty, yet I could still feel the warm lingering presence of her soul. Her body was just a material vessel that she used until it had become too weak for the rest of her eternal journey.

For months after her death, I could not escape the grasp of my daily thoughts and reflections on her life and the recurring sadness of her absence. Feeling the need to embrace my new reality, I made a conscious decision to block these thoughts as they arose.

Shortly after, she appeared to me in a dream and asked, "Ah wah mek yu kip ah call mi an hang up di fone?"*

I awoke startled but, in that moment, convinced that her spirit still lingered even after death.

Sometime later, while stricken with a bad case of influenza and in a partially awakened state of stupor or dream around 2 a.m. one morning, she appeared above me in the form of an apparition. As I struggled to, and finally did, become more lucid, her apparition, or figment of my dream, disappeared. Real or imagined, in that moment, I knew from my sixth sense that she would be ever present, watching over me.

LIFE LESSONS

1. A mother's love is the steel of a child's foundation, without which they topple beneath the tremors of adversity and the gale-force winds of life's storms.

2. In the river of parenthood, seed the current with resourcefulness and entrepreneurship; then your children will never thirst.

---

* Translation: "Why do you keep calling me and hanging up the phone?"

3. Few virtues are as scarce as self-sacrifice. If you are its beneficiary, you are blessed beyond measure.

4. Philanthropy is the acknowledgment that we are all one connected consciousness: as you do unto another, you do unto yourself.

5. Activism begins with recognizing that leadership is not equally bestowed. If you are among the gifted, step forward when humanity calls.

6. Role models are society's roots; without them, the whole tree weakens.

My mother, Kerean Jones, around the late 1950s.

My mother, Kerean Jones, and I, around the early 1980s.

My mother, Kerean Jones, around the early 1990s.

(This page intentionally left blank.)

PART II

FINDING MY WAY

(This page intentionally left blank.)

CHAPTER 8

Classrooms That Opened My World

Learning, from within and beyond the walls

Jamaica's Education System: 1970s to 1980s

I understood from an early age the importance of education and that it was my best route to a prosperous and meaningful life. I often heard repeated by my mother and others the common maxim that "silver and gold may vanish away, but a good education will never decay." As a child, I saw my siblings attend primary through high school with unfailing fervor, followed their example, and developed my own passion for learning. Before I relate my personal path through Jamaica's public education system, I'll explain its overall structure.

During my childhood, government-provided schooling was compulsory for children ages six through sixteen and modeled on the British education system. Early childhood education, while not compulsory, was provided by community-operated basic schools or government-operated infant schools, which children began attending around age three. Community-operated schools were regulated by the government and received partial funding if they met certain standards.[33]

At around age six, children transitioned to grade one of primary school. At the conclusion of each academic year, students completed school-administered examinations in reading, writing, and mathematics. Their performance was evaluated and ranked in comparison to their peers. From the ages of ten to twelve, in grades five and six, children were expected to sit the Common Entrance Examination (CEE), a prerequisite for entry into high schools and the government's means of allocating limited spaces.

High school lasted five years, designated as forms one through five, equivalent to U.S. grades seven through eleven. In fifth form, students sat either the Caribbean Secondary Education Certificate (CSEC, also known as CXC) or the University of Cambridge's General Certificate of Education (GCE) O-level exams in a broad range of subjects. GCE O-level exams were gradually replaced by CSEC, with the full transition completed in the late 1980s.

Following the fifth form, a student could optionally continue for two additional years, designated the lower and upper sixth forms, equivalent to U.S. grades twelve and thirteen. At the end, they sat GCE A-level exams, eventually fully replaced by the Caribbean Advanced Proficiency Examination (CAPE) in the early 2000s. Students who opted to attend sixth form were mostly those who planned on going to college or university.

Children who failed the CEE often faced dire prospects. Their options were: remain in primary school and repeat the exam the following year; attend an all-age school; attend a "new secondary" school that was less academic and more vocationally focused; attend a private high school; or end their education. Most private high schools were generally viewed as less desirable than public high schools and often had fewer resources. The limited access to public high schools disproportionately affected children from economically disadvantaged backgrounds.[34]

After my journey through the system, the government enacted major reforms in 1992 and 1999 through the Reform of Secondary Education (ROSE) program and the Grade Six Achievement Test (GSAT), which replaced the CEE. These efforts, along with an increase in the number of public high schools, expanded access and enabled nearly all primary school students to receive a quality secondary education.

Subsequent reforms included the rollout of the National Standards Curriculum (NSC) in 2016 and the replacement of the GSAT with the Primary Exit Profile (PEP) in 2019. These changes further modernized the system by emphasizing competency-based assessment, critical thinking, and twenty-first-century skills, while maintaining near-universal secondary enrollment.[35]

My Basic and Primary Schooling

My first school, which I started at around age three, was just a quarter mile from home: Miss Estelle Basic School, named after the single teacher who ran it. The one-room building was made of cinder blocks with an unfinished concrete floor, wooden doors and windows, and a sloped roof of galvanized zinc sheeting. Each desk was attached to a bench that seated three children. I'd estimate there were twenty to thirty students total, and the school day ran from 8:00 a.m. to 2:00 p.m.

Here, I learned the alphabet, how to count, simple addition and subtraction, nursery rhymes, social skills, one- and two-times multiplication tables, childhood games, and a few mantras. From the street, passersby could hear the discordant sounds of children's voices chanting their lessons, with Miss Estelle leading the way like the conductor of a choir in training.

One of the mantras we were required to recite daily, with rhythmic melody, became a profound guiding principle for the rest of my life. Whenever lofty goals seemed unachievable, or challenges obscured my path, I recalled this refrain: "Good, better, best, never let it rest, until your good is better and your better best."

I was always accompanied to and from school, usually by our live-in household helper. When our last helper left in 1971, my mother transferred me to the Mandeville Infant School, conveniently located just a short walk from her place of business. I completed my early childhood education there. At age five, I moved on to Richmond Primary School, about a mile and a half walk from home.

In grade one, the curriculum largely repeated what I'd learned in early childhood education. New skills—like cursive writing and more challenging arithmetic—arrived in grade two. Fueled by a growing enthusiasm for learning, I rose to third place in my class by the end of grade three. That momentum carried me to second place in both grade four and grade five.

I was so passionate about school that many mornings I was the first to arrive and had to wait for the gates to be opened. The few occasions I attempted to avoid school—mostly unsuccessfully—were whenever the Ministry of Health was scheduled to arrive and administer the dreaded vaccinations.

The curriculum placed heavy emphasis on composition writing to improve students' mastery of English and their ability to communicate ideas clearly and effectively. I still recall the daunting summer assignment after grade four: we had to write twenty compositions, each at least three pages long. That rigorous training laid the foundation for my ability to think critically, write descriptively, and argue persuasively—skills that would serve me well throughout my academic and professional life.

In grade five, at age nine, I was one of about ten students selected to join grade six students in sitting the CEE. Along with the other exam candidates, I attended special classes after regular school hours, where we were taught more advanced concepts in preparation for the exams.

Prep classes for CEE Math—the greatest challenge for most students—were taught by the school's most feared teacher, Mrs. J. She was short, somewhat stocky, of light complexion, wore her hair in a bun, and had a commanding voice that pierced through the air like a nail being hammered into wood. She quickly meted out corporal punishment to students who were inattentive or failed to complete assignments on time.

Thankfully, my grade five teacher, Mrs. B, taught with compassion, patience, and understanding—providing me an effective counterbalance to Mrs. J's bluster.

Around January 1978, I sat the CEE, hoping for a high score that would secure me a place at Manchester High School (MHS)—anecdotally the top-ranked high school in the parish, with far more students competing for its limited first-form slots. This was the first of many life-changing exams I would face. On exam day, my nervousness gave way to confidence, especially in the math section, which felt easy thanks to Mrs. J's rigorous teaching.

In June 1978, the list of successful students for the entire country, categorized by assigned high school, was published in the only national newspaper at the time, *The Gleaner*. I was at school when the news broke—I passed for MHS just as I had hoped.

Mrs. B was the first to inform and congratulate me, excitedly hugging me tightly. I was the only student from grade five and one of only five students from my school who were successful. Happily, my older niece was one of the four who passed from grade six. As for Mrs. J, her congratulations were somewhat muted, as she seemed disappointed that a classmate, her favorite grade-five candidate, was unsuccessful.

School of Hard Knocks

Beyond academics, primary school took me out of my protective infant bubble. To survive, I had to learn how to avoid altercations with the more disorderly and aggressive students, who routinely instigated fights. These rabble-rousers often issued threats to fellow students that they would be attacked after school. These threats often escalated into actual fights, with a crowd of students gathered to watch the spectacle like a sanctioned boxing event. Sometimes the clashes grew to involve entire student districts pitted against one another.

Unfortunately, one such inter-district rivalry pitted my district, New Hall, against Belretiro. The showdowns usually erupted at the street intersection where the main road branched toward each district. They often started with traded insults, escalated to fistfights, and ended with both sides pelting rocks across the divide like a medieval battle.

My mother, aware of this reprehensible juvenile misbehavior, warned me not to be a spectator or participant in any after-school mayhem. In obedience, I often had to dash from school at the ring of the final bell, usually with my cousins Chris and Tyrone in tow, running at breakneck speed until we had passed the battle intersection.

What I couldn't avoid were the bullies—mostly older students who targeted the younger and frailer ones. In grade two, I became the target of a grade-six boy named Byron. For several weeks, whenever our paths crossed on the walk home from school, he'd mischievously slap the side of my head, tug at my clothes, or rough me up however he pleased. It usually ended with him demanding, and me handing over, whatever money or food I had on me.

One day, I'd finally had enough. As Byron approached to grab my arm, in a reflex reaction, I swung my metal lunchbox with all my strength—connecting with his forehead and opening a gash. Blood poured down his face as my cousins and I ran as fast as we could.

I assume he dropped out of school after the incident, as I didn't see him again until years later when he surprisingly approached me on the street. He showed no anger, just smiled, pointed to the large scar on his forehead, and said, "Ah yu gi mi dis, yu memba?" He'd apparently accepted the fact that he'd picked on the wrong target too many times. As the Jamaican saying goes, "Duppy kno ahuu fi frighten,"* but in this case, he clearly had exhausted his window of opportunity.

My High School Academic Passage

In September 1978, I began my journey at Manchester High School (MHS), impeccably dressed in the mandatory khaki uniform. The school's brown-and-gold diagonally striped tie hung taut around my neck, emblazoned with the shield and motto "Sic Luceat Lux" ("Let your light so shine"). It was a proudly worn hand-me-down from my older brother Gerry. A few months earlier, I'd been diagnosed with hyperopia (farsightedness), and now the prescription eyeglasses perched on my nose made me feel like the classic little nerd. I didn't mind. I was ready.

I was finally a proud student at MHS, one of Jamaica's oldest and most prestigious institutions, founded in 1855 and celebrated for its academic rigor and strong extracurriculars.

The incoming first-form class numbered between 200 and 250 students. We were assigned in ascending age order to eight form rooms (the Jamaican equivalent of U.S. homerooms). As the youngest boy, I landed in the youngest form, with about twenty-eight students, and effectively became the youngest boy in the entire school of roughly 1,300. My fellow young classmates provided an aspirational and highly competitive environment.

For the first time, I was enrolled in distinct subjects, each with its own schedule: English Language, English Literature, History, Religious Education, Physical Education, Spanish as my first foreign language, Music, Family Circle, and the ones that interested me most—Integrated Science, Geography, and Mathematics.

Despite little or no parental academic supervision, mounting distractions, and frequent last-minute cramming (as I described in Chapter 5), I somehow managed to hold my own. I ranked fifth, eighth, and twelfth in my class across my first three terms.

---

* Translation: Byron: "You gave this to me, do you remember?" Saying: "A ghost knows who to frighten," which means assailants pick on those they think are weak or easily intimidated.

In the second form, French joined my roster of subjects, and I excelled—partly because I was captivated by the elegant sound of the language in my European French teacher's voice. Then came a descriptive writing assignment in English. My teacher's praise gave me a significant boost: I scored second highest in the class. Looking back, I credit that moment with sparking my lifelong love of writing. Though I claim no mastery and still have much to learn, it's a skill that has served me well in my academic and professional life.

In the third form, the school held a career day, bringing in professionals from diverse fields to introduce, discuss, and guide us toward a wide range of possible careers. For most of us, it was the first time we'd ever spoken one-on-one with such accomplished individuals—an aspirational expansion of our worldview.

In fourth form, more specialized subjects were introduced, and Integrated Science was split into its three core components: Physics, Chemistry, and Biology. With guidance counseling, we were expected to have at least a general sense of our future career path—whether in the liberal arts, business, or the sciences. We then chose subjects where we had performed well, those aligned with our chosen path, and started preparing for GCE and CSEC exams, which we would sit at the end of fifth form.

For the reasons I alluded to in Chapter 5, I decided to pursue becoming a Doctor of Dental Surgery (DDS) instead of my childhood dream of being a Doctor of Medicine (MD). This meant committing to a core science track, with other subjects added to round out my schedule.

A scheduling conflict between chemistry and French ended my pursuit of fluency in a foreign language—at least for the near future. Physics quickly became my favorite subject, fueled by a growing curiosity about the physical laws of nature. My British physics teacher, Mr. T, with his unorthodox and awe-inspiring teaching methods, only deepened that fascination.

In fifth form, while some classmates aimed to sit exams in nine subjects, I took an easier path—partly out of laziness, partly to spare my mother the exam fees for subjects I considered nonessential. Knowing that UWI required only five passes for admission, I focused on six core subjects and passed all of them: GCE O-level Physics, Biology, and Chemistry, plus CSEC Mathematics, English, and Geography.

In a last-minute registration decision, I added Art, expecting it to be light work. The GCE O-level exam included coursework—pieces of art completed during the year—and two final exam sittings. The exam included no theory—just painting a landscape from memory or imagination and drawing a preserved dead fish as a still life. I scored a "D," which was not a shocker—simply confirming that fine art wasn't my calling.

Following high school graduation at age fifteen, I advanced to sixth form and pursued GCE A-levels in Zoology, Chemistry, and Physics, along with the somewhat mandatory Use of English (or General Paper). I was determined to attend the University of the West Indies (UWI) for undergraduate studies after completing the two years of sixth form.

In my final year of sixth form, I made my first visit to the UWI Mona Campus—located in St. Andrew Parish, near the border with Kingston—and was immediately captivated by its beauty. That visit cemented my resolve to attend. I applied after sixth form and was admitted to the Faculty of Natural Sciences to pursue a Bachelor of Science degree. I regarded it as both an honor and a profound responsibility to be the first in my immediate and extended family to gain admission to Jamaica's only university at that time.

High School Beyond the Curriculum

High school exposed me to a much broader cross-section of society than primary school. My classmates came from more diverse economic and social backgrounds, and through this small world, I began to see the deep economic and social stratification that shaped Jamaica as a whole.

I started noticing roughly three tiers among my peers, although the boundaries sometimes blurred. At one level were wealthier classmates, mostly from private prep schools and two-parent households. Their parents were educated professionals, business owners, or held lucrative jobs at one of two bauxite mining companies (Alcan and ALPART). They were driven to and from school by chartered taxis, parents, or walked from some of the wealthy neighborhoods of Mandeville, where they mostly lived. They often talked about their vacations in Florida, private tennis lessons, and access to the town's country clubs.

Next were those who came from public primary schools in or near town and from two-parent homes. Their parents were mostly educated civil servants, such as teachers and nurses, with steady jobs that afforded them a stable, if modest, life. Many lived close enough to walk to school, were driven by parents, or traveled by ride-share taxis. They weren't as affluent as the first group, but they benefited from strong parental guidance and a clear focus on planning for tertiary education and long-term careers.

Rounding out the trio were the students who came from rural public primary schools, often from single-parent homes with limited financial resources. They sometimes had to help their families earn income by working in small family businesses or farms, or doing odd jobs. Ride-share taxis or minibuses were their only means of getting to and from school. Their parents lacked tertiary education—and often secondary education—which, combined with financial constraints, usually meant less emphasis on sending their children to college. This was the group from which I came.

Apart from a few classmates who were standoffish, I recall getting along well with everyone else. Still, I consciously kept a clear line between my life on campus and off. Friendships—especially with those from wealthier backgrounds—stayed at school. I worried that our unequal economic circumstances could lead to awkward or embarrassing situations outside those walls. When invited to house parties, I usually politely declined. I had no one to drive me there, and no easy way to get home afterward.

Unlike some classmates who lingered at school after the final bell, I usually made a quick exit unless something compelling was happening, such as an inter-school football match or athletics meet. This was partly because I wanted to help my mother at her shop, just a short walk from campus, or get home to indulge in my favorite hobby: riding my bicycle. My friends would sometimes tease me good-naturedly about how eagerly I left campus.

Over time, I came to realize this was a smart strategy for steering clear of the after-school vices and their consequences—detention, suspension, or worse. I often heard rumors of classmates hiding in empty classrooms to smoke cigarettes or ganja, engage in hormone-fueled encounters, and face punishment when caught.

Around third form, during breaks throughout the day, I started to hang out more with a growing circle of male friends. Since most of them already had nicknames, I knew it would be only a matter of time before I was given one. In the Jamaican tradition, I knew it could go either way—flattering or humiliating.

One day, during idle banter, I decided to share the story of the fearsome day I encountered Spaddy, which I detailed in Chapter 4. As soon as I concluded my narration, one friend declared that I deserved the name "Spaddy." There was instant, unanimous agreement, and the nickname stuck through high school and sixth form—though it evolved along the way.

As an ode to my signature Lionel Richie-inspired hairstyle, I was sometimes called Spaddy Richie or Lionel Spaddy. The variant, Spaddy General, was my favorite. Considering the possibility of far more humiliating nicknames, I embraced all without complaint. To this day, my high school friends still mostly call me Spaddy.

At some point, I made it known to my friends that my signature hairstyle was cut by me, not a barber. Word spread, and soon I had a lunchtime side hustle: cutting classmates' hair for $5 each.

My only school reprimand came in fourth form, when I decided to join the infamous "Bread Posse." The Bread Posse was a group of boys who would team up at lunchtime and head to a nearby bakery in town to purchase piping-hot loaves of bread and beef patties. After procuring the treats, we would then enter the nearby golf course at the Manchester Country Club—through an unsecured area—find a shaded area beneath a tree, and commence the lunchtime feast.

One day after lunch, at the suggestion of one or more ringleaders, we all marched in single file—like soldiers returning from battle—through the town back to campus. Reports of this unsanctioned parade of students, clearly identifiable by our uniforms, immediately reached the principal. Luckily, we escaped with just a strong reprimand and a warning of more serious consequences if it was repeated. Suffice it to say that my involvement with the group ended abruptly.

As school terms turned into years, I grew more confident and social—volunteering for class debates, joining the cadets (briefly), and attending end-of-year school parties. In fourth form, I joined three male classmates to perform a reggae dance at the annual variety concert. I also signed up excitedly for a duet with a female classmate to sing Peabo

Bryson and Roberta Flack's "Tonight I Celebrate My Love." Unfortunately, after a couple of practice sessions, she backed out before the show. But the singing bug had already taken root—more on that in later chapters.

At the start of sixth form, the faculty selected me as a prefect. The prefect body was small—led by a head boy and head girl—and selected for past good behavior and academic performance. Our role was to support the teachers in maintaining discipline, serve as role models and mentors for younger students, and help with various school activities.

I was assigned as a prefect for a first-form class of about twenty-five to thirty students. My role included helping them with assignments and maintaining order each morning before their form teacher arrived. Looking back, this was my first real taste of leadership—and the beginning of developing the skills needed to become an effective leader.

My First University Year

In September 1985, at age seventeen, with a student loan and some financial support from my mother, I matriculated at the University of the West Indies (UWI) and began my Bachelor of Science degree. I had been admitted to the second year, with the expectation of completing the program in three years. I registered for courses in Physics, Chemistry, Zoology, and others mandated by the university.

UWI was established in 1948 as an external college of the University of London and became fully independent in 1962. Until 1991—two years after I graduated—it retained the British three-term structure (Autumn, Spring, and Summer). Final exams covered the entire year's syllabus for multiple courses in each subject and were crammed into a roughly one-month window at the end of the academic year.[36]

In my first year, I chose to live off campus—boarding with family friends, first in Duhaney Park and later in Pembroke Hall—which turned out to be a mistake. The main problem was the chaotic, unreliable, and poorly regulated minibus system run by private operators. I faced long waits as overcrowded minibuses passed by, often with commuters hanging out of the doors, before one finally stopped that I could board. Then came the midway transfer at Half Way Tree, repeating the same frustrating wait. As a result, I frequently missed morning lectures and tutorials.[37]

Effectively, the twelve-mile commuting nightmare to and from campus gobbled up three hours of my day, leaving me drained by the time I returned home. In those moments of exhaustion, I drew encouragement and fortitude from two Jamaican maxims: "Ef yu waan gud, yuh nuoz haffi run" and "Di hotta di bakkle, di sweeta di victory."*

Like many undergraduates, I was navigating my first true foray into independence within a vastly different environment. Beyond the logistical hurdles of the commute, I was now fully responsible for the domestic trifecta of grocery shopping, cooking, and laundry—all while attempting to carve out time for the rigors of study.

Living so far from the Mona campus left me feeling isolated. While it shielded me from the distractions of campus parties and late-night socializing, it also cut me off from the benefits of joining study groups. Living among housemates who were not enrolled in tertiary studies further fragmented my focus. Though I was no stranger to a lack of parental academic supervision, university required more self-governance and focus than high school, which I was slow to master.

By the time my final exams approached, I was playing catch-up. I somehow got up to speed and passed my physics, zoology, and mandatory university courses. However, I suffered the first—and what would remain the only—consequential academic failure of my life. My failure in chemistry was a humbling blow; it meant my degree would now span four years rather than the three I had originally envisioned.

I spent the summer of 1986 in a state of rigorous self-examination, deconstructing my missteps and forging a resolve to return to the Mona campus, committed to succeeding at any cost.

The first and most obvious change I needed was to live within walking distance of—or on—campus. I chose the former, applied, and was accepted to board at the United Theological College of the West Indies (UTC), right across the street from UWI's rear entrance. Besides the proximity to UWI, boarding included dinner, and the accommodations consisted of four-bedroom cottages, each with a

---

* Translation: "If you want good, your nose has to run," and "The hotter the battle, the sweeter the victory," both imply that great success and reward require overcoming significant challenges.

shared bathroom, which I preferred to the large communal bathrooms in UWI's residence halls.

My Last Three Undergraduate Years

I returned to campus with a plan to successfully conquer my remaining three years. With my commuting challenge out of the way, I would endeavor to attend all lectures and tutorials, join a classmate or group for study marathons, and make better use of the now-accessible libraries and facilities.

Having already passed the labs, I registered to repeat the theory sections of second-year chemistry, along with the mandatory university courses. Motivated mainly by intellectual curiosity—and to fill out the rest of my schedule—I signed up for geology, which began at the second-year level. That decision would ultimately prove to be one of the most well-timed choices of my life.

From the very first geology classes, I realized my intellectual curiosity would be well served. Every topic and concept ignited my excitement, and I excelled. By the second term, my professors noticed my aptitude and enthusiasm, and I began connecting with third- and fourth-year geology students.

I was encouraged to apply for the annual scholarship awarded by the Geological Society of Jamaica to a third-year student. I submitted my application on time, stayed focused, and—after the year-end geology exams—finished at the top of my class. I also passed the repeated second-year chemistry.[38]

In the summer of 1987, along with a few other applicants, I was interviewed for the scholarship by a panel that included representatives from the sponsoring companies. Not long after, I learned I had been selected as the recipient. At the time, the scholarship was worth JA$10,000 per year and renewable for my fourth year if I maintained at least a B average.

The scholarship covered my boarding, tuition, books, and food expenses in full. This freed me from student loans and extra financial help from my aging mother, who was then a permanent resident in the United States.

In my third year, with geology as my major and zoology as my minor, I maintained my strong academic focus and performed well. At the end, I was rewarded with the renewal of my scholarship. That momentum carried me through my fourth and final year.

My most challenging and rewarding academic experience came in my final year of geology. As a geology major, I undertook a major research project that included four weeks of summer-break fieldwork, followed by laboratory analyses and a comprehensive final report.

In my final term, I submitted my 156-page project report titled "The Geology of the Essex Hall Area – Above Rocks Inlier, Jamaica" and defended my findings before the faculty. I earned an "A" for the project and graduated in June 1989, receiving my Bachelor of Science degree with Second Class Honours (Upper Division)—roughly equivalent to an A- average.

My initial failure in chemistry inadvertently steered me toward geology, earned me a prestigious scholarship, and led to my degree with honors. That unexpected reversal of fortune fundamentally reshaped my philosophy on failure. I came to see setbacks not as dead ends but as opportunities to pivot toward even greater things—a guiding principle I've carried with me ever since.

University Beyond the Curriculum

Like my earlier transition from primary to high school, university exposed me to an even more diverse cross-section of society. My classmates came not only from varied economic and social backgrounds in Jamaica, but also from other English-speaking Caribbean islands.[39] For the first time, I encountered a vibrant mix of cultures, accents, and personalities. This immersion into a truly multicultural environment proved invaluable later, when I immigrated to the United States.

I was fortunate to have around fifteen to twenty high school friends and acquaintances who were either at UWI or the nearby College of Arts, Science and Technology (CAST).[40] Additionally, the university's welcoming atmosphere helped me expand my circle within both academic and social groups.

Moving from the Mandeville area to Kingston felt, in essence, like a country boy coming to town. I left behind a small town's cool climate and fresh air for the big city's sweltering heat, humidity, and smog. Transportation shifted from familiar ride-share taxis to overcrowded, poorly regulated minibuses. Despite these challenges, I quickly adapted—embracing new entertainment options and facilities, and occasionally giving in to the city's alluring temptations.

My first visit to a strip club came in my first year at UWI, when a housemate invited me to what he called a "nice club." As I stepped inside, this naive country boy instantly understood what he meant: naked women on stage, men ogling from arm's length.

Shocked, I quickly retreated to the far back corner. My housemate called after me, "A weh yuh a guh? Cum ya suh, wey di gyal dem deh."*

On another occasion, a housemate invited me to a house party. I scored my first dance with a Kingston girl and, full of excitement, launched into my signature high-stepping, arm-swinging countryman skank.

She looked unimpressed—dismayed, even—by my lack of finesse in the intimate rub-a-dub style. She pulled me closer, leaned in, and whispered, "Jus rent a tile nuh mon."†

Suffice it to say, this country bumpkin had just damaged his prospects.

True to the Jamaican saying that "Chicken merry, hawk deh near,"‡ disturbing news came in February 1986, shortly after I started my second term at UWI. The Jamaican government, led by Prime Minister Edward Seaga, announced the imposition of a cess on students attending UWI and CAST.

The cess required that students, starting the next academic year, pay 10 percent of the tuition covered by the government. This move would end thirteen years of tuition-free education at UWI and CAST, which was implemented in 1973 under the prior prime minister, Michael Manley. For most students, including me, who were already struggling financially to pay for their tertiary education, this change hit hard. A storm of protests erupted across both campuses.[41]

---

* Translation: "Where are you going? Come here where the girls are."

† Translation: "Please, just rent a tile," which refers to the intimate, close-quarters, stationary dancing style known as rub-a-dub, where a couple occupies only a small space, like that of a single floor tile.

‡ Translation: "When the chicken is merry, the hawk is near," which means that in moments of joy, unexpected potential dangers and challenges may loom.

I threw myself fully into the student protests—boycotting classes and joining marches. The most powerful was a two-hour, five-mile trek from campus to the Ministry of Education, involving hundreds of students from UWI and CAST. Our improvised chants rang out in outrage as we waved handmade banners and placards, demanding an end to what we saw as a grave injustice and financial burden on students.

We soon expanded our efforts, rallying support from other tertiary institutions across the island. We believed UWI and CAST were only the beginning and that the "cess" would spread to other colleges if unchecked. Along with a fellow UWI student, I volunteered to carry our message to the Church Teachers' College in Mandeville.

With the cooperation of the college faculty, I delivered a resounding speech to a packed auditorium of students, calling for collective resistance to preserve free tertiary education. The response was rousing: thunderous applause, a standing ovation, and a flood of questions. My colleague and I left convinced we had their full moral support.

Months later, despite the unified efforts of students from UWI and CAST—some even tear-gassed and arrested—the cess was imposed as scheduled. Regardless, we had taken a brave, defiant stand, and I learned even a just cause can lose.

In my second year, after moving onto UTC's campus right across from UWI, I finally found a better balance between academics and extracurricular life. UTC organized friendly competitions by room letter (A through D) in each cottage, encouraging social interaction and harmony among students. I eagerly joined in, representing my room in chess and dominoes. My next big singing opportunity also arrived—this time, I wasn't going to miss out as I had in high school.

Near the end of each school year, UTC held a variety concert where students could showcase their talents. I signed up and performed Pinchers's *Hackle Mi Body* in front of a packed auditorium, using a large boombox and cassette tape to play the backing rhythm track and singing over a borrowed microphone.[42]

At the end of my performance, the packed auditorium erupted in roaring applause and gave me a standing ovation. What made it even more rewarding was that most of the audience were theology students—often skeptical of secular music. Over the following week, several UTC students approached me, asking me to join their choir, but, being non-religious, I politely declined each time.

It is also here on the UTC campus that I experienced the unsettling power of the earth shifting beneath me—my first and second earthquakes. As a geology student, I had the unique privilege of access to the UWI Earthquake Unit—Jamaica's main seismic monitoring and research hub. Yet, the intellectual intrigue of examining the fresh seismometer recordings was always tempered by a visceral, deep-seated fear.[43]

Kingston and its surrounding areas lie in a high seismic hazard zone due to their proximity to a major fault system. The region's subsurface—mostly loose alluvial sand and gravel—also makes it vulnerable to liquefaction during strong shaking. This combination has led to devastating historical earthquakes, most notably the 1692 Port Royal earthquake, which sank much of the city, and the 1907 Kingston earthquake, which leveled large parts of the capital and claimed thousands of lives.[44]

My first earthquake was a mild harbinger of what was to come. One morning in the shower, I felt the sensation of my cottage moving and naively thought someone was outside shaking the building—only to learn later it was a microearthquake that registered 1.2 on the Richter scale.

The second was far more intense. One afternoon during a final-exam study session in the library, my girlfriend (future wife) and I were suddenly jolted and tossed in our chairs as bookshelves swayed and tables slid across the floor. We held each other tightly; by the time we scrambled for cover, it was over—but that minute felt like an eternity. We had just endured a 4.4 earthquake, classified as "light" on the Richter scale.

In my third year, I moved from UTC to a private residence near campus for the first two terms. For my final term, I secured on-campus accommodation at UWI's Chancellor Hall. This shift to more communal living brought both positive and negative experiences. On the positive side, it fostered greater camaraderie, such as studying late with friends and fellow boarders. On the negative, I had to carefully time my use of the large communal bathroom, which—despite morning cleanings—was often in poor condition by day's end.

The most impactful event of my university years was meeting my first love and becoming engaged to my future wife at age twenty—the circumstances of which I'll detail in the next chapter. My engagement came just before my final academic year, as Jamaica struggled to recover from the devastation of Hurricane Gilbert—a Category 4 storm with sustained winds of 130 mph that made landfall on September 12, 1988. I did not experience the hurricane firsthand; I was in the United States at the time.

On my return to Jamaica, I saw the tragic aftermath of Hurricane Gilbert—the slow recovery due to limited resources, and the disproportionate suffering of those with the least means. Amid the devastation, however, there were still powerful signs of hope and resilience in the unbroken spirit and ingenuity of my fellow Jamaicans. UWI's facilities—classrooms, laboratories, and student housing—also suffered widespread damage, delaying the start of classes by about four weeks.

As fate would have it, while I was away, my fiancée found an apartment on the grounds behind the U.S. Embassy on Oxford Road—just four miles from campus. Each morning, I passed long lines of fellow Jamaicans waiting with visa petitions in hand, hope shining in their eyes—lines swollen in the wake of Hurricane Gilbert. By early afternoon, joy lit the faces of the fortunate few whose dreams came true, while rejection shadowed most. I had lived that same hope and heartbreak myself, which I'll detail in a later chapter.

My journey—from the simplicity of basic school through the rigors of university—gave me a wealth of knowledge and skills: some from within classroom walls, many more from the world beyond. Collectively, these experiences acted as the guide rails that shaped the direction of my life and career. I remain profoundly grateful for the challenges that tested me and the opportunities that allowed me to thrive.

LIFE LESSONS

1. Find your lifelong mantra. Let it anchor you, honor every small win, and keep you aimed at becoming your best.

2. Some failures are blessings in disguise. They redirect us toward paths far richer than any success could have carved. In the throes of despair, trust that the universe knows best.

3. Never waste a second chance to reach your zenith; a third is not guaranteed.

4. Disasters are inevitable and often unpredictable. Survival hangs on the thin line where preparation meets luck. Prepare well, then discharge the rest to the universe.

Richmond Primary School in 2010 (attended 1973–1978)

Manchester High School (attended 1978–1985)
Photograph courtesy of Kevon Clayton, 2026, Instagram: @portraitsbykevon

Partial view of the UWI, Mona Campus (attended 1985–1989)
Photo courtesy of Rush Raymore Reviews-Jamaica (YouTube), taken in 2022.

(This page intentionally left blank.)

CHAPTER 9

More Than Just a Feeling

Making the choice to love

During my adolescence, prior to my second year at university, I had a few short-lived intimate relationships. None, however, aroused in me the profound feeling that I understood as being in love, nor was I actively seeking such a bond. I was content in my emotional independence, unaware that change was on the immediate horizon. That dramatic shift came during my second week living on the campus of the United Theological College of the West Indies (UTC).

At around 5 p.m. one weekday, accompanied by a cottage-mate, I joined the dinner queue at the cafeteria. Standing ahead of us was the lady who—without knowing it—was about to capture my heart.

Before I was even fully aware of her presence, my cottage-mate said, in his strong Vincentian accent, "Eric, I like that girl for you."

I assumed it was part of an ongoing joke we ran and brushed him off, but he looked at me with all seriousness and said, "This time I'm not joking."

I then turned to fully observe her form and comportment, catching a view of her face as she glanced around. Looking back at him, I said, "I like her for me too."

She was fair in complexion, with beautiful, beaming eyes, radiant cheeks, and sported a pixie cut hairstyle like Anita Baker's. She stood at around five feet tall but was propped up a few more inches by her chic pumps. She was casually but attractively dressed in a pair of tight-fitting jeans and a short-sleeve blouse that accentuated her physical assets. She seemed to exude quintessential femininity.

Bravely, I stepped up to her and introduced myself with as much charm as I could muster. The smile she gave me in return was warm and vibrant; her voice was soft and confident: "Hi, I'm Lisa. How are you?"

During a long dinner conversation, I learned that she was a postgraduate student at UWI's Norman Manley Law School, age twenty-two—four years my senior—and spoke English almost exclusively, with weak, faint attempts at Patois. By the end, I sensed winning her heart would be difficult, but I was determined to try.

Over the next few months, I thoughtfully pursued her: timing my visits to the cafeteria to coincide with her dinner hours, inviting her to campus events, and showing care through small, considerate gestures. Eventually, she told me she thought I was a player trying to "conquer" an older girl, that my infatuation would fade, and she preferred to stay just friends. I walked away feeling dejected. In the days that followed, I quietly considered my options.

The answer was clear to me: I could not be her platonic friend. Being around her and unable to express the deep attraction and passion I felt would have been torturous. I told her so. She brushed it aside as youthful immaturity, but she would come to realize I was serious. From then on, I stopped coordinating my cafeteria hours with hers and made every effort to avoid her. I honestly wasn't trying to test the old saying that "absence makes the heart grow fonder"—I was simply protecting my heart and making room for other possibilities.

Aware of my persistent avoidance, she unexpectedly came to my cottage one evening—with a friend of hers providing moral support—to ask me to the Law School's Christmas party. Not wanting to embarrass her with a rejection in front of her friend, I responded unenthusiastically, "Well, if you insist, then yes."

I was under no illusion that this meant a change in her platonic stance, and I fought to keep my emotions in check the night of the party. After, we parted for the four-week Christmas break.

During the break, I met someone new and tried to push Lisa from my mind—but it was of no use.

When I returned to UTC in January 1987, I continued avoiding her. One day, she timed her approach and intercepted me, asking with feigned innocence, "Why are you avoiding me?"

I answered calmly, "Didn't I explain months ago that I can't be your platonic friend?"

She again brushed me off with her simplistic "Stop being so immature." The exchange again left me convinced—she still wasn't ready to see me as anything more.

A couple of weeks later, needing clothes pegs to sun-dry my laundry, I hesitated but went to borrow some from a former female classmate who lived in the same cottage as Lisa. When I knocked, Lisa opened the door.

I explained I was looking for her roommate to borrow some clothes pegs, but she wasn't home. As I turned to leave, Lisa called out, "Stop being silly! Please wait—let me lend you mine."

Later that evening, when I returned the borrowed items, she invited me inside with a warm voice: "Please come in."

This was my first time entering her room, and—though brief—it led to my long-awaited first kiss. I felt my unfulfilled desire was about to blossom into something real—coincidentally on Valentine's Day.

But this was not going to be a sprint; it would be a slow, careful walk until she was convinced I was truly ready for a serious relationship.

After weeks of slow, incremental progress, I ached for her passion and could no longer contain the intensity of my hushed desires. So, I poured my heart into a written declaration of love—twelve poetic stanzas—and delivered it to her.

I allowed myself to be completely vulnerable, guided only by emotion, because winning her heart was worth the risk. In those lines, I confessed my constant yearning to be near her, the heavy ache of her absence, and how difficult it was to say goodbye—even if just until the very next day. I told her these novel feelings had crumbled my protective walls and left me terrified. I spoke of her alluring attributes, and that, with her, I felt the true manifestation of love for the first time.

I endured a sleepless night waiting for her response, which arrived early the next morning: a heartwarming, handwritten declaration of her own love, mirroring mine.

She now seemed convinced of my sincerity and equally desirous of a committed relationship. The most profound stanza in her response spoke of her recognition that my desire for her went far beyond lustful passion—she saw it in my eyes. And in my words, she heard more than the vain flattery that fell from other men's lips—something deeper, something the eye alone could not see.

From that moment on, we were inseparable—spending nearly all our free time together. I came to know her immediate family and close relatives, and we shared holidays with each other's families, weaving our lives more closely together.

She graduated from law school in June 1988 and began practicing as a government attorney. As a natural progression of our deep, mutual love and commitment, I proposed. We got engaged in late September 1988 and lived together for the last three terms of my final academic year.

Living with Lisa brought me emotional stability, tranquility, and exuberant happiness—further fueling my drive to study hard and finish strong. After earning my degree, I returned to the United States in early June 1989. We married in December 1989—the rest of our story unfolds in a later chapter.

LIFE LESSONS

1. True love cannot manifest without the willingness to be open and vulnerable to unreciprocated desire. Still, the immeasurable reward outweighs any disappointment.

CHAPTER 10

A Religious Evolution

Navigating faith, logic, and consciousness

Jamaica's Religiosity

In the 1970s era of my childhood, I was enmeshed in a society where religious beliefs and practices were dominated by Christianity and its abundant Protestant denominations. I heard of Catholicism only as it related to schools of Catholic origin or those that were still under Catholic control. I did not personally know anyone who attended the relatively few Catholic churches.[45]

Among the Christian denominations were those of European origin, which included the Anglican (Church of England), Baptist, Methodist, Presbyterian, and Moravian. Those of U.S. origin included the Church of God, Pentecostals, Church of Christ, Seventh-day Adventists, Jehovah's Witnesses, and the Church of Jesus Christ of Latter-day Saints (Mormons). Those that were strongly influenced by and incorporated African spiritual beliefs and practices included the Revival Zion, the Church of God, the Pentecostals, Pocomania, Kumina, the Ethiopian Zion Coptic, the Native Baptists, the Spiritual Baptists, and Obeah. Rastafari is not included here, as Rastafarians consider it a way of life—not a religion—which I'll discuss later in this chapter.[46]

Given the foregoing, it's no surprise Jamaica is said to hold the Guinness World Record for the most churches per square mile—an anecdote I've heard since my youth. Ironically, the island also claims the world record for the most rum bars per square mile. This is a paradox that I'll leave to you, the reader, to unravel.*

My Early Religious Education

I was raised by my mother in the Christian tradition, attending Sunday services with her and my siblings at the Richmond Church of Christ. Before every meal, I recited the same memorized grace: "For health and strength and daily food, we praise thy name, O Lord. Amen." Each night, I repeated the familiar bedtime prayer: "Now I lay me down to sleep, I pray the Lord my soul to keep. And if I die before I wake, I pray the Lord my soul to take. Amen." At school, morning devotions and prayers were required, always rooted in Christian tradition. Religious Education, based on Christian beliefs, was also a mandatory subject during my early high school years.

I learned at a young age, through the "hell and brimstone" sermons—commonly preached from the church pulpit—that failing to abide by the commandments and the teachings of Jesus Christ would condemn me to eternal hell upon his second coming. These messages underpinned the church's proselytizing mission of winning converts but instilled more fear than joy in my consciousness.

Around age eight, after most of my siblings had converted to the Seventh-day Adventist denomination, I followed suit. Surprisingly, while my mother remained with the Church of Christ, she never opposed my decision. I assumed it was because her own father was an Adventist. Her understanding that I would attend church weekly seemed to outweigh any reservations she may have had.

While the trademark "hell and brimstone" messages were also routinely delivered by the Adventists, there were marked differences in how they interpreted Bible scriptures and prophecy. Much of this interpretation was based on the teachings of Ellen G. White (1827–

---

* The claim that Jamaica has the most churches per square mile is frequently attributed to Guinness World Records, though the specific criteria and whether it remains an active record have varied across editions and are difficult to verify in current official listings. The claim of the most rum bars per square mile is a well-known anecdote in Jamaican culture, frequently repeated in travel literature and among the locals.

1915), who was the co-founder of the church and considered a prophetess.

True to its name, the church followed the Ten Commandments literally in its day of worship—the seventh day, Saturday, as the Sabbath. There was also a strong emphasis on healthy living—preferably vegetarian—and on the imminent return of Christ. This Second Advent, they believed, would come once the church's message (the truth) had reached every person on earth—seemingly within a few years rather than decades.

There was a strong sense of camaraderie among the members, who tended to spend almost the entire Saturday together. Morning services were followed by Saturday afternoon Bible studies, and after sunset, social gatherings lasted for hours. I learned to pray from my own heart rather than just reciting memorized words, and I attended Richmond Seventh-day Adventist Church with real fervor. For the most part, I embraced the belief system wholeheartedly.[47]

After moving to the Hillside District, I found myself surrounded by four branches of the church—all within walking distance. The most impressive chapel, which I often attended, stood on the campus of the nearby West Indies College, a Seventh-day Adventist institution. My fervor—and even a year-long stint as a strict vegetarian—continued until around age thirteen. Yet at no point did I feel compelled to take the ultimate step of baptism.

A key source of my underlying hesitation was the church's messaging against "earthly" aspirations. The belief was that material possessions could distract from divine worship—and were ultimately pointless given Christ's imminent return. I came to hold a different view: God expects us to fully steward our talents, and if that results in earthly prosperity, we should use it to help those who are less fortunate.

Perhaps fueled by raging teenage hormones, I found myself increasingly distracted during Saturday sermons—my attention drifting from the pulpit to the girls in attendance. While I believed in the existence of God, I began to quietly question the blind acceptance of biblical narratives and prophecies, many of which clashed with my growing sense of logic. Church attendance started to feel disingenuous, so at age fourteen, I stopped going.

Despite my departure from the church, I still held deep convictions rooted in certain core teachings of Christ—those that echoed my innate sense of goodness. Humility, compassion, and charity—as beautifully embodied in the Beatitudes and stories like the woman at the well, the Good Samaritan, the washing of the disciples' feet, and the widow's offering—continued to guide my path.

Concepts Beyond Christianity

Up to the time of my departure from the church, my understanding of God was shaped entirely by Christian doctrine. I had very little exposure to other religious beliefs, atheism, or agnosticism, and only a superficial awareness of Rastafarian values. That limited perspective was now on the verge of a gradual, quiet transformation.

One of the artisans who supplied goods to my mother's shop, Bongo Jerry, was a Rastafarian. His genuine and friendly nature drew me into long conversations whenever he made deliveries. Through those talks, he patiently shared the principles of his faith and gently dispelled the negative stereotypes that had previously clouded my understanding.

Rastafariani uses and interprets the Christian Bible in its own unique way. Most adherents view the movement not as a religion in the conventional sense, but as a way of life. At its heart is the belief that Haile Selassie I, Emperor of Ethiopia, is God incarnate—the Second Advent of Jesus Christ. The faith is deeply Afrocentric, rejecting Western societal values and the oppression of the African diaspora while advocating for repatriation to Africa.[48]

Bongo Jerry taught me about Rastafarian humility, healthy, organic living, the avoidance of destructive vices such as alcohol, cigarettes, and other drugs, the sacred use of ganja, deep respect for women as empresses, and the enduring principle of "one love" for all humanity. I left every conversation with newfound enlightenment, useful knowledge, and an "irie" feeling.

Around age fifteen, a girl I was actively courting in high school told me matter-of-factly that she was an atheist. Until then, I had thought atheism was some abstract idea from a distant land—not something that existed in Jamaica.

Utterly stunned, I asked, "What do you mean? How could you not believe in God?"

In a calm, nonchalant way, she replied, "Don't worry, I respect your beliefs—this doesn't mean we can't be friends."

But I couldn't return the same respect. I quietly withdrew my interest and began distancing myself from her.

That brief encounter stayed with me longer than I expected. It planted a small seed of curiosity about belief systems I had never seriously questioned—curiosity that would grow quietly over the next couple of years until it met the wider lens of university.

During my undergraduate years at UWI, my scientific education deepened the cognitive dissonance I already felt between logic and faith. In a general requirements course called "The Development of Civilization," I learned that other monotheistic religions predated the Judeo-Christian traditions. This stood in stark contrast to the Christian doctrine of my youth, which presented Judaism as the first true monotheism, followed by Christianity as the salvation of humankind from earlier "sinful" polytheism and idolatry.

Through logical reasoning and the evidence I encountered, I came to accept Darwin's theory of evolution by natural selection over the Biblical creation account. Through my geological education, I learned the science of radiometric dating, which established the Earth's age at 4.5 billion years—far older than the 6,000–10,000 years suggested by literal readings of scripture. In many informal debates about the origin of the universe, I found science silent on what—if anything—preceded the Big Bang. My Christian friends, in turn, could not explain who created God. On both sides, I realized, we faced limits we could not cross.[49]

By this point, the logic of science had taken precedence over every conflicting Biblical narrative. I found myself left with an agnostic conviction: I neither knew nor denied the existence of God, nor could I say whether such a thing could ever be known.

Extrasensory Perception

My earliest exposure to claims of ethereal energies came from the duppy stories I heard as a child (shared in Chapter 3). Because they were others' experiences, I viewed them abstractly, with no real impact on my developing beliefs.

My first personal experience that triggered thoughts of extrasensory capabilities—beyond our five senses—happened in late August 2001. I awoke from a dream so vivid and impactful that I sat up in bed with my heart pounding and my hair standing on end. In it, I saw one of the iconic World Trade Center (WTC) towers engulfed in flames. The intense foreboding I quickly attributed to having worked inside the WTC from 1992 to early 1994. I calmed myself—after all, I no longer worked there—and dismissed it as an irrational nightmare before going back to sleep.

On the morning of September 11, 2001, shortly after entering my office in lower Manhattan, I heard rising chatter, sirens, and an announcement to evacuate the building immediately. A plane had crashed into the north tower of the WTC, just several city blocks away. As we gathered in Battery Park, a second plane hit the south tower. From there, I watched smoke pour from near the tops of both buildings.

Around 10 a.m., the crowd began running south toward the Staten Island Ferry Terminal. Enveloped in clouds of dust and ash that turned a bright day to dusk, I joined the stampede. News spread that the south tower had collapsed. I waited in the crowded terminal until the air cleared somewhat and the skies brightened, as I planned my nearest escape route by foot from Manhattan.

Just as I started to leave the ferry terminal, I saw a fresh cloud of dust and ash approaching—I quickly retreated. The North Tower had just collapsed. About a half-hour later, with a pungent odor and soot still permeating the air, I joined thousands walking toward and across the Brooklyn Bridge. Cell networks were overloaded, so I kept walking for several miles before I could finally call for a ride home.[50]

After showering off the soot and acrid odor that still clung to my skin, I sat down to watch the news. As footage replayed the flames bursting from the side of one tower, I froze. The images matched my dream almost exactly.

This experience triggered deep introspection. Why had such a catastrophic event been partly revealed to me weeks earlier—not symbolically, but literally? What could I have done with such an incomplete premonition, and who would have found it credible or useful? Those unanswered questions stifled any desire to contemplate or further explore extrasensory perceptive possibilities. However, nine years later, what I experienced following my mother's death on December 20, 2010—which I described in Chapter 7—compelled me to reopen and examine deeper questions about consciousness and God.

My Concept of God

My inner sense now tells me that death involves a twofold transition: the physical body's contents—molecules, atoms, and bounded energies—disperse into the environment according to the second law of thermodynamics, while nonphysical consciousness—our subjective experiences, memories, thoughts, beliefs, and awareness—departs the body intact. I see consciousness and soul as deeply intertwined. While we are alive, our soul expresses itself as our consciousness in the physical world, but also provides a channel of communication with a nonphysical realm. When we die, our soul transitions to permanently join this nonphysical realm.[51]

Perhaps that other realm is a collective consciousness—the realm of the sixth sense—that the brain can access only when it is not bound by waking consciousness, through intuition or dreams. It may have been through this collective consciousness that an element of the horrific attack on the World Trade Center was revealed to me beforehand.

These beliefs—fueled by my instincts, extrasensory perceptions, and philosophical exploration—have shaped my current concept of God, which is by no means unique. I believe God is an all-encompassing universal consciousness manifested in all conscious mortal beings, yet eternally immortal in itself—the realm of the sixth sense. Thus, I am spiritual but not religious. This belief does not conflict with my acceptance of scientific logic, as science still grapples with fundamental questions about where consciousness resides and what happens to it upon death.

Admittedly, I have yet to deeply explore many of the world's religions and their beliefs. Yet, I respect every person's path—whether religious or atheistic beliefs—so long as it fosters personal fulfillment, elevates well-being, and causes no harm to others. I sense that while we view reality through different lenses, we are all connected by a shared consciousness.

On matters of God, consciousness, and the meaning of life, I will always keep an open mind. Human scientific knowledge of the physical universe remains limited by our current frameworks—general relativity and quantum mechanics. I suspect that within and beyond these frameworks lie other undiscovered mysteries. As someone shaped by science and inspired by the rise of artificial intelligence, I believe AI may one day help reveal those unknowns—perhaps by expanding our capacity to probe what we cannot yet grasp. Until then, I will seek to find comfort in the uncertainty.

LIFE LESSONS

1. Respect any religious belief or practice, provided it uplifts the spirit, improves well-being, and makes society more humane. Anything less simply hasn't earned your reverence.

2. Arguably, no one—religious, atheist, or agnostic—has enough evidence to defend their deepest convictions by logic alone. In the final step, everyone places faith in uncertainty.

3. Stay stubbornly open to the universe's ethereal possibilities and never stop searching for truth.

4. Trust the universe in all its grandeur. It is infinitely intelligent and will guide humanity to its ultimate destiny.

CHAPTER 11

Crossing Borders, Planting New Roots

Aspiration, immersion, and transculturation

My Path to Permanent Immigration

Many Jamaicans, lacking generational wealth and eager to improve their lives, saw immigration to the United States as their beacon of hope—a land offering economic and educational opportunities beyond what was possible at home.

Two decades after the 1965 U.S. Immigration and Nationality Act first eased immigration restrictions, President Ronald Reagan signed the Immigration Reform and Control Act (IRCA) on November 6, 1986. This law granted legal status to many undocumented Jamaican pioneers who had arrived years earlier. Once legalized, they could petition for immediate relatives, further accelerating the wave of Jamaican migration to the United States.[52]

By 1977, two of my siblings had already immigrated to the United States. Their remittances—cash sent home and barrels filled with clothes, shoes, and American food—only deepened our fascination and longing to follow. Showing up to school with those new gifts quickly drew the familiar chorus from classmates: "Barrel come!" In the early 1980s, when my mother began making periodic visits to the U.S., she brought back gifts and firsthand accounts of low-cost goods and services, further amplifying the appeal. She also permanently immigrated to the United States in 1985.

At around age eighteen, I set out from Mandeville before daybreak one summer morning for the U.S. Embassy in Kingston, hoping to secure a non-immigrant visitor visa. I joined the long queue of hopeful applicants filling out forms and, hours later, was finally called for my interview with a consular officer.

Everything seemed to be going smoothly until she asked, “Are your parents married and living together?”

I answered truthfully, “No.”

She immediately turned away to consult a colleague, then returned a minute later with the denial.

Disappointed, I walked away knowing the Jamaican truth: “Evri dawg hab im day an evri puss im four o’clock.”* This simply wasn’t my path—something better lay ahead.

Around October 1987—about a year and a half after my visitor visa denial—my mother’s petition for my permanent residency reached the U.S. Embassy. I was notified of the steps to complete before my interview.

Earlier that year, on May 15, 1987, the U.S. Public Health Service had added a controversial requirement: mandatory HIV testing for all permanent visa applicants, with a positive result barring entry. Though I believed I had no reason to worry—and I was proven correct—the fear surrounding those early days of HIV testing was inescapable.[53]

On the morning of my interview, I was directed to a different section of the embassy, bypassing the long queue of hopefuls seeking visitor visas. I had reviewed the list of requirements meticulously—multiple times—and felt thoroughly prepared. This moment was my opportunity to pursue the American dream, for which I had long aspired. I was ready.

The process was quicker than I imagined. By afternoon, I had my approval and a sealed envelope to present to U.S. Immigration upon arrival. I was overjoyed—feeling privileged, deeply grateful, and truly blessed. Later that day, I called my mother to share the news. She was equally jubilant, and I thanked her profusely.

---

* Translation: “Every dog has his day and every cat his four o’clock,” meaning that everyone will get their opportunity at some point, so be patient.

Landing in America

In December 1987, after completing the first term of my third year at UWI, I set foot on American soil for the first time. I landed at John F. Kennedy (JFK) Airport in New York City on a cold winter night, handed my sealed envelope to the immigration officer, and was fingerprinted. The coincidence—or perhaps destiny—was not lost on me: the same JFK whose portrait had hung on our dining room wall in childhood was now the gateway to the life I had long dreamed of.

As I stepped out of customs, my eldest brother, Gerry, was waiting with a warm coat, ready to face the frigid winter air outside. I slipped into his car, and he drove us toward Brooklyn, where my mother anxiously awaited my arrival.

My senses were on alert as I glanced in every direction, eager to absorb as much as I could of the "promised land." As we exited the highway and traversed the streets of Brooklyn, I was struck by the graffiti, the monotony of red-brick building facades, seemingly battle-scarred high-rises, and the shuttered shopfronts and corner stores. I was astonished—perhaps naively—this was nothing like the image I had carried in my mind. My thoughts drifted to movies I had watched, such as *Beat Street*, which had portrayed similar urban scenes; yet, seeing them in person felt utterly different.

I was still adapting to the sights of Brooklyn when we reached my mother's humble one-bedroom apartment on the first floor of a pre-World War II red-brick building in the Flatlands neighborhood. I stepped inside, and the moment I saw her, I was elated—hugging and kissing her for the first time in over two years.

As we chatted, my mother sensed my "fish out of water" feeling and asked gently, "Son, yu nuh happi fi dey eir?"

I swallowed hard, mustered as much excitement as I could, and answered, "Yes, Mama, a wey mek yu aks mi dat? Yu kno sey mi glad fi si yu. Mi jus a try git used tuh di place."*

In the days that followed, I opened up and admitted my initial trepidation.

---

* Translation: Mother: "Son, aren't you happy to be here?" Me: "Yes, Mama, why did you ask me that? You know that I'm happy to see you. I'm just trying to get used to the place (environment)."

Brooklyn became my new home—except for the terms I would spend back at UWI completing my degree. My mother did everything she could to make me feel settled, and I gradually began to adjust. With family, I started venturing beyond Brooklyn to Queens and Long Island. But it was Manhattan that finally shattered my sense of a general lack of grandeur.

On my first subway ride, accompanied by a niece, I emerged from a station in Manhattan looking skyward—transfixed by the towering midtown skyscrapers all around me. In a quiet sigh of relief, I whispered to myself, "Finally, this is the United States I envisioned."

Days later, my sister Olive took me to the top of the Empire State Building. From that height, I gazed in amazement at the vast sprawl of New York's five boroughs and the neighboring state of New Jersey. This was the "Big Apple" in all its splendor—from Manhattan's gleaming opulence to the rough-and-tumble streets of the outer boroughs. This was now my new home, with all its opportunities and challenges still waiting to be explored.

I greeted my first snowfall with pure excitement—seeing and touching snow for the first time felt like magic. The novelty of a cold winter thrilled me, and I gave little thought to the downsides I'd discover in years ahead. On Christmas Day, I celebrated my twentieth birthday in the United States with family and friends—the first of many to come.

Bearing gifts for my girlfriend, I returned to Jamaica in mid-to-late January 1988 to start the next term at UWI. The fantastical myth of an America of abundance for all had given way to a more realistic view: like Jamaica, inequality was stark, with poverty and squalor often just steps from centers of wealth and power. Only through hard work and dedication could the American dream truly be realized.

In late May 1988, at the end of the school year, I returned to the United States—this time to Florida, where two of my brothers lived. I was hell-bent on getting a job as soon as possible. Within days, I was interviewed and offered a position at a nearby McDonald's restaurant.

A couple of days before my start date, I called my mother to tell her about the job. Her reaction caught me off guard—she broke into sobs:

"But Junior, mi hab mi hawt set sey yu ongle wudda tan dey fi tuu week, den cum tan wid mi ah Brooklyn fi di rest addi summa."*

I was torn between the opportunity and her longing. In the end, I chose her—I turned down the job and flew to New York.

I was still determined to find a summer job—ideally one that paid better than McDonald's. I bought newspapers and scanned the classifieds. Aha! There it was: "Make up to $13 per hour as a foot messenger in Manhattan." That was nearly four times the $3.35 minimum wage at the time. I called immediately and arranged an interview for the next morning.[54]

I arrived, filled out the application, was interviewed, hired on the spot, and told to report the next morning. The job involved delivering mostly envelopes and small handheld packages. Pay ranged from $2 to $5 for most small deliveries (as told to you when assigned), with subway tokens provided only for trips over ten city blocks. Larger packages could earn up to $10.

I showed up promptly the next morning and was sent off on my first two deliveries by foot—a round trip of about twelve blocks that earned me roughly $5. When I returned, I was assigned another two or three, but I noticed the seasoned veterans were getting ten or more each time. That pattern held with every trip back.

The temperature that day hovered around 85°F or higher, with thick, oppressive humidity hanging in the air. By about 2 p.m., I had already spent roughly $12 on food and water to fuel my long treks across the city—about half my earnings so far.

At the end of the day, my feet were swollen as I boarded the subway back to Brooklyn. Riding home, I muttered to myself, "Dem tink mi ah Ali Button wuk fi nutten?"†

I concluded that the advertised "up to $13 per hour" was clearly meant for long-term messengers, not students doing temporary summer work.

---

* Translation: "But Junior, I had my heart set that you would only stay there for two weeks, then come and stay with me in Brooklyn for the rest of the summer."

† Translation: "Do they think I am an Ali Button that works for nothing?" In Jamaica, "Ali Button" refers to someone who works hard with little or no reward, essentially being exploited.

The next morning, with my feet still swollen and aching, I decided to quit my first U.S. job after just one day. A few days later, I collected my paycheck—$26 after taxes and deductions. That measly sum drove home the hard truth many low-skilled immigrants face: surviving often means juggling multiple low-paying jobs to make ends meet.

For the rest of the summer, I got occasional work at an advertising consultancy owned by my brother Gerry. I also did some sightseeing, visiting the top of the World Trade Center and the Museum of Natural History. In late September 1988, I returned to Jamaica for my final year at UWI, which started later than usual because of the damage Hurricane Gilbert had caused on campus.

Full Immersion

After completing my Bachelor of Science degree, I left my fiancée in Jamaica in June 1989, planning to return in December for our wedding. After landing at JFK, I went straight back to my mother's apartment in Brooklyn with grit and determination to succeed—no matter what it took. With a wedding just six months away, I needed a job immediately. I updated my resume—thin on work experience—and began the hunt.

I was joining the hundreds of thousands of fellow hardworking Jamaican immigrants who called New York City and the surrounding regions home. The community had earned a reputation for an outstanding work ethic—a cultural hallmark so strong that it was often parodied by comedians. This was most famously captured in the TV sketch comedy show *In Living Color*, where the recurring "Hey Mon" sketches featured a Jamaican family named Hedley. The patriarch often proudly listed his dozen-plus jobs and mocked anyone with "only one job" as lazy.

During that era, Jamaican immigrants had labor-force participation rates that often surpassed those of the native-born population. They worked across a wide range of sectors—service industries, transportation, construction, and manufacturing—and a significant portion held professional and technical roles, especially in healthcare, education, management, and business. This reflected both the education and skills many brought from Jamaica and their steady career advancement over time. They undeniably strengthened the U.S.

economy by generating more tax revenue, filling critical labor shortages, and boosting GDP through higher productivity and consumer spending.[55]

While searching for a job better aligned with my education and expectations, I took a practical retail position to cover immediate expenses—one with flexible hours that let me attend interviews. I was hired at a nearby Alexander's Department Store (a major New York-area chain that closed in 1992), working the cash register and sales floor.

During this time, I also applied for my driver's license and passed after the second road test. Accustomed to driving on the left in Jamaica, I failed the first test when—after a three-point turn on an empty road—I continued driving in the left opposing lane, startling the examiner.

By late August, I had two significant job options: an offer from an environmental consulting company and an invitation to interview with a New York City government agency. I chose the consulting position because a trusted acquaintance who already worked there recommended me. It also aligned more closely with my field of study and offered the promise of overtime—exactly what I needed to maximize my income.

After orientation at the company's Manhattan office (my home base), I was sent to the head office in Boston for a week of training. My first field assignment was to inspect and oversee a hazardous materials abatement project at an airline terminal at JFK Airport. Once again, the coincidence struck me: the same JFK whose portrait had hung in our childhood dining room was now the site of my first real professional step in the United States.

I quickly mastered my assigned duties to my supervisor's satisfaction and began racking up overtime. Within a few weeks, I was offered an additional twenty-four hours of overtime per week at a nearby terminal. To make commuting between JFK and my mother's Brooklyn apartment manageable, I needed a car. Just three months after arriving in the United States, I bought my first new car—a black Volkswagen Jetta—with my brother Gerry cosigning the loan.

I was now on my way—working upwards of seventy-six hours a week and earning time-and-a-half or double time for overtime. Naively oblivious to the dangers of driving while sleep-deprived, I had my first near-tragic accident—less than a month after buying the car—on the drive home from work around 12:30 p.m. one weekday.

It was a hot day, so I rolled up the windows, cranked the air conditioning, slid in one of my favorite reggae cassettes, and pumped up the volume. I exited the airport and merged onto the Belt Parkway heading west.

About fifteen minutes later, a loud pattering on the hood jolted me awake. Opening my eyes, I saw bulrushes being flattened in front as the car veered off the right side of the highway. I reacted instantly, yanking the wheel to steer back onto the shoulder. The sharp jolt blew out both left-side tires—sliced by the pavement's jagged edge.

Finally, the car came to a stop. I sat there in total shock—heart racing, hands shaking. After a few minutes, I calmed down enough to step out and check the damage. Miraculously, the body had no dents—just scuffed paint from the bulrushes. The two left-side tires and hubcaps were ruined. Realizing how much worse it could have been, I released a long, quivering sigh of relief.

This was a stark warning: balance material gains with well-being and recognize that unknown hazards can strike at any time. I reflected on the lyrics of Bob Marley's *Rat Race*, which warns against being trapped in endless, questionable pursuits—and the danger of complacency: "When you think it's peace and safety, it's sudden destruction."[56]

I asked myself, "What if in that split second that I fell asleep, the car had veered left instead, and crashed into adjacent-lane traffic or the median rail?" Thankfully, that was not my destiny.

Reflections After My First Six Months

I adapted to the fast-paced hustle and bustle of New York City surprisingly well—much faster than I had imagined. I felt increasingly battle-tested navigating the streets and highways by car and the winding branches of the subway system by train.

Financially, the overtime hours I worked ensured I would have enough for our planned December wedding. I had also learned the importance of building credit through responsible use of revolving accounts and timely bill payments, so I applied for and received my first credit card with a $1,000 limit.

1989 marked the first year of George H.W. Bush's Republican presidency, with Democrats holding the majority in both houses of Congress. That same year, he appointed Colin Powell—the son of Jamaican immigrants—as the twelfth Chairman of the Joint Chiefs of Staff, the first African American to hold the position.

I watched the activities and pronouncements of both political parties, noting their sharply contrasting ideologies. I began to observe and experience the often subtle, sometimes overt differences in how minorities of various races were treated. I listened to heated debates about affirmative action and meritocracy—issues I would later explore in greater depth, contrasting them with my Jamaican experience.

One of my most welcome early discoveries was the ease and efficiency with which I could obtain basic services. There was no need to "know someone" at a utility company to have electricity, telephone, or cable installed promptly. I experienced no power outages. Mail arrived reliably, though I was baffled by the daily flood of junk mail. Public transportation was affordable, accessible, and generally punctual—despite frequent reports of subway crime.

I quickly discovered the low-budget immigrants' dream spots for cheap clothes and necessities—Fulton Street Mall and 86th and Pitkin Avenues in Brooklyn—where prices seemed almost too good to be true. I soon learned the hard way that "you get what you pay for," as some clothes barely survived a single wash. Unhealthy, cheap junk food was everywhere, available on almost every block, and basic groceries remained relatively affordable.

I felt geographically unlimited by the sheer scale of the continental United States—3.12 million square miles, stretching roughly 2,800 miles from east to west—compared with Jamaica's 4,227 square miles and 146-mile length. The vast network of wide highways that crisscrossed the country stirred in me an irresistible urge to hit the open road, an exploratory freedom unimaginable on an island one could drive across in just a few hours.

That summer, I drove with friends from Brooklyn to Toronto, Canada—roughly 500 miles—my first time crossing into another country by car.

That feeling of being unbounded resonated deeply with my inner psyche, whispering of limitless possibilities. I embraced my new American frontier with excitement.

Yet I would never forget my roots. A warm, nostalgic affection for Jamaica—the land of my birth, adolescence, and early adulthood—would remain with me always. I took great pride in being Jamaican and carried our proud saying wherever I went: "Wi likkle, but wi tallawah."*

I learned that the United States wasn't perfect, yet I recognized that its history had been one of steady progress toward a more perfect union. I saw this progress in its twenty-seven constitutional amendments, as well as landmark legislation such as the Social Security Act of 1935, the Civil Rights Act of 1964, the Voting Rights Act of 1965, the Fair Housing Act of 1968, and their subsequent amendments—all reflecting the nation's evolving social, political, and economic needs.[57]

After six fully immersive months in the United States, I made a firm decision: as soon as I completed the five-year residency requirement, I would become an American citizen. I'll share the details of that process in a later chapter.

By late December 1989, my long separation from Lisa had become unbearable. With all the wedding plans finally in place, I boarded the plane for Jamaica with uncontainable excitement. I was ready to start a family, and the United States would be our home.

LIFE LESSONS

1. Let initial rejection stir resolve, not despair, for far greater opportunities always lie ahead.

2. Never be seduced by extravagant promises of grandeur in places, people, or things. Believe only what your own experience confirms.

3. If opportunity is the door, determination, grit, and hard work are the only keys that ever fit the lock.

4. Never let success or contentment lull you into complacency. What follows can undo everything.

---

* Translation: "We are small, but we are mighty," meaning that we are capable of achieving great things despite being a small nation.

5. Sleep can kill you quicker than speed, the moment it finds you at the wheel.

6. Let 'Why?' be your litmus test for cheap or expensive alike. The low price may betray you tomorrow; the high price may betray you today.

7. Be fiercely proud of where you began. Those struggles, lessons, and triumphs forged the resilient achiever—you.

(This page intentionally left blank.)

CHAPTER 12

Choosing Paths, Making Turns

The big decisions of early adulthood

Marriage and Transition

After a sixteen-month engagement, I got married in December 1989, just after my twenty-second birthday. It marked the beginning of a transformative journey—married life—a lifelong commitment filled with hope and the aspiration of building a family rooted in love, understanding, and fortitude.

The ceremony and reception were held in Montego Bay, with many family members and friends in attendance. We honeymooned for a couple days before returning to the United States.

Unlike me, Lisa had never aspired to live in the United States. She agreed to come only with the understanding that once I completed postgraduate studies and we had saved enough money, we would return to live in Jamaica. We even set a timeframe of ten to twelve years.

For the time being, we stayed in my mother's apartment while searching for our own place. Luckily, within a couple of months, a one-bedroom apartment became available in the same building. Both my mother and I were delighted by our proximity.

We signed a one-year lease at $475 per month and moved into a fourth-floor apartment in a building with no elevator. I had a six-month head start on acclimatization and did everything I could to make Lisa's transition smooth. It proved far more difficult than either of us had expected.

We hit our first bump in the road during our initial meeting with the immigration attorney I had hired to file for Lisa's permanent residency. Naively, I had assumed that because Lisa was born in

England and held dual Jamaican and British citizenship, she would quickly receive a work permit after I filed. However, that benefit applied only to spouses of U.S. citizens, not to green card holders. She would not be allowed to work until her own green card was issued, which could take up to a year. Still, to practice law, she first needed to pass the New York Bar exam, which she could take while she waited.[58]

"Chubble nuh set like rain,"* as we say in Jamaica—and more problems soon followed. My unfamiliarity with winter driving led to a major front-end collision. It happened on a snowy Sunday evening just before dusk. I was driving about thirty miles per hour when an accident occurred roughly a hundred feet ahead. I slammed on the brakes, the car slid, and we braced for the inevitable collision—ending up in a four-car pileup.

The insurance company assessed the damage at $5,500. For context, I had bought the car for roughly $15,000. As expected, my insurance premium later rose sharply.

After two weeks of borrowing a friend's car to get to work, I finally picked up my vehicle from the body shop with a deep sigh of relief. Days later, my streak of bad luck continued. I was pulled over on the Belt Parkway by a police officer.

"Do you know why I stopped you?" he asked.

"No, sir," I replied.

"You were traveling at sixty-seven miles per hour in a fifty-mile-per-hour zone. Please hand me your driver's license and registration."

As he walked back to his patrol car to process the ticket, I was overcome with grief. My driver's license was still less than six months old, so a speeding ticket meant an immediate suspension. I threw up my hands in distress as tears rolled down my face. Lisa did her best to console me.

The officer, realizing my predicament, soon returned and saw me visibly shaken, tears streaming down my face. "What's wrong?" he asked.

"Sir, I just recently got married. I just got the car back from the repair shop after a bad front-end collision, and if I lose my license, I won't be able to get to work."

---

* Translation: "Trouble doesn't set like rain," which means that, unlike rain, which one can forecast, problems can arrive unexpectedly.

He walked to the front, surveyed the repaired damage, and then handed back my documents. "Well, it seems they did a good repair. I'm letting you off with a warning this time. But man up—you can't look weak in front of your wife."

In my first encounter with a U.S. police officer, I learned that they were capable of compassion. The fact that he was African American was simply an observation; it played no part in how I assessed the outcome. I'll explore this subject more deeply later.

Further Education and Early Career Choices

As the months passed, we settled into a routine. I worked long hours and took every overtime shift I could get, while Lisa attended prep classes for the Bar exam. Still, one significant issue loomed over us.

Up to that point, I had not abandoned my plan to attend dental school—the path we had agreed upon at the time of our engagement. The plan had been simple: Lisa would work full-time while I worked part-time, prepared for the Dental Admissions Test, and applied to dental schools. But as her wait for a green card stretched on, I was lured by something closer at hand. My employer offered partial tuition reimbursement for employees pursuing a Master of Science degree in fields related to the company's core business.

The opportunity to earn a postgraduate degree at such a low cost was one I didn't want to pass up and regret later. As we say in Jamaica, "Di fos wata hag si im walla."* So I set about convincing Lisa of the merits of changing our plans—at least for the short term. Student loans would cover the difference between the tuition and my employer's reimbursement.

I applied to the Department of Civil and Environmental Engineering at Polytechnic University in Brooklyn and was accepted into their Environmental Health Science master's program. I attended evening classes that ran from six in the evening until as late as ten at night, all while working a demanding full-time job that frequently required overtime on weekends and overnights.[59]

---

* Translation: "The first water a hog sees, he will wallow in," which advises that it is better to seize opportunities as they come instead of waiting for an ideal one.

I welcomed the difference in academic structure—two semesters per year in the United States instead of the three terms I had known at UWI, and semesterly exams rather than annual ones. Studying for just one semester's material at a time was far less challenging than for an entire year, as I had endured as an undergraduate.

Surprisingly, I discovered that the quality of laboratories and equipment did not exceed that of those I used at UWI, despite the relatively high tuition. This, along with other observations, made me proud of UWI and deepened my appreciation for the first-class education it provided.

On the job, I was receiving prime assignments with major clients and earning glowing performance reviews and accolades from the firm's principals. Yet financial and promotional recognition did not keep pace. So, upon completing my MS, I decided to look for opportunities elsewhere. I'll explain more fully down the road.

The Unexpected Pregnancy

We were regularly asked by family, friends, and well-wishers, "When are you going to have a baby?" We usually replied that we were waiting until 1994, giving ourselves time to settle in properly. We repeated that answer while celebrating Christmas Day with family in 1991—only to discover, just days later, that Lisa was pregnant, much earlier than we had planned.

This surprising discovery brought a mixture of joy, anxiety, and trepidation. We had planned to delay parenthood because we first wanted to buy a home better suited for raising a child. Now that Lisa was pregnant, the four flights of stairs in our apartment building suddenly became a serious problem. We found ourselves on an accelerated timeline.

We worked hard and saved enough money for the down payment on a spacious one-bedroom co-op apartment in a more modern, elevator-equipped building—just a mile from my mother and two blocks from a subway station. The purchase price was $37,000, making it an affordable and popular choice for first-time homebuyers at the time.

We gratefully moved into our new home a few months before Lisa was due to give birth. Now twenty-five years old, I asked myself rhetorically: Could I have bought a home at this age if I had stayed in Jamaica? Based on expected earning potential and housing costs, I knew the honest answer was no.

I dutifully accompanied my wife to her obstetrician visits whenever I could, but I unfortunately missed her first sonogram. On my return home that evening, Lisa—who rarely told jokes—decided to test her comedic skills on her gullible husband.

She greeted me at the door with bright, beaming eyes, rosy cheeks, and an unusually girlish excitement.

"Guess what? I'm so overjoyed I still can't believe it!" she exclaimed.

"What? What happened?" I asked eagerly. "Is it a boy?"

"No," she replied with a playful grin. "We're having twins!"

I quickly sat down, completely stunned by her elation.

"Do you know what this means?" I asked. "How are we going to afford this? It means doubling our childcare expenses for everything."

I went on and on, laying out all the rational concerns and planning we needed to start immediately. Lisa responded with nothing but calm, nonchalant replies.

Finally, after she decided I had suffered enough, she smiled and said, "I'm only joking. We're having a boy."

For the next few months, we eagerly awaited our son's arrival. As Lisa approached and then surpassed her due date, she glowed with flawless skin, her pregnant belly swollen like a balloon ready to pop.

In late August 1992, the obstetrician determined that her overdistended uterus would likely prevent normal labor contractions and recommended a Cesarean section two days later.

On the scheduled delivery day, we drove to St. Mary's Hospital in Brooklyn—nervously excited. Lisa was about to undergo surgery, bring our son into the world, and our lives would change forever.

The hospital's policy prevented me from being in the delivery room because of the C-section. So I paced the corridors, with the feeling of a thousand butterflies fluttering in my stomach.

"Mr. Jones," a nurse called out. "Come, let me introduce you to your son. You have a healthy, bouncing baby boy."

As the nurse placed my ten-and-a-quarter-pound, twenty-two-and-a-half-inch-long son in my arms, I was overcome with pride. Tears of joy rolled down my cheeks.

She assured me that Lisa was doing well and would be ready to see me soon. He was easily the biggest newborn I had ever seen. When they later placed him in the nursery bassinet among the other babies, he looked twice their size.

Two days later, we brought home our new treasure—our son, Roger. Lisa's mother traveled from Jamaica to help her adjust to motherhood and shared her wisdom on caring for a newborn.

As a new father, I was fiercely vigilant and protective. I'll continue sharing my story of becoming a father and raising children in the pages ahead.

A New Job and Career Trajectory

Through careful observation—which I'll share more about later—I noticed that the public sector offered minorities clearer, more merit-based paths for advancement. I therefore focused my new job search there.

Six weeks after completing my MS in January 1994, I was hired as an Environmental Protection Specialist by a major public service agency. I'll refer to it simply as "the Agency" from here on.

The offices were conveniently located—just a twenty-minute train ride from home. I quickly settled in, and my presence and value were soon recognized. The accolades were no longer only empty words as I had experienced in the private sector; they now came with annual promotions and matching salary increases.

I oversaw environmental regulatory compliance for facilities and major capital projects, and acted as the Agency's liaison to city, state, and federal environmental agencies on subsurface issues.

After two years, I compared my experiences in the private and public sectors and confirmed my initial observations: the public sector treated minorities more fairly. This was where I would remain.

I had originally planned to stay at the Agency for only four years before moving on to the federal level, ideally the U.S. Environmental Protection Agency. In the end, I abandoned that idea. I was satisfied with my upward mobility and the Agency's excellent benefits.

In 1995, the Agency introduced an employee tuition reimbursement program—another educational opportunity I eagerly embraced. I reasoned that a graduate degree in public administration would strengthen my qualifications and accelerate my trajectory in public service. I applied to Baruch College, part of the City University of New York system, and was accepted into the Master of Public Administration (MPA) program.[60]

LIFE LESSONS

1. The path to success is rarely the one planned. Detour signs of great opportunity will appear; the wise recognize them, and the brave change course.

2. Acting on anecdotes and intuition is reckless when the facts are within reach.

3. A well-timed confession of your struggles could be the one key that unlocks true compassion and forgiveness.

4. Dead-end road? U-turn. Dead-end job? Same rule.

(This page intentionally left blank.)

PART III

TRIALS AND TRANSFORMATION

(This page intentionally left blank.)

CHAPTER 13

Touched by Societal Inequities

Realizing the costs of difference

The Jamaican Experience

I grew up in a predominantly Black, multi-ethnic Jamaican society where I had no firsthand experience of racism against any racial group. Yes, there was evidence of classism related to economic status, and subtle undertones of colorism—which I sometimes heard mentioned—but I rarely, if ever, personally witnessed it.

In my experience, no citizen was deprived of an opportunity on the basis of race. As previously mentioned in Chapter 1—and it is worth reemphasizing—ethnicity was never used in hyphenated constructs where one's ethnicity preceded nationality. Whether of African, white, Indian, Chinese, or multi-ethnic ancestry, we all first and foremost identified ourselves simply as Jamaicans.

In history classes, we learned of the atrocities of the Spanish after Christopher Columbus arrived in 1494 and the eventual genocide of the original Jamaicans, the Taíno (also known as the Arawaks).

We also learned of the atrocities of the transatlantic slave trade—the horrific Middle Passage that brought enslaved Africans across the sea to the Americas—and their subsequent sale as chattel to labor on sugar plantations. This brutal system of African enslavement, which began under the Spanish and was later intensified by the English, lasted more than 300 years before full emancipation was granted on August 1, 1838.

The visceral revulsion I felt while reading history books about this dreadful past was eclipsed by the visual imagery of the television series *Roots*. Watching it as a child opened my eyes to the stark brutalities inflicted on the enslaved—the stripping of their identities and their fierce struggle to preserve a sense of self through their names and cultural heritage.[61]

Following the abolition of slavery, social inequities and racial bias persisted. With the help of missionaries and civil rights advocates, the formerly enslaved continued to demand their rights through activism in both Jamaica and Britain.[62]

With the help of Christian missionaries, several "Free Villages" were established, offering former slaves an escape from the harsh, low-wage conditions on plantations and a genuine path to land ownership and economic freedom. These settlements were often supported directly by Nonconformist missionaries, particularly Baptists and Methodists. The villages enabled land purchase and fostered both economic and spiritual independence from the plantation system. The first such village was Sligoville, founded by the Baptist Missionary Society in 1835.[63]

A pivotal moment came with the Morant Bay Rebellion of 1865, led by Paul Bogle, a Black Baptist deacon, and George William Gordon, a mixed-race politician and activist. The uprising was fueled by deep post-emancipation grievances: widespread poverty, crushing taxes, and the denial of political rights, especially the severely restricted voting franchise.

Both leaders were arrested, tried, and hanged. In the brutal suppression that followed, hundreds more were executed, thousands were flogged, and countless homes were destroyed.

The rebellion forced the British government to recall Governor Edward Eyre because of the brutality of the reprisals and to impose sweeping reforms. In 1866, the old Jamaican Assembly—dominated by white planters—was abolished, and Jamaica was converted into a Crown Colony under direct British rule. Judicial reforms, infrastructure improvements, and limited land redistribution soon followed.

Yet full voting rights would not be granted until 1944, and independence, achieved through continued activism and struggle, finally came in 1962.[64]

I was born in the age of independence, 129 years after the end of slavery. Yet my genealogical research revealed a complex reality: during slavery, some of my ancestors included both free Whites and enslaved Africans. This dichotomy forced me to confront a painful truth—I was connected to both the victims on one side and the free and privileged on the other.

Thankfully, as I noted in Chapter 1, my research also revealed that my white great-great-grandfather, who lived in Jamaica during slavery, was a carpenter and not a slaveholding planter. As for his own forebears and their occupations, it is perhaps fortuitous that no information surfaced—lest it be the dreaded kind.

Following independence, initiatives to address systemic inequities continued. However, these measures did not explicitly target race as a criterion. Instead, they took the form of equity reforms—affirmative action policies designed to support economically disadvantaged groups, promote equal access to quality education, and enhance opportunities for social mobility.

One significant example of these initiatives was the 1963 implementation of a policy that reserved 70 percent of free high school places for students from public primary schools who passed the Common Entrance Examination (CEE), while allocating only 30 percent to those from private preparatory schools. At the time, prep school students—invariably from wealthier families—were consistently outperforming their poorer counterparts and claiming most of the available slots. The policy's aim was to expand educational access for disadvantaged children, and it proved largely successful, though it was later reformed.[65]

I grew up in the 1970s and 1980s, seeing Black professionals in esteemed positions throughout society. The overwhelming majority of doctors, attorneys, judges, pharmacists, politicians, professors, teachers, nurses, and managers were of African descent. Collectively, they provided ample role models and vivid examples of Black excellence.

Most small businesses, often part of the informal economy, were Black-owned. However, almost all the large and more profitable private enterprises—banking, tourism, manufacturing, and mining—were still controlled by Jamaica's ethnic white, Chinese, Lebanese, and Syrian minorities as well as by foreign corporations.[66]

The African-American Reality

Unlike Jamaica, where slavery was abolished in 1838 by an act of the British Parliament without civil war, the process in the United States was markedly different. Slavery in the United States was not abolished until twenty-seven years later, on December 6, 1865, with the ratification of the Thirteenth Amendment to the Constitution. This freedom was secured through a bloody Civil War that claimed the lives of 620,000 to 750,000 soldiers.[67]

Despite the legal end of slavery, its legacy persisted in American society through the Jim Crow laws of the late nineteenth and early twentieth centuries in the South. These laws, enacted by Southern states, enforced racial segregation and, in effect, prolonged discrimination as well as the social and economic inequalities endured by formerly enslaved people.[68]

It wasn't until the Civil Rights Movement of the 1950s and 1960s, and the constitutional and legislative victories it produced, that significant advances were made in the fight against racial discrimination and segregation.

In 1954, the U.S. Supreme Court declared racial segregation in public schools unconstitutional in the landmark case Brown v. Board of Education, which originated from lawsuits brought by Black families. African Americans and their allies—led by luminaries such as Martin Luther King Jr.—fought tirelessly to secure passage of the Civil Rights Act of 1964 and the Voting Rights Act of 1965, which dismantled legal segregation and protected voting rights nearly a century after emancipation.[69]

Upon immigrating to the United States and acclimating to life here, I observed stark contrasts between the contemporary Black experience in Jamaica and that in the United States. In the United States, anyone with any African ancestry was considered Black first, before any other defining characteristic.

Black Americans constituted a minority group of roughly 12 percent of the population, yet were disproportionately underrepresented in the more lucrative and prestigious professions. At the academic and professional conferences I attended, I noticed the relative scarcity of Black professionals and the rarity of Black presenters. This disproportion was even more pronounced in both small and large business ownership.[70]

I saw media images of the bleak conditions in often crime-ridden inner-city housing projects, which were disproportionately occupied by African Americans as a vestige of historic segregation. The media and some politicians frequently portrayed residents of the projects—and Black communities more broadly—as largely dependent on government welfare, with the claim that families had more children to receive larger benefits. If true, it was not difficult to deduce that such welfare dependency could diminish incentives for employment and perpetuate a cycle of sustained poverty.

The truth was that this mainstream narrative was an exaggerated and unfair stereotype. At the time, only a minority of the African American population received welfare—roughly 13 to 17 percent at its peak—while comprising about 12 percent of the U.S. population. Of those recipients, only 2 to 5 percent were long-term dependents.[71]

I observed the enactment of the Personal Responsibility and Work Opportunity Reconciliation Act of 1996, which ended indefinite welfare dependency and promoted employment through time limits and work requirements. I saw this legislation as a constructive step toward countering the persistent, broadly unfair stereotype, and reflected on the more than sixty years that had passed before such reforms were implemented.[72]

I listened as Black people from Jamaica and other countries—who were benefiting from the past struggles and the legislative and constitutional achievements of African Americans—made disparaging comparative statements. They argued that they made better use of opportunities in the United States than African Americans did, often citing their own patterns of working multiple jobs, earning undergraduate and postgraduate degrees, and achieving home ownership at higher rates.[73]

From my perspective, many Black immigrants arrived from countries where Black people constituted the majority and held positions at every level of society—from teachers and doctors to politicians and business owners. That widespread visibility of Black success and self-determination often gave us a different psychological starting point than many native-born African Americans.

As a minority group, African Americans have been shaped by centuries of systemic racism, segregation, and disenfranchisement. Neither path—immigrant nor native-born—was easy, but the contrast between them was striking and, I believe, helps explain some of the differences in outlook and outcomes. While many African American luminaries existed, they often seemed distant from the inner-city Black population centers, where sufficient role models appeared to be lacking.[74]

While the United States implemented various affirmative action programs to address persistent inequities, its approach differed from Jamaica's earlier economics-based model. Rather than focusing on class or economic disadvantage, these programs often involved race-based quotas and targeted recruitment. They were—and continue to be—attacked by some as not merit-based and, in effect, a form of "reverse discrimination." Beneficiaries of affirmative action, including Black immigrants, were often stigmatized as "token Blacks." Yet opponents of these programs rarely acknowledge the persistence of systemic, race-based inequities that undermine true meritocracy, where equally or more qualified Black people are frequently overlooked.[75]

While many Black people have succeeded despite persistent biases, the absence of effective mechanisms to correct those biases leaves the economically disadvantaged—disproportionately Black—with little realistic chance of advancing through merit alone. In my humble opinion, the path forward should begin, as Jamaica demonstrated, with an economics-based means test to ensure that high-quality education is accessible to the less fortunate.

With access to the best education, the economically disadvantaged and racially sidelined can rise to become masters of their own destiny, creating more business owners who, in turn, provide meritorious opportunities for others. I continue to hope that our shared humanity will one day rise above politics and race to create real, lasting change and truly equal opportunity.

Navigating a Career Amid Inequality

I embarked on my first career-defining job with enthusiasm and dedication. I believed that exemplary performance would serve as a stepping stone toward realizing my American dream of a successful career—this was my unwavering commitment. With my Jamaican mindset, I harbored no preconceptions about potential bias, assuming I would be judged and rewarded solely on merit.

In my third month on the job, I experienced my first significant, thought-provoking encounter. As recounted in Chapter 11, I was working upward of thirty-six hours of overtime per week in anticipation of my upcoming wedding. This apparently caught the attention of the white general manager, who, in a private aside, asked me in a condescending tone, "So what are you doing with all this money you're making?" Stunned, I muttered the truth and walked away, feeling that my privacy had been violated. I pondered his motive for this strange and offensive intrusion, which proved to be the first in a pattern that would continue.

As I noted in Chapter 12, my employer consistently confirmed my merit through exceptional written performance reviews and accolades from the firm's principals—up to the president himself. I recall the operations manager once saying to me, "Everything you touch turns to gold." Because I often finished in-house-administered certification exams before my coworkers, achieving among the highest scores, he once asked, "So how does it feel to be so smart?"

On one occasion, the company's president—for whom I had personally managed a project involving high-profile clients—was visiting the New York City office. By chance, our paths crossed, and we met in person for the first time. In front of the general manager and the operations manager, he told me how elated he was to meet me and to thank me personally for the high quality and thoroughness of my work. I listened as both managers chimed in, echoing his sentiments.

Despite these written and verbal acknowledgments, as the years passed, I received no salary increases or promotions commensurate with my glowing reviews and accolades. I often observed white colleagues being treated far better in this regard.[76]

A defining moment came in my fourth year of employment. A white employee with less tenure—for whom I had provided on-the-job training—was promoted to a title above mine, complete with a salary increase.

In true "stand up for your rights" Jamaican fashion, I immediately marched into the operations manager's office. "Please explain this to me," I demanded.

Flushed red, he offered an incoherent defense before concluding, "Don't worry, it will be addressed."

He offered no merit-based reason for promoting this junior staffer ahead of me, leaving me to conclude—given my excellent performance reviews—that none existed. I wondered whether it was his race, his country of birth, or some other bias that had given him the promotional advantage.

A few days later, I received a letter announcing my promotion from Staff Geologist to Senior Geologist. Eagerly scanning the page for the corresponding salary adjustment, I was dismayed to find my pay unchanged.

Once again, seething but controlled, I stormed back into the operations manager's office. Before I could speak, he preempted me: "I know why you're here, but the company is going through difficult financial times, and we can't give out salary increases right now. It will be reconsidered in the future."[77]

I walked away flabbergasted. Soon afterward, I learned from the few other Black employees that they, too, had experienced similar treatment. I immediately resolved to seek employment elsewhere. This episode also spurred me to examine more closely the dynamics of Black and minority employment, including their opportunities for advancement.

I discovered that only in the public sector did Blacks and other minorities hold significant representation in managerial ranks relative to their population shares, and that they also enjoyed greater pay equity. I also came to understand the power and protective role of labor unions in safeguarding workers' rights, as well as their strong presence in the public sector. Consequently, if I wanted to improve my odds of being recognized and promoted based on merit, the public sector would be my best option.[78]

Despite my decision to leave my private-sector employer, I was determined not to depart without a principled act of defiance. My opportunity arrived a couple months later, when the company invited all employees to an all-hands meeting. The invitation read, "All employees are encouraged to ask any questions, express any concerns you may have, and make suggestions for improvement." This would be my chance to right a wrong—or, at the very least, to expose it to all the branch's employees.

The day arrived, and the conference room was filled with management and staff. Eventually, the floor was opened for questions, and I waited for my turn.

The general manager signaled, "Eric, you're next."

I stood and posed the following scenario: "Imagine two employees. The first has consistently received excellent performance reviews; the second is a more recent hire who was trained by the first. What would justify promoting the second employee above the first?"

The room fell deathly silent; the faces of the principals leading the meeting flushed red. As we say in Jamaica, "Mi tro mi caan, mi nuh call nuh fowl,"*

The general manager, instead of answering the question, responded in a muttering tone: "But I thought the operations manager discussed this issue with you?"

Without replying, I met his gaze directly and walked out of the room.

A few months later, after receiving a job offer from the Agency—as described in the previous chapter—I handed in my resignation letter. My private-sector career had lasted a few months shy of five years.

As I will relate in more detail in a future chapter, my assessment that the public sector would offer greater merit-based recognition and advancement proved true for nearly thirty-one years. Yet I hold enormous respect for Blacks and other minorities who succeed in the U.S. private sector. In their own way, they are pillars of resilience and living proof of their rightful place in that world. In my case, I chose to step away from the prospect of repeatedly confronting discriminatory practices. I understood the sacrifices I was unwilling to make to achieve my career goals, and for that reason, I have no regrets.[79]

Grappling with Social and Political Issues

On August 23, 1989, a few months after returning to the United States from the University of the West Indies, I experienced my first rude awakening to the reality that racially motivated tensions and atrocities remained very much alive. Print and broadcast media reported the fatal shooting of Yusuf Hawkins, an innocent sixteen-year-old Black male, who had been attacked by a white mob in Bensonhurst, Brooklyn, along

---

* Translation: "I threw my corn, I didn't call any fowl," meaning I made a general statement about misconduct, and the guilty person revealed themself by acting guilty.

with his friends. I witnessed the large-scale protests that followed, demanding justice. I felt fear and began to question whether I had made the right decision to immigrate. [80]

After the initial shock had subsided and hope began to displace despondency, on March 3, 1991, I witnessed on television one of the most horrific atrocities of my life. The video footage of four white Los Angeles Police Department (LAPD) officers brutally beating Black motorist Rodney King played in seemingly endless loops. The images of him lying on the ground, hands raised in futile attempts to shield himself from the blows, etched dark and inescapable memories in my mind.[81]

There was no time for my psyche to recover. Just six months later, in August 1991, long-simmering tensions erupted into riots in Crown Heights, Brooklyn, after a seven-year-old Black child was struck and killed by a car driven by a Hasidic Jew. Violent retaliation followed, resulting in the fatal stabbing of a rabbinical student.[82]

Less than a year later, on April 29, 1992, the four LAPD officers who had brutally beaten and severely injured Rodney King were acquitted by a jury with no Black members. Widespread riots, looting, and arson erupted across Los Angeles, resulting in dozens of deaths, thousands of injuries, and roughly $1 billion in property damage. Television screens seemed perpetually filled with coverage of the apparently endless unfolding chaos.[83]

By this time, my wife, Lisa, was in her second trimester of pregnancy, and these events weighed heavily on her mind. She began to seriously question the wisdom of raising our soon-to-be-born son in the United States. She often recalled her parents' decision to return to Jamaica from England—when she was two years old—precisely to shield her from racism. I had little with which to counter her concerns and often nodded in acknowledgment without committing to an untimely departure. Lisa ultimately returned permanently to Jamaica in 1996; the details surrounding that decision I will relate in a subsequent chapter.

Soon, my first personal encounter with racial profiling unfolded, confronting me directly with the stark hazards of simply commuting while Black. After a late-night work shift on a project site in Manhattan, I hailed a cab for the ride home to Brooklyn around 2 a.m. The driver was a white woman with whom I had coincidentally travelled on a couple of prior occasions.

All seemed to be going well as we exchanged small talk until we reached Flatbush Avenue, about three miles from my apartment. At a stoplight, a white man pulled up beside us, stared menacingly at me in the back seat, and asked the driver if she was all right. When she asked why and motioned for him to move on, he began following us instead. Thankfully, she lost him by accelerating and weaving through traffic. Upon reaching my apartment, I quickly paid the fare and hurried inside—shaken.[84]

Reprehensible racial incidents—at least those that attracted widespread media attention—would sadly resurge after periods of relative calm, and a couple more gut-wrenching events warrant mention. On June 7, 1998, James Byrd Jr., a Black man in Jasper, Texas, was brutally murdered by three white supremacists. He was beaten, chained by the ankles to the back of a pickup truck, and dragged for three miles along an asphalt road until his body was dismembered.[85]

Seven months later, on February 4, 1999, four New York City police officers fired forty-one shots at Amadou Diallo, an unarmed West African immigrant, striking him nineteen times and killing him. The officers were acquitted the following year in a trial that ignited widespread protests over police brutality.[86]

In 1998, while purchasing my first home, I had a front-row seat to witness the phenomenon of "white flight." Together with my second wife, I bought a house from a white family in a relatively quiet but predominantly white Brooklyn neighborhood where middle-class Caribbean immigrant families had begun purchasing homes. All the houses near ours were occupied by white families. Within one to two years, however, every one of them had sold and left—a pattern that repeated itself on every block throughout the neighborhood.[87]

White flight was often fueled by false narratives, one of the most salient being the belief that property values would plummet once minorities moved in. To test this assumption, I researched the 2025 estimated value of the home we purchased in 1998 (and sold in 2006) and compared its appreciation to that of a similarly priced home in Staten Island, to which the seller and most of the other white residents had relocated.

I found that our Brooklyn property had appreciated approximately 400 percent, compared with about 340 percent for the Staten Island equivalent. In fact, many Brooklyn neighborhoods from which whites had once fled later experienced gentrification—only to see many of those same residents return years later.[88]

Fast-forward to February 10, 2007, when hope filled the air with Barack Obama's launch of his improbable campaign for president of the United States. At first, like many others, I harbored strong doubts that he would even survive the Democratic primary, let alone prove electable in the general election. Yet on August 27, 2008, he defied all expectations and secured the Democratic Party's nomination as its presidential candidate for the November 4, 2008, election. Enthusiastically, I contributed cash to his campaign almost weekly and listened to nearly every publicized speech.

On election night, I sat glued to the television, breath held, as returns and state projections streamed in. Sooner than anticipated, around 8 p.m., the major networks began declaring Barack Obama's victory. I remained transfixed, overwhelmed by a surge of emotions too profound to articulate—as tears streamed down my face. I sat numb for several minutes—then erupted in celebration—calling friends and family and receiving calls in return well into the early morning hours.

I felt convinced, like so many others, that Barack Obama's election marked the next watershed moment for race relations and equality since the civil rights victories of the 1960s. In fact, he had won not only overwhelming support from Black voters and other minorities but also approximately 43 percent of white voters.[89]

In retrospect, hope had clouded the reality that deep, entrenched systemic biases and inequalities could not be dismantled by one man over the course of a two-term presidency. I watched as the opposition did everything in its power to obstruct his agenda and constrain his accomplishments. How history will ultimately judge his legacy remains to be seen—particularly regarding the tension between symbolic inclusion and meaningful structural change.[90]

Around the same time, smartphones equipped with increasingly better cameras became ubiquitous, instantly empowering bystanders to record acts of brutality. Atrocities that might otherwise have remained hidden were now brought to light with growing frequency. Police beatings, fatal chokings, and shootings of unarmed Black people—

sometimes shot in the back or as young as twelve years old—were captured on smartphones and shared widely. Some footage even originated from the police's own body cameras.

As each incident was broadcast by the media, I felt a mix of anger, sadness, and—admittedly—at times hopelessness. High-profile police-involved killings included Oscar Grant (2009), Eric Garner (2014), Michael Brown (2014), Tamir Rice (2014), Walter Scott (2015), Alton Sterling (2016), Philando Castile (2016), Johnnie Rush (2018), Atatiana Jefferson (2019), Dreasjon "Sean" Reed (2020), George Floyd (2020), and Jacob Blake (2020). Civilian white supremacists and vigilantes were also among the assailants in cases such as Trayvon Martin (2012), Dylann Roof (2015), and Ahmaud Arbery (2020).[91]

I witnessed the birth of the Black Lives Matter movement in 2013, following the acquittal of the man who shot and killed Trayvon Martin. I observed the protests grow increasingly multiracial, with white, Latino, and Asian American participants joining in large numbers. In these crowds, I saw the goodness of humanity and our collective yearning for justice and brotherly love—regardless of race.[92]

In most of the listed police-involved cases (e.g., Garner, Brown, Rice, Sterling, Castile, Reed, Blake), grand juries, trials, or prosecutors resulted in no indictment, acquittal, or declined federal charges. Convictions were secured in only a minority of instances (e.g., Grant, Scott, Jefferson, Floyd). Outcomes in the vigilante cases were mixed: acquittal in the Trayvon Martin case (2013) and convictions in the Dylann Roof case (2017) and the Ahmaud Arbery cases (2021–2022).[93]

In another political pendulum swing, on January 20, 2021, I witnessed Kamala Harris—daughter of a Jamaican immigrant father—become the first woman and first African American vice president of the United States. Two years later, on January 18, 2023, Wes Moore, son of Jamaican immigrants, was sworn in as the first Black governor of Maryland—the third Black person ever elected governor in U.S. history.

These political milestones sparked new hope amid despair and stirred immense pride throughout the Jamaican diaspora. These luminaries, among many, continued to believe that real change was possible and staked their political careers on that conviction.

Reflections

There is a Jamaican saying which states, "Jackass sey di worl nuh level,"* yet I often wonder whether I have become personally immune to its unevenness. Have I unconsciously begun to see obvious injustices as a sad, unavoidable part of daily life—sidelined like a spectator at a sporting event, offering moral support but not taking any real active role? While I applaud the socio-political leaders of the Jamaican diaspora, have I unwittingly fallen into the Black immigrant trap of viewing the African American struggle as somehow separate from our own?[94]

Was Jamaica's son and national hero, Marcus Garvey, right in asserting that people of African descent would never be fully accepted or achieve true equality in Western society? Was he correct in believing that only success independent of white society could bring true respect—and thus the need for repatriation? Garvey famously argued, "A race without authority and power is a race without respect."[95]

I have often heard the claim that most racial and other biases are unconscious rather than deliberate. Yet whether unconscious or intentional, both are acutely and chronically harmful. For anyone genuinely committed to eradicating bias from their behavior, I believe there is one straightforward introspective question: Would you treat someone the same way—in any given circumstance—regardless of their race? If the honest answer is no, then does it truly matter whether the bias is unconscious or deliberate? In either case, only conscious, deliberate effort can begin to remedy this persistent malady.[96]

In the words of Nelson Mandela:

> *No one is born hating another person because of the color of their skin, or his background, or his religion. People must learn to hate, and if they can learn to hate, they can be taught to love, for love comes more naturally to the human heart than its opposite.*[97]

---

* Translation: "The donkey says that the world is not level," which is a recognition of the inequalities that we should be prepared to face as we travel through life.

Beyond the negative, I have had many personal experiences that testify to the goodness in the average American. Regardless of race, political persuasion—conservative or liberal—or role as police officer or civilian, I have personally witnessed genuine humanity in my fellow citizens. I will never forget the night in Manhattan in 1993 when, around 10 p.m., I accidentally locked my keys in the car, leaving my one-year-old son, my wife, and me stranded. I called 911, and within five minutes, two white police officers arrived to help.

With empathy for our predicament, they quickly pried open the driver's door using a slim jim. As my wife secured our son in his car seat, one of the officers removed his hat and showed me a photograph of his own family tucked inside the lining. He was a father with a loving family, whom he cherished and for whom he held great aspirations—just like any other parent. He kept them close to his heart, both literally and figuratively, always mindful of the extreme dangers inherent in the profession he had chosen.

I recall one night in 1995, around 2 a.m., when a white police officer stopped me for speeding on a lonely highway on my way to Buffalo, New York. Before he could explain the reason, I politely apologized. "Good night, officer. I'm truly sorry for speeding, but it was out of fear because of how deserted the road is at this hour."

"So where are you headed?" he asked.

I told him, and he inquired which route I planned to take. He then offered to show me a shorter path that would save more than an hour of travel time. I accepted, and he carefully traced the route on my paper map. Without issuing a ticket, he simply cautioned, "Please drive carefully and have a good night."

I have worked successfully in roles as both an employee and a supervisor with colleagues of many races, including white coworkers. Supervisors from various racial backgrounds have also played significant roles in the positive trajectory of my public service career. They saw my potential and merit first—above my ethnic and immigrant background—offered me opportunities, and cheered my achievements.

I recall anxiously awaiting the moment I became eligible and immediately applying for U.S. citizenship. I studied zealously for the civics test on U.S. history and government and aced it. On September 7, 1994, I attended the naturalization swearing-in ceremony at the U.S.

District Court in downtown Brooklyn. That year, I was one of 12,216 Jamaicans who became naturalized U.S. citizens.[98]

As I looked around the room, I saw faces representing seemingly every ethnic group and nationality from around the world—99.6 percent genetically the same.[99] Every face beamed with pride and anticipation of becoming American. I, too, was overcome by that profound joy, hope, and pride in becoming a Jamaican-American. I have never lost that pride, and I continue to hope and believe that a better day lies ahead for all Americans—regardless of race, color, creed, gender, or national origin.

LIFE LESSONS

1. African slavery came in three forms—chains on the body, chains on the mind, chains on the wallet—only the first was broken.

2. Conscious and unconscious racism are two sides of the same coin, wielding the same power and inflicting the same pain.

3. Civil rights should be like the air—free, limitless, and owed to every lung that draws breath.

4. Critics decry affirmative action while pretending merit is color-blind—it never was and may never be.

5. A rainbow shows, in every color at once, that the storm has ended. We are the human rainbow; united, we can end the hurricane of division.

6. Standing up for your rights is never just for you; it catalyzes change that benefits many.

7. Like an undammed river, hope without buildup generates no power.

8. Unity, however elusive, is the engine of every great success. Division is the broken wheel that derails everything else.

CHAPTER 14

The Battles Behind the Vows

When the fortitude of love erodes

The Seeds of Discontent

When I proposed to Lisa in the summer of 1988, I was ready to make a lifelong commitment to the woman I envisioned as my forever partner. In that moment, I realized my love for her was unconditional—no tragedy or affliction could ever separate us. That promise and devotion were deepened and formalized by our marriage in December 1989.

Her immigration to the United States to join me was part of the agreement we reached at the time of our engagement. As noted in a previous chapter, however, Lisa never truly desired to live in the United States. Her upbringing differed markedly from mine: she grew up in a small, close-knit family where both parents were always present, with only one sibling and a doting father.

Her parents were staunch Jamaican patriots who had repatriated from England to Jamaica. By their example, they taught their children to remain on the island and devote their future careers and endeavors to its development. Her father was a prominent Jamaican luminary and a multi-term parliamentarian.

We had both agreed that a timeframe of ten to twelve years in the United States would be necessary to accomplish our—or more accurately, my—goals. My primary objective was to study and earn a Doctor of Dental Surgery (DDS) degree, then work and save for several years to buy a home in Jamaica and establish a dental practice there. We envisioned that Lisa's career as an attorney would advance in tandem once she passed the New York Bar exam.

As previously detailed in Chapter 12, our plans encountered unforeseen delays and were ultimately altered. Lisa's delayed receipt of her green card required me to work full-time—often with overtime—to cover all our expenses. This left no room for the rigors and financial demands of full-time dental school. Consequently, I adjusted course: I completed a partly employer-paid MS degree and later enrolled in an employer-paid MPA degree program.

The earlier-than-planned birth of our son and the recurring racially motivated incidents triggered ongoing discussions about where best to raise our child. While I agreed with Lisa that a Jamaican society free of racial tensions and related inequities would be ideal, I also believed that—with vigilant guidance and careful parenting—he could be raised equally well here in the United States.

In contrast to Lisa's, my upbringing had been marked by far more challenges and struggles, so I was better equipped to maneuver and adapt to our shifting circumstances. For Lisa, however, the changes in direction, the racially tense environment, and her ongoing difficulties adjusting planted the seeds of discontent.

Navigating Private Battles

My changes in academic and career pursuits forced me to reexamine the ten- to twelve-year timeframe I had committed to. I concluded—though I admittedly did not immediately share this with Lisa—that it was no longer realistic. I doubted my ability to achieve economic security for our family in Jamaica on my new career path. Over time, I began to suggest that we consider longer-term permanency in the United States, but on each occasion, she ignored or deflected it.

After Lisa received her green card and began her search for full-time employment, the opportunities she found fell short of her expectations. She eventually accepted a position in the legal department of a bank, where she drafted and reviewed real estate contracts and oversaw loan closings.

To her chagrin, the role required extensive travel across the five boroughs of New York City, Long Island, and Westchester County. Her unfamiliarity with the streets and highways—during an era when paper maps were the primary means of navigation—only heightened her frustration. Despite these challenges, she persevered, though not without voicing her complaints.

I recall Lisa returning home late one evening following a work assignment in Westchester County, more than forty miles away. Shortly after she walked in, she burst into tears—visibly shaken as she recounted losing her way after making a few wrong turns. She ended with an anguished outburst: "I hate this country; I don't want to be here any longer!"

I did my best to calm her, promising that from then on I would rehearse any long-distance route with her the night before an assignment. I kept that promise. Whenever the need arose, I strapped our infant son into his car seat and drove her on route-rehearsal trips to familiarize her with the roads.

Lisa felt professionally stalled, and her discontent continued to deepen. In contrast, during her relatively short one-and-a-half-year legal career in Jamaica as a government attorney, she worked on a wide range of high-impact legal matters and was occasionally mentioned in the press. This was a far cry from now, when she felt like a small fish in an ocean overflowing with attorneys—a sentiment that ominously echoed a forthcoming reckoning.

By this point, Lisa was no longer ignoring the issue of how long we would remain in the United States but raising it with increasing frequency. In my attempts at deflection, I would often counter—unconvincingly—with, "But we agreed to a ten-to-twelve-year timeframe."

She usually responded with sarcasm: "Oh really, Eric Jones? If you cared about me, you would make me happy by returning to Jamaica as soon as possible."

The stage was now set for the defining battle of our marriage. In retrospect, my repeated invocation of the timeframe was perhaps an attempt to delay the inevitable or a belief that she simply needed more time to adjust and assimilate to life in the United States.

Our conflicts eventually eroded our physical relationship. By May 1995, Lisa told me she no longer wanted intimacy. She stated it in a way that left no room for discussion and showed no interest in counseling or any other form of resolution. I chose to give her time and space by sleeping in the living room of our one-bedroom co-op—an arrangement that continued for nearly a year.

The sting of her decision—whether justified or not—drove me to occasional, unexplained weekend absences, perhaps an immature attempt at revenge. I was failing at my marital promise of a happy, loving, and lasting marriage. Through these struggles, I often reflected on my father and feared that I was embodying elements of his worst examples in my own life.

Raising issues around our differences—known before marriage but once deemed inconsequential—suddenly felt important. In retrospect, this was perhaps my way of finding fault with Lisa to offset my own failings. From the beginning, I knew domestic and cooking skills were not her forte, yet I respected her efforts, remained patient, and gladly shared those responsibilities. That patience was now wearing thin, and I unfairly elevated this issue to a level of importance it did not deserve.

I grew increasingly worried about how the underlying tension in our home might affect our two-year-old son and did everything I could to compensate. Each day, I picked him up from daycare and devoted one-on-one quality time to him. Yet I knew that witnessing his parents live in harmony was also vital for his emotional development—something I was failing to provide.

The Beginning of the End

Although it was clear that Lisa's greatest desire was to return to Jamaica, she took no independent steps toward that goal. I assumed the challenge felt too overwhelming for her to face alone, or that she believed acting on it would hasten the end of our marriage. I watched as she grew more withdrawn and distant, our occasional conversations now limited almost entirely to our son's care.

One Saturday around midday, I returned from grocery shopping and heard what sounded like two adults conversing inside the apartment. Unaware of any planned visitors that day, I opened the door with heightened curiosity and stepped inside. I found Lisa vacuuming the carpet, talking to herself at an elevated volume to be heard over the noise.

Alarmed and unsettled, I asked, "Are you okay? Why are you talking to yourself?"

Seemingly embarrassed, she retorted, "This is my way of resolving my problems."

I had no training in psychology, but I could see that the combined pressures of her stalled career, our faltering marriage, and her unabated longing to return to Jamaica were taking a dangerous toll on her mental health. I believed immediate action was necessary, so that afternoon I sat down with her and discussed a plan for her return.

I proposed that she reach out to her former employer in the Jamaican government to explore returning to her old position. I offered to buy her a newer car and have it shipped to Jamaica, along with furniture to furnish an apartment. I suggested that I remain in the United States until I had saved enough to buy a home in Jamaica, during which time I would visit her and our son periodically, and she and he would visit me in return.

Effectively, I proposed we attempt a long-distance marriage and transnational parenting—an arrangement not uncommon among Jamaican immigrants living in the United States.[100]

As we began putting the plan into action, I saw a bit of sparkle return to her eyes and a new glow to her countenance—the tension between us visibly eased. For Lisa, however, a return to physical intimacy remained out of the question. Within just a couple of weeks, her former employer offered her a position at a level above the one she had left. Her father later secured an apartment for her in the same complex where we once lived—behind the U.S. Embassy in Kingston.

Leading up to Lisa's return, my greatest trepidation was being separated from my son for extended periods. I worried about how my absence would affect him—the lack of a constant father figure in the home. How would I feel coming home each day to a lonely apartment, without his enthusiastic hugs, the patter of his little feet, or the sight of his effervescent toddler exuberance?

Despite Lisa's profound love for our son, I worried that she lacked the same resilience and strength my mother had shown—qualities I believed essential for compensating for a father's absence. My only consolation was the favorable U.S. dollar-to-Jamaican dollar exchange rate, which would allow me to cover the cost of his education at one of Kingston's esteemed private preparatory schools.

In March 1996, all preparations for Lisa's return were complete. The final step was to drive the car I had bought for her to Florida, from where it would be shipped at half the cost of shipping from New York. Lisa and our son would then fly from Florida to Jamaica.

I drove most of the way, with our three-and-a-half-year-old son comfortably secured in the back seat. When fatigue set in, I asked Lisa to take over so I could nap. Touched by the hands of fate—or sheer luck—I awoke just in time to intervene, averting an accident that could have injured or killed my entire family.

In need of refueling, Lisa decided to exit the highway and began crossing a poorly lit intersection—unaware of a tractor-trailer approaching at high speed. I shouted "Stop!" and she slammed on the brakes just in time as the truck roared past. We sat there for several minutes, shaken, while she trembled behind the wheel—with our son still fast asleep in the back seat, undisturbed by my outburst.

A couple of days later, Lisa and our son left for Jamaica, and I flew back to New York to face the challenges of adjusting to my new solitude. I called her several times each week to check on their adjustment and our son's daycare arrangements. In her voice, I heard a zeal and fervor that echoed the days of our courtship and engagement. True to my promise of frequent visits, I flew to Jamaica in June 1996, three months after their departure.

Unaccompanied by our son, Lisa picked me up from the airport in Kingston. Our first stop was to retrieve him from daycare. She was now in her element—radiant, beautiful, and more relaxed than she had appeared in the years leading up to her return. In that moment, my hopes for a successful long-distance relationship swelled.

As we pulled into the daycare center's parking lot, my anticipation of seeing and holding my son again was overwhelming. He rushed toward me, and I scooped him up into a tight, unending embrace. As we exchanged a few words, it became clear that his assimilation had been rapid. In just three months, he was already speaking fluent Patois and asked, "Daddy, a weh di cyar deh?" *

I stayed with them throughout my two-week vacation, dropping Lisa off and picking her up from work on weekdays and taking the family to visit relatives and recreation spots across the island over the weekend. Yet Lisa remained unready to resume the physical intimacy

---

* Translation: "Daddy, where's the car?"

we once shared. Despite this, I left Jamaica still hopeful that our long-distance relationship could succeed.

I continued to call Lisa frequently. As planned, I met them in Florida in December 1996 and took them to many attractions in South Florida. I admired—and felt deeply satisfied with—our son's growing intelligence and development, and I concluded that Lisa had done an excellent job caring for him in my absence.

However, I came to realize that distance and time had not healed Lisa's persistent lack of intimacy. For the first time, I began to contemplate the end of our marriage. Frigidity had permanently replaced love and passion; no spark of reignition appeared. My hope for a successful long-distance relationship seemed dashed. We had grown apart, and there was seemingly no bridge that could span the divide.

About a month after my return to New York, I tested Lisa's commitment to our marriage by raising the possibility of divorce. Perhaps because of her religious beliefs, the stigma of divorce, or concern that our son would be raised outside of wedlock, she reacted angrily to the suggestion. Yet she offered no remedy or promise to rekindle the intimate bond we once shared.

In my view, I now faced a difficult choice between two clear options: returning to live in Jamaica with Lisa or pursuing a divorce. Returning offered no guarantee of a renewed intimate and loving relationship, and I still saw no economically viable career path for myself in Jamaica. Consequently, I chose divorce. I reconciled myself to the fact that the most painful consequence would be the absence of my daily physical presence in my son's life. Therefore, I devised a plan to minimize that absence—one I hoped could be incorporated into our divorce agreement.

The Divorce

In February 1997, I hired an attorney to draft the Stipulation of Settlement for our divorce and sent it to Lisa for review. As an attorney herself, she reviewed it quickly and returned it with the requested changes. The stipulation was finalized and signed in March, and the court issued our final Judgment of Divorce a few months later. From courtship to divorce, our relationship had lasted roughly ten years.

Among the salient agreements we reached, the most important concerned my parental visitation rights. On this issue, Lisa was fair and lenient, for which I was deeply grateful. She retained custody, but our son would spend all summers and occasional Christmases with me, and I could visit him in Jamaica whenever I chose.

Beyond monthly child support—with annual incremental increases—I agreed to cover all his clothing, medical needs, and 70 percent of his private school tuition. This was a commitment I would never falter in fulfilling. The unspoken lessons learned from my father's dereliction of duty would not be repeated with my son.

We also agreed that upon our son's high school graduation, at around age sixteen, he could join me in the United States to attend college and live under my custody. This arrangement became one of the most important events of my life—one I will explore in detail in my chapter on becoming the father I never had.

For me, the divorce meant I had failed at my dream of a lifelong marriage and of providing my son with a harmonious, nurturing two-parent home. I had failed to honor my vows to have and to hold Lisa—for better, for worse, for richer, for poorer, in sickness and in health—to love and to cherish, till death do us part. Yet I understood the reality of irreconcilable differences and remained grateful to Lisa for the true, profound love we once shared.

LIFE LESSONS

1. When core values collide, a marriage survives only through self-sacrifice. Someone must love more than they need to win.

CHAPTER 15

Starting Over on an Uncharted Path

More impulsive than wise

The Rebound

I met the woman who would later become my second wife one month before Lisa's departure in March 1996. She was a commission-based sales representative named Marge—two years my senior—whom I encountered while making a major purchase. Our shared Jamaican roots sparked friendly banter. She gave me a discount on the item, and I took her business card in case I needed to make a future purchase.

Months later, driven by the loneliness of Lisa's absence, I began to build a friendship with Marge. The relationship remained platonic for some time, but as the finality of my marriage to Lisa became undeniable, it gradually deepened into intimacy.

Marge's actions and words made me feel as though I embodied the qualities she had always longed for in a man—I felt idealized. If I fell ill, she would leave work early to tend to me. She showered me with compliments and inundated me with pager alerts, phone calls, and voicemails day and night. Her frequent calls even inspired me to write and record a song in the studio. In a later chapter, I will describe my artistic and entrepreneurial pursuits, which Marge supported unwaveringly.

I did not allow myself the time needed—after a ten-year relationship and a painful divorce—for meaningful emotional introspection. Instead, I plunged headlong into another committed relationship. What could possibly go wrong? I asked myself with only superficial musings. I figured I had nothing to lose: I was enjoying the company of an attractive, emotionally generous woman who seemed eager to please me in every way.

Going into Second Gear

Around the time Lisa signed the divorce stipulation in March 1997, Marge was planning to move to a new apartment. Impulsively, I invited her and her toddler daughter, Simone, from a previous relationship to come live with me.

Her domestic prowess now shone fully—she was a phenomenal cook, rising before dawn each weekday to prepare lavish Jamaican breakfasts for me. Nothing was off the menu: ackee and saltfish, fried breadfruit, mackerel with green bananas, fried dumplings—you name it, she made it. She also packed a hearty cooked lunch for me to take to work. Gradually, I gained weight, eventually feeling overweight. To shed the pounds, I returned to my former dietary habits, and thankfully, she took no offense.

She catered to my every need, showered me with gifts, and made me feel like a king. At the same time, I observed how effortlessly she excelled as a mother to her toddler—all while holding down a full-time job. I reflected that Lisa had not, would not, and most likely could not have managed all these things simultaneously.

Eventually, I began meeting and getting to know some of her friends and coworkers. It soon became clear that Marge was the very definition of a social butterfly and extrovert—a stark contrast to my more reserved, introverted nature. She was deeply connected throughout the Jamaican diaspora, seemingly at every level. No matter where we went, it seemed someone always knew her.

A few of her male coworkers, after meeting me, would ask, "How do you deal with her?" They then explained that she could be somewhat combative and that few dared challenge her. This stood in stark contrast to the demure, docile, loving, and doting woman I knew at home. In their presence, she often countered that she operated differently at home than at work. In private, when I asked Marge why they saw her that way, she answered candidly: in her experience, it was the only way she could survive in the cutthroat, male-dominated world of commission-based sales.

In retrospect, Marge articulated a clear rationale for her dual personality: she possessed both feminine sensibilities and distinctly masculine traits. This differed markedly from the even-keeled demeanor I had known in Lisa, who remained consistent regardless of her surroundings. That contrast hinted at the potential for conflict should her work persona ever spill over into our home.

As is common with couples getting to know each other, we had many conversations about our upbringings, past relationships, jobs, and dreams for the future. Yet I often walked away from these talks with lingering unanswered questions or a persistent lack of clarity—and with the growing realization that we held markedly different values. I imagine Marge recognized these differences as well.

I had a habit of wanting us to look into each other's eyes for a sustained period—perhaps as my way of peering into her soul while she peered into mine. Marge, however, never allowed it. After a few seconds, she would invariably turn away, repeating her familiar refrain: "It makes me feel shy."

Despite my tentative reservations, life with Marge and her daughter, Simone, was good, and I again felt the warmth of a real family. While I awaited the court's formal final judgment of divorce from Lisa, thoughts of marrying Marge began creeping into our conversations—a step I often downplayed as unnecessary. Eventually, I decided to take the leap. My "yes" was rooted in the kindness and passion Marge had shown me.

While I felt plenty of affection for Marge, it never approached the depth I had known with Lisa. I rationalized that my love for Lisa had been fueled by the unjaded intensity and novelty of first love—a once-in-a-lifetime experience unlikely to be recaptured. Still, I believed that if Marge and I stayed on the same path, my affection for her would continue to deepen over time.

Driven by positive aspiration, I set aside my misgivings about how our incompatibilities might affect the future. Perhaps because of lingering immaturity in matters of marriage, I focused only on what I liked about our life together and ignored the signs that could threaten the relationship's long-term health.

My Second Marriage

As I write about my second marriage and its challenges, I am simply sharing my truth as I lived and remember it. I believe that the success or failure of any marriage rests on good and bad decisions made, in whole or in part, by both partners. Inherent incompatibilities in values and behavior inevitably set off a cycle of triggers and responses between the two individuals. For good reason, I have chosen to omit certain significant details—most likely understating the true difficulty of the challenges.

One morning in late 1997, Marge and I exchanged our marital vows before a city clerk and two witnesses in downtown Manhattan. There were no invited guests, no fanfare—just a quiet, understated ceremony. We celebrated afterward over lunch with one of the witnesses at an Indian restaurant in Queens. I still remember her silky, low-cropped hair framing her beautiful face and the modest but elegant white dress she wore. It was a joyful, pleasant occasion and, for me, a new beginning down an uncharted path. I imagined that for her—her first marriage—it embodied the fulfillment of long-held dreams and ambitions.

For additional space and comfort—and as a sound investment—we decided to save toward the purchase of a two-family home. As related in Chapter 13, in 1998, we bought one in a comparatively quiet neighborhood of Brooklyn. We were now on our way to greater financial security, with the rental income nearly covering the monthly mortgage. I felt optimistic about our future and reflected that perhaps my earlier misgivings had been unwarranted.

This growing tranquility was derailed about six months after we moved into our home, when our buried incompatibilities finally surfaced. The red flags I had once ignored now fluttered openly in the wind. An incident occurred that echoed the forebodings I had pushed to the back of my mind. I found the episode troubling enough to begin contemplating a swift end to our marriage. After two weeks of tearful apologies and promises, I did some soul-searching and relented.

What followed until the sixth year of our marriage—in a rarely interrupted cadence—was a metaphorical roller-coaster ride. After each heated verbal clash, the ascent from the bottom began with apologies and commitments not to repeat past mistakes. Sadly, like clockwork, once we reached the peak of renewed peace and happiness, the calm proved fleeting. We would plunge again under the gravity of our incompatibilities, back to the bottom of the valley below.

The inescapable truth was that this recurring discord had become a permanent dynamic in our relationship. I consoled myself with the self-indoctrination that no marriage was perfect and that incompatibilities would exist with any woman. At the same time, I looked inward and examined how my own actions and reactions—such as my tendency to raise my voice in defense of my position during arguments—helped escalate the conflicts.

At one point, I decided to adopt the adage "A happy wife, a happy life" and stay quiet whenever I sensed a quarrel in the making. It worked for a while, but eventually it became another source of her annoyance. She would ask, "Why are you ignoring me?" I soon realized I was trapped in a no-win situation and concluded that I was incapable of providing—or ensuring—her fundamental happiness.

To Marge's credit, no matter the state of her emotional well-being or the interpersonal trials we faced, she never faltered in her domestic, parental, or work responsibilities. She rarely accepted my help with household chores, always sourced and prepared whatever meal I desired, cared for Simone with unwavering devotion, and maintained her status as a top-performing employee. She often pointed to these qualities as reasons I should overlook or endure the maladies that plagued our marriage.

Our longest stretches of joy and peace typically came during the long summers, when both Simone and my son, Roger, were in our care and my mother was visiting. I suspected Marge never wanted my mother to witness our turmoil—or give Roger any reason to report back to his mother that we were at odds.

Through it all, I pressed forward with my career and entrepreneurial pursuits. Lured by a booming real estate market, I set out to buy a second house and rent out the first entirely. It was a newly constructed two-family home just blocks from our original one. I worked closely with the builder to convert it into a single-family residence. We now had five bedrooms and a large, partially finished basement that would later be completed and transformed into offices for my company.

We moved into the new home in 2002, and Marge was elated—exuberant with pride. As the effervescent social butterfly, she excitedly showed off the house to a daily parade of her friends and coworkers.

For months, we lived in harmony. Absorbed in furnishings and decorations, Marge seemed to find nothing to derail our tranquility. The roller coaster was cruising along level ground at last, and I savored the respite from discord. Unfortunately, true to the Jamaican adage "Fyah deh ah mus-mus tail, im tink ah kool breeze,"* the bumpy ride soon returned with greater force as issues previously unknown came to light.

Ultimately, the stress of a rocky marriage took its toll and led to its demise. Although concerns over the financial impact of divorce delayed the inevitable, the outcome felt unavoidable. The details of that decision—the greatest challenge of my life—I will agonizingly share in a later chapter titled "Uncharted Path, Unavoidable Storm."

LIFE LESSONS

1. When the bond between two hearts breaks, do not reach for another's heart until you have studied the pieces of your own.

2. Adults rarely recast their mold. Incompatible values and habits don't vanish because we wish them to; they simply wait in the dark.

3. On life's journey, ignore a warning sign only if you are ready to live with the wreckage.

4. Transparency is the warmth that keeps love alive. Without it, everything freezes.

5. If someone cannot hold your gaze, believe the eyes, not their words.

6. When a relationship turns into a roller coaster, get off before the coming derailment.

---

* Translation: "Fire is at the mouse's tail, but he thinks it's a cool breeze," which signifies someone having a false sense of security amid looming turmoil by misinterpreting the signs.

- -

CHAPTER 16

Becoming the Father I Never Had

Raising children with love, resolve, and presence

- -

Development of My Core Paternal Values

My father's conduct offered no role model of fatherhood I could later emulate. I endured the agony and disappointment of his misguidance, moral bankruptcy, absence, broken promises, and financial neglect—and I pledged that I would never inflict the same on my own child.

My exemplary role model for parenthood was my mother. She taught me by example that children should be raised with a moral compass, love, integrity, humility, compassion, respect, and generosity. She understood the importance of education and provided whatever resources were needed. She never dictated the careers we should pursue but asked only that we strive to be the best in whatever path we chose. From her, I learned the value of honesty, resilience, sacrifice, and self-reliance.

When I thought about becoming a father, I decided that the values my mother had taught me would be my guide. I imagined that if I could come anywhere close to her parental prowess, I would be a good father. I would heed the wisdom of the Jamaican proverb, "Ben di tree wen ih yung; wen ih hul, ih wi bruk."*

From around age eighteen, I decided I wanted only one child—an intentional choice for fatherhood. I rationalized that the optimal amount of time I should devote to raising each child might be

---

* Translation: "Bend the tree when it's young; when it's old, it will break," which means children are best taught at a young age, as the older they get, the harder it is to correct their behavior.

compromised by my competing career ambitions. I also never wanted to deprive any of them of educational opportunities because of personal financial constraints.

My Early Days of Fatherhood

Continuing from Chapter 12, the initial days after bringing home my beautiful baby boy, Roger, resembled the careful receipt and handling of precious cargo. Having felt a bit insecure about my ability to manage very small, fragile infants, I found Roger's robust weight of ten and a quarter pounds reassuring. With pride and profound love, I fully shared in the tasks of changing his soiled diapers, bathing him, feeding him, and soothing him during his moments of discomfort. I recall the many sleepless nights and the toll they took on us as new parents.

He developed quickly. By around one month old, he was already holding his own feeding bottle. At about three months, I found him on his back, holding a magazine open taut above his face—his tiny hands gripping the edges firmly while his eyes darted from side to side, as if he was reading. His attention span was remarkable: by six months, he could sit through an entire one-hour television show with hardly a distraction. I taught him the alphabet, and by age one, he was identifying letters and attempting to write them on his erasable board. He began speaking early, and before age two, he was recognizing words—his favorite being "pizza."

In preparation for the "terrible twos," I read one of the renowned books on the subject and mentally braced myself for the challenges ahead. Like clockwork, soon after turning two, Roger woke up one morning with an entirely new personality. My calm, cheerful toddler seemed to have transformed overnight. Frequent tantrums, mood swings, and the defiant "no" became the new norm.

I observed how Roger sought to assert his independence, often darting off in a store or supermarket while his mother or I chased after him—giggling and dodging our grasps with delight. Fortunately for us and his daycare center, the terrible twos phase lasted only about six months. After that, he returned to his calm, attentive self.

I fondly remember taking Roger to see his first full-length movie, *Toy Story*, a few months after his third birthday in November 1995. I watched in amazement as his eyes remained glued to the screen for nearly the entire ninety minutes. The next day, he was accurately recalling and narrating scenes that had captured his imagination.

The Painful Separation

For reasons narrated in Chapter 14, I was first separated from my son when his mother returned to Jamaica with him in March 1996. The pain of that separation was heart-wrenching. Each day after work, I came home missing his exuberant, effervescent greetings, his warm hugs, and the sound of his giggly voice. The enchanting pitter-patter of his feet from room to room was gone. For weeks, his absence brought a sadness from which I struggled to emerge. Though my extended absence from his life stemmed from circumstances unlike my father's, I wrestled with justifying the difference.

I eagerly awaited my first trip to see him in Jamaica, planned for three months after his departure. For me, the visit was an opportunity to assess how well he was adjusting to my absence in his new environment and the quality of his daycare.

Upon arrival, the joy of reuniting with him felt as though a full year had passed. I spent every day of my two-week vacation with him, undistracted by work or anything else. Buoyed by the sense that he was adjusting well, I returned to the United States with a deeper sense of contentment.

Our next meeting that year would be in Florida for Christmas. That Florida vacation would be the last time spent together as a family, with him and his mother.

From that point onward, and in accordance with our divorce agreement, Roger spent every summer and, on occasion, Christmas vacation in my care. Until he was eight, I either flew to and from Jamaica each year to escort him myself or sponsored a relative to accompany him.

During the summer of 1997, before his fifth birthday, Roger asked me in a quiet moment, "Daddy, are you getting a divorce from Mommy?"

I was startled, never having imagined that he knew or understood what it meant. I responded as compassionately as I could, hoping to ease his evident concern.

"Yes," I said, "but Mommy and Daddy will always be there for you. We love you more than you can ever imagine."

He burst into tears as I hugged him tightly, suddenly grasping the painful weight of my decision and uncertain how it might shape his future.

The first time I decided to let him fly unaccompanied—in the care of a flight attendant—was gut-wrenching. After hugging him tightly and releasing him to her, I watched him walk down the jet bridge, small hand in hers, as tears streamed uncontrollably down my face. For the next few hours, I remained on edge, nerves in a bundle, until his mother assured me he had arrived safely and was in her custody.

The Arrival of My Stepdaughter

I was blessed with the unexpected gift of raising a daughter when my second wife, Marge, brought her two-year-old daughter, Simone, into my life. She was a beautiful, well-behaved, and loving child, and we gravitated toward each other immediately. Her mother told her I was Uncle Eric, but the name fell on deaf ears—the only one she ever used was Daddy. I imagined she saw in me a man worthy of being her father, and I saw in her a daughter to care for, protect, and love.

Occasionally, during our marriage, Marge suggested that I formally adopt Simone, perhaps seeing how deeply I cared for her daughter. I chose not to, for two reasons: the rocky nature of our marriage and the fact that Simone had a biological father who, by all accounts, was a decent man who wanted to be part of her life. He actively sought his visitation rights, which I helped facilitate. On designated Saturday mornings, Marge would drop her off with him on her way to work, and I would pick her up in the afternoons.

With Simone, I was able to do things I had been deprived of doing with my son—watching her occasional school performances, helping with math homework, and assisting with science projects. Outside of daycare or school, she was usually in my care during evenings when her mother worked late. She was also with me on Saturdays as I ran errands or handled business. Most people assumed she was my biological child.

Simone exemplified unconditional love. Aside from a poor appetite, she rarely needed to be reprimanded. She held no grudges—

quickly forgetting any discord or correction and returning at once to her loving nature. Although she witnessed numerous quarrels between her mother and me, she remained neutral, gravitating toward both of us equally.

At around age four, Simone taught me an unforgettable lesson during one of my routine Saturday errands. I had apparently forgotten the Jamaican saying "Lickle pig hab big iez."* Stopped at a crosswalk, I watched a very large person stroll past and, in an inappropriate jest, muttered, "Look at the fatty." What followed was a gentle but piercing reminder from Simone that negative thoughts and statements—even when unheard by the person they target—still carry consequences.

From the back seat, securely buckled in her car seat, Simone immediately burst into tears. Between sobs, she said, "Daddy, that is so mean. You shouldn't call anybody fatty."

I felt a rush of shame and quickly apologized. "I'm so sorry, Simone. I should not have said that, and I promise not to do it again."

In her usual loving way, she wiped her tears and replied, "Okay, Daddy, I forgive you."

Summers Filled with Fatherly Joy

Spending the summer months with my two children brought me profound joy. Roger and Simone embodied what it meant to have near-perfect children. Marge and I would often watch them in awe—an uncompromising friendship, inseparable and harmonious. I have no recollection of any real discord between them. They made parenting seem effortless.

I invested time teaching them the value of always striving to do and be their best. In them, I instilled the mantra I had learned as a child: "Good, better, best, never let it rest, until your good is better and your better best." I encouraged them not to be content with exam grades simply because they compared favorably with their peers, but to measure their performance against a single standard—100 percent. Both

* Translation: "Little pig has big ears," means that children are listening, so parents should be careful not to say negative or adult-themed things in their presence.

were high-performing students, so there was no need for additional tutoring outside of school.

They understood the value of love, respect, generosity, courtesy, and gratitude—either through quiet observation or their innate sensibilities—and needed little or no reinstruction. I taught them the worth of hard work by example, as they watched my rigorous schedule: a full-time job followed each day by returning home to manage my business. They often sat in my home office, keeping me company as I worked, and accompanied me on weekend business errands.

We unfailingly celebrated both their birthdays. Simone's came before the summer, while Roger's fell after—when he would already be back in Jamaica—but we always marked his before he left. Each summer, he arrived with an almost empty suitcase, which we filled with clothes and gifts on his departure—thanks in part to Marge's generosity and evident love for him.

For their entertainment, I devoted two weeks of vacation each summer to taking them on adventures: Disney World, Universal Orlando, SeaWorld, Hersheypark, Colonial Williamsburg, Busch Gardens, Six Flags Great Adventure, Splish Splash, the Poconos, various parks, fairgrounds, zoos, and movie theaters.

The final long-distance summer trip I took with both children was in 2006. On our way to Canada, we stopped at Niagara Falls and rode the Maid of the Mist to the base of the falls. In Toronto, I took them to the top of the CN Tower. After a couple of days there, we continued on to Montreal, where we spent two more days.

A Painful End to a Summer Tradition

Upon returning to the United States from Canada on July 15, 2006, my children were exposed to one of my most distressing experiences—a lesson in injustice. I pulled up to the border-crossing checkpoint and handed the required documents to the immigration officer. After a few moments, a second officer approached my car door and asked me to accompany him to the back of the vehicle.

I assumed he wanted me to open the rear hatch for an inspection of the contents, so I quickly complied. He then asked me to place my hands behind my back, and moments later, I was in handcuffs. "Why am I being handcuffed?" I asked.

Without explanation, he began escorting me toward the office, the improperly installed handcuffs cutting into my wrists. "I can't leave my kids like this," I exclaimed, seeing the agony on their faces and tears rolling down their cheeks.

"Someone will take them inside," he replied.

The walk to the office building was a few hundred feet. As I winced from the pain of the handcuffs, another officer rushed toward us and demanded that the detaining agent remove them. Inside the building, I was escorted to a holding room and asked a few questions.

As I expressed my outrage at being handcuffed, an agent asked cynically, "So you've never been handcuffed before?"

"No, I haven't," I responded emphatically.

I was released after about ten minutes with little in the way of an apology, but with an explanation that "Eric Jones" was a common name and they had needed secondary processing to confirm my identity. Finally reunited with my children—who had been my primary concern throughout—I explained what had happened and assured them I would seek a formal apology. It was a lesson by example: they should always stand up for what is right.

On July 30, 2006, I wrote a two-page letter to the U.S. Customs and Border Protection (USCBP) detailing what had transpired, expressing my belief that the treatment was unjust, and requesting improved procedures to prevent it from happening again. On October 26, I received a detailed two-page response and a formal apology from the Area Port Director. It assured me that any employee misconduct would be investigated and that appropriate disciplinary actions would be taken if any policies were violated. I was also provided a letter to present to a supervisor at any port of entry, in case an officer decided that secondary processing was necessary.

The Growing Distance from My Stepdaughter

Following my divorce from Marge (as detailed in a chapter ahead), my time with Simone became increasingly infrequent. This was further exacerbated when I moved from New York to New Jersey in 2009. Even so, I endeavored to stay in touch by telephone, offering academic advice and guidance whenever I could.

Later that year, Simone graduated from junior high. For Father's Day, she gave me a gift that touched me deeply: a photograph of us taken at her graduation, with these words superimposed across it:

> *Recently, I've been feeling like our relationship is a little distant. Sometimes it kills me because I feel like a part of me is missing. But then I think about the past, all the laughs, cries, frowns, and smiles that we shared.*
>
> *Sometimes when I think about it, it's just a little overwhelming to bear, because I love you so much. I have always felt incomplete without you, and I know you feel the same way, too. In my heart, no one could ever take your place.*
>
> *Whenever I'm with you, I always feel safe. Whenever I see you, I never want to say goodbye. I'm not going to lie; there have been several times when I have actually sat there and cried. I love you with all my heart, but losing you would be something that would tremendously tear me apart.*

It was a painful realization for both of us that circumstances and distance were gradually weakening our once-strong father-daughter bond. Instinctively distancing myself from her mother after our divorce also played its part.

I continued to advise Simone throughout high school on curricula, university choices, and potential careers—sometimes over lunch near my job in Manhattan. I never discouraged her dream of becoming a Hollywood actress, but I encouraged her to choose a major that would offer greater job security. She finished university with the highest honors, and I proudly attended her graduation, watching her receive her Bachelor of Arts degree *summa cum laude*. Overall, the parental credit for her success goes to her mother, Marge.

I celebrate each of her victories as she climbs the professional ladder and walks the path of her marriage. I hope one day her deferred dream of becoming a Hollywood actress will come to fruition. While we continue to communicate occasionally, I wish our relationship were closer—a distance I hope time will bridge. Yet I will forever be proud of her, whether from near or far.

Path to Full Custody of My Son

Back in Jamaica, Roger excelled through preparatory school, and I made it a point to call him once a week without fail. I was never late with tuition payments or child support, which I dutifully increased each year. I proudly watched him graduate, finishing fifth in his class. He aced the Grade Six Achievement Test (GSAT) and gained admission to what is arguably the best and most sought-after public high school in Kingston. In quiet moments, I speculated that perhaps his life in Jamaica—even in my absence—had turned out to be the right decision.

His exceptional performance continued through the first two years of high school, but by the third, he began to falter. Perhaps drawn into bad company or simply testing the boundaries of his independence, he drifted—and his mother felt a father's intervention was needed. I increased the frequency of my calls and administered tough love. Thankfully, he got back on track, improved his grades, and maintained strong performance through the remainder of high school. Beyond academics, he played on the basketball team and joined an entrepreneurial society.

He passed his Caribbean Secondary Education Certificate (CSEC) exams in eight subjects—five with grade ones and three with grade twos. Both Lisa and I overflowed with pride at his graduation in July 2009.

Shortly before he finished high school, Roger expressed his desire to attend college in the United States. This would place him in my full custody. His mother was not opposed to his decision—a recognition that, at sixteen, he now had this right as stipulated in our divorce agreement.

Now living on my own, following my second divorce, I felt confident in my ability to be a single parent. For me, defining the nature of our relationship and setting appropriate boundaries loomed large. Accordingly, upon his arrival, I asked Roger whether he preferred a strict father-son relationship or a friendship rooted in mutual trust. Not surprisingly, he chose the latter. Cool, I thought—I now had a son and a friend.

As Roger matured through early adolescence, it became clear that his personality was markedly different from mine. Now in my permanent custody, I had to navigate those differences—for which I was not fully prepared. Unlike the adolescent challenges I had faced and the independence I had learned, he had grown up more privileged and more dependent. His mother had never endured childhood or adolescent hardships herself, so she may have been unable to teach him certain survival skills. Those were the very skills I could not successfully instill during his two-month annual summer visits.

For the first few months, I focused on helping him acclimate to his new environment and lifestyle. I had no household help, as he had been accustomed to—so he needed to learn to do his share of chores. For the first time in his life, he would rely on the subway for his commute to college—no more chauffeuring as he had enjoyed in prep and high school. He did not know how to cook even the simplest meals, so I taught him the basics. Effectively, I now filled the role of both father and mother, much like the dual role my own mother had played in my life.

It didn't take long to realize that my role could not be friend first and father later. He needed tough love and a strong father figure. I had to guide him and instill the important lessons and conduct that had so far eluded him, through no fault of his own.

Guiding His College Journey

The plan I proposed—and with which Roger agreed—was to enroll him in a New Jersey county community college for the fall of 2009, complete his associate's degree, and then transfer to a four-year college to earn his bachelor's. He was quickly accepted based on his CSEC grades, high school transcript, and admissions placement test. He finished his first semester with a perfect 4.0 grade point average.

For his second semester, I transferred him to another county college with an easier commute—within walking distance from home. He again excelled, earning another 4.0 GPA and induction into the Phi Theta Kappa Honor Society. On October 15, 2010, I accompanied him to the induction ceremony, filled with pride and hope for his continued academic success. A modest scholarship soon followed, which helped offset a portion of his tuition for the next semester.

For the spring 2011 semester, Roger made the President's High Honor List, and by the end, he needed only a few more credits to complete his associate's degree. However, he convinced me it was time to move on to a four-year college—specifically a New Jersey state university where his credits would transfer seamlessly.

Under my watchful eye and guidance, I grappled with Roger's teenage vices—not uncommon among his peers—and saw that he still lacked the maturity for full independence. I concluded he was not ready to live on campus, which sparked our first major dispute. Ultimately, he unhappily acquiesced, was accepted for the fall 2011 semester, and commuted by train for the thirty-five-minute trip to campus. Not all his credits transferred to the major he chose, so completing his bachelor's degree would take longer than planned.

Inspired by the achievements of Jamaican-Canadian billionaire Michael Lee-Chin, Roger chose to major in finance. When he was around ten years old, I once asked him, "So what do you want to be when you grow up?"

He replied, "Banking."

When I pressed for more specificity, he retorted,

"No, Dad, I don't want a job in a bank; I want to own the bank."

I soon learned that he had been inspired after watching an interview with Lee-Chin, who had recently acquired a major bank chain in Jamaica.[101]

To help develop his independence, I insisted that Roger seek a part-time job. He had already held a short-lived summer internship, but now he needed something more permanent. I figured he could easily find work at any of the numerous establishments within walking distance of home. Yet each time I suggested a place, he returned saying they were not hiring. Eventually, I took charge: I walked him directly to the manager of a nearby supermarket—and he was hired on the spot as a part-time cashier. To his credit, he held the job faithfully until he finished university.

He quickly made friends on campus and, before long, was indulging in parties and sleepovers—all to the detriment of his grades. As a result, I increased my vigilance and control over his activities. We had many heated verbal battles, often triggered by his excuse-filled rebuttals to my observations and corrective instructions.

All my efforts to keep him focused finally paid off when, in May 2014, I sat in the stadium for his graduation ceremony and watched him receive his Bachelor of Science degree. In that moment, I felt more pride, joy, and a sense of accomplishment than I had when receiving my own degrees.

The Time for Emancipation

For the first few months after graduation, he was more laid-back than I expected of a recent college graduate. He was applying for jobs and going on occasional interviews, but not with much principled determination. To inject more urgency into his search, I gave him a deadline: find work or join the U.S. Navy. The alternative frightened him, and before long, he found a job.

Observing him as he went to and from work each day, I could see that he was developing a good work ethic. Over the next couple of years, he changed jobs a few times, each move bringing a better position and higher salary. Yet he showed little financial responsibility. Instead of saving, he spent freely on entertainment and other vices—at a rate far exceeding my own, even though he earned considerably less. My attempts to offer financial guidance fell on deaf ears.

At home, his lifestyle choices were affecting my well-being and growing increasingly problematic. I concluded that the only real remedy was his emancipation and independence: living on his own would force him to budget for life's expenses and take charge of his own destiny. At age twenty-five, I gave him one year to save money and plan his transition from partial dependency to full independence. After many stark reminders, he moved out a year later, in March 2018, and has lived independently ever since.

In him, I still see so much untapped potential and innate brilliance, and I hope—and believe—he will access it before too long. Unlike me, who never lived independently before my first marriage, I hope his years of independence will prepare him well for that future. When he ultimately finds the woman of his dreams, may their marriage be lifelong, filled with tranquility and happiness.

While we communicate, although not as frequently as I desire, physical distance limits how often we see each other. It's a poignant realization that children eventually become adults with their own visions and aspirations and must ultimately travel their own paths.

Reflections

I've sometimes wondered whether my mother would be satisfied with how I fulfilled my paternal responsibilities—whether I fell short by her standards. Yet I believe, and hope, she would be proud that I raised my children with a moral compass, love, integrity, humility, compassion, respect, generosity, gratitude, and a commitment to education. I also believe she would understand that if their resilience in adversity sometimes falls short, it is because they had an easier path—and that ease came at the cost of the tougher forging she knew so well.

I imagine she would judge me harshly for not providing my children with a two-parent home throughout their childhood and adolescent years—regardless of the reasons. I suspect she would be most critical of my failure to meet her exacting standards of parental self-sacrifice. In this respect, I acknowledge that I have been an imperfect vessel, operating within limits that may have been, in part, self-imposed.

In the end, it is my hope that my children appreciate the positive contributions I have made in their lives, find at least some traits in me worth emulating, and forgive me for any fatherly imperfections.

LIFE LESSONS

1. Children need two parents the way an airliner needs two pilots. One might land the plane, but is it worth the risk?

2. Love has many dialects—most are gentle. Tough love is the one that sounds like anger but delivers rescue.

3. Your children learn parenting from you. So, what kind of parents are you teaching them to be?

4. A child is a sponge with eyes and ears. They see and reenact your actions, hear and remember your words.

5. To a child, separation and divorce feel like an unconscious rejection of half of who they are.

6. An absent parent is the missing piece of a child's life puzzle. The picture will never be complete.

7. Blessings often come in small packages. So does the child you accept who is not your blood but becomes yours by choice.

8. A child's unbridled honesty is a mirror you cannot dodge—look, listen, learn.

9. Stand tall against injustice today, so your children never have to stoop tomorrow.

10. Celebrate your children's successes, but teach them to mine strength from every failure.

11. A parent's last great gift is emancipation. Holding on only impedes the flight you taught them to take.

My son, Roger, and stepdaughter, Simone, 1999.

My children and I, 1997.

(This page intentionally left blank.)

CHAPTER 17

Dreams Deferred, Not Denied

What it means to wait well

The Essence of My Dreams

Throughout my life, my deepest aspirations have often taken shape in moments of solitude. I have pursued the conventional markers of success—academic achievement, a meaningful career, a committed marriage, and responsible parenthood. Yet beyond these worthy pursuits, I have harbored quieter dreams rooted in creativity, self-improvement, and the simple joys of living. Some of these dreams evolved not through deliberate planning but were ignited by unexpected opportunities and shifting circumstances.

These dreams have provided a constant source of meaning in my life, undimmed even when they seemed distant or the path to them uncertain. Yet I have remained a pragmatic visionary—knowing when to pivot, defer, or patiently await the right moment. I largely attribute this balance to an upbringing shaped by challenges, which instilled in me resilience and adaptability.

As detailed in previous chapters, my academic and career aspirations have at times pivoted—redirected by shifting circumstances and the embrace of unexpected opportunities. I fell short of my dream of a single, lifelong marriage, yet I always hoped to avoid becoming a serial monogamist. My dream of parenthood was realized, though shy of my optimal goal: full-time presence in my children's lives.

Following the painful departure of my first wife, Lisa, with my son, in March 1996, I took stock of my unfulfilled aspirations. My career was advancing steadily upward, and my second master's degree was progressing, yet a longer list of dreams remained: to become a recording and performing artist; to master the guitar; to speak a foreign language fluently; to catch up on my reading of great literary works; to become a published author beyond academia; to engage in meaningful volunteer and philanthropic work; to serve as a mentor; to learn to ski and to golf; and to witness a live volcanic eruption on the island of Hawaiʻi. At twenty-nine, I still had time to pursue them all—if paced thoughtfully. Some would need to be deferred, but none, I resolved, would be abandoned.

A Musical Upsurge

My copious consumption of reggae and dancehall music began in childhood and continued through adulthood, undiminished by my immigration to the United States. Then, around July 1996, I experienced an inexplicable surge of artistic creativity. The standing ovation I had received following a singing performance—as recounted in Chapter 8—had lain dormant in my subconscious for years but was now rising insistently to the surface. Like many Jamaicans, I felt the infectious rhythm and bass that define our musical heritage, urging me toward self-expression.

Over the next few months, I wrote twenty-five songs. I purchased a semi-professional microphone, composed melodies, practiced my phrasing and timing over popular reggae rhythm tracks, and recorded amateur versions onto cassettes.

Thanks to the burgeoning Internet, I located and joined a reggae networking organization, through which I discovered a small Jamaican-owned recording studio that could help bring my passion to life. I visited the studio for the first time one evening in early September 1996, intending only to meet the owner. Four hours later, I had recorded my first song, titled "*How Wrong*." The lyrics are as follows:

Chorus:
How wrong, wrong, wrong, wrong
S-o-o-o wr-o-o-ong
How wrong, wrong, wrong, wrong
S-o-o-o wr-o-o-ong

Verse 1:

How wrong for man to abandon his children
All over the world, children are suffering
Crying from hunger, crying for love
I've taken some time to examine the cause
How could you expect the children to make it alone

Chorus

Verse 2:
I've prayed to Jah to help find a solution
For so long we have been in this situation
Living a lie, struggle and confusion
Let's put our thoughts together and set up a plan
Fathers return to your children
Give them a helping hand

Chorus

Verse 3:
Look into yourself, take responsibility
Set an example for the youths to follow
For the children to strive, they need the tools of life
Educate them, now teach them the right
So that they can realize their destiny

Chorus
[Repeat Verse 1]
Chorus

I later drafted an agreement with the studio to record a nine-track album titled *Together in Inity*.* I adopted the artist name "Ejandi," a name I coined from my initials "EJ." However, after completing five songs, I abandoned the project.

Long, futile waits for scheduled recording sessions that never started, combined with the nightly sixty-mile round-trip, wore down my

---

* Translation: The word "Inity" was coined by Rastafarians and adopted into the Patois lexicon as a replacement for "Unity," and emphasizes spiritual and social togetherness.

patience and deepened my frustration. Regrettably, I did not own the sixteen-track analog tape that held the recordings, so I walked away with only a digitized, unmastered version of my first song, *How Wrong*, and rough cuts of the other four on analog cassettes.

My musical ambitions also encountered a stark reality check when I contacted an artist manager. I told her enthusiastically, "I have a demo song I'd like you to listen to."

She replied, "Before you send it, I have some questions. If you currently have a full-time job or career, are you willing to give it up to pursue your artistic dream?"

Without waiting for my reply, she continued, "Becoming an artist demands immense sacrifice, patience, and often disappointment and financial hardship. Are you truly ready for that?"

For a prolonged moment, I was speechless. Then I said, "Let me think about it and call you back."

The truth was, I didn't need time to think about it. I would not—could not—abandon my ongoing academic and career pursuits. I had obligations and responsibilities that took precedence, so this dream had to be deferred to an indefinite future. In the meantime, I would keep the flame alive through karaoke whenever the chance arose.

Shortly afterward, a new dream—sparked by fresh opportunity and shifting circumstances—began to unfold. It transformed my longing to become an artist into a determination to become an entrepreneur in the music industry. In the next chapter, I provide rich details about this substantial entrepreneurial endeavor.

Waiting Well

Postponing my unfulfilled ambitions indefinitely demanded both confidence and sustained patience. The hardest choice came in 1997, when I decided to take a hiatus from pursuing my second master's degree to make room for my entrepreneurial venture. I believed that delaying academia would prove less regrettable in the long run than letting my entrepreneurship window of opportunity close. I understood that the creative zeal and seemingly boundless energy required to launch and sustain such an endeavor could diminish with age.

Later that year, the wheels of my authorial ambitions began to turn. Thoughts and ideas were jotted down loosely, but I deliberately postponed serious pursuit due to pressing time constraints. As for my longstanding desire to become multilingual, I continued to wait passively for the right spark to ignite that fire.

As for my longing to catch up voraciously on the literary works I considered essential, I began slowly. Eventually, between 2009 and 2015, I reached and sustained the reading pace I had always desired. Since then, I have continued at a slower but steady rate, made easier by the convenience of e-books and audiobooks.

My dreams of volunteerism and mentorship, learning to ski and to golf, playing the guitar, and witnessing a live volcanic eruption would remain dormant for years but would eventually come to fruition, as you will read in the pages ahead. Recording and releasing an album, along with philanthropy that extended beyond charitable donations, would remain unfulfilled—but never forgotten—dreams.

LIFE LESSONS

1. Aspirations are the fuel of a meaningful life. When the tank runs dry, so does the soul.

2. A dream is a lush green valley you envision but cannot reach until you've climbed every mountain that stands in the way.

3. When a dream starts feeling like a nightmare, wake up. There are other aspirations that let you sleep.

4. On my deathbed, let it be that I pursued every worthy dream, won some, lost some, but regretted none.

My first studio recording session in 1996.

CHAPTER 18

Finding Pioneering Purpose

Taking risks and the pursuit of vision

The Entrepreneurial Spark

Until she immigrated to the United States at age fifty-seven, my mother's livelihood depended on the success of her small entrepreneurial enterprise. By every measure, I considered her a successful businesswoman. She never relied on bank loans to grow or sustain her business, and she never once faltered in meeting her financial obligations to the wholesalers who extended her credit for merchandise.

In my teenage years, I spent much of my summer and Christmas breaks helping in my mother's shop, where I developed a real knack for sales. When she left me in charge, I frequently surprised her with the high volume of sales I generated—far exceeding her expectations. On her behalf, I often negotiated terms, made wholesale purchases from vendors, and accompanied her on business trips to Kingston.

Though I was more academically inclined and never particularly aspired to become an entrepreneur, her example must have planted a seed—one that lay dormant for years, waiting for the right moment to sprout into action.

After deferring my dream of becoming a recording and performing reggae artist—yet still deeply drawn to the music industry—I discovered a promising niche. At the time, I subscribed to a popular music mail-order club, but its monthly catalogs rarely included reggae CDs. Living in Brooklyn, I had to travel to a handful of Jamaican-run record stores scattered across Brooklyn, Queens, or the Bronx to find the music I wanted. This limited access became the spark that ignited my decision to launch my own company.

After obtaining dual employment authorization from the Agency where I worked, I registered and launched Ejaness Reggae Comprehensive in November 1996—a sole proprietorship run from my home. Like my artist name "Ejandi," I created "Ejaness" using my initials "EJ" as the root.[102]

Throughout the following narrative, I will use "I" and "we" interchangeably to acknowledge the contributions of those who worked under my leadership. I also use "reggae" as an umbrella term to encompass all genres of Jamaican music, including dancehall, lovers' rock, dub, rocksteady, and ska.

The company's ambitious mission was "Building a Reggae World," realized by making reggae music merchandise more readily available in every corner of the globe. Achieving this vision in the long term would require an online music store, but until I found a suitable web developer, we would begin locally with paper catalogs.

The initial sequence of tasks included locating wholesale distributors, designing the catalog, and then printing and distributing the first edition, which I titled *Reggae—Rule the World*. Our promotional strategy was straightforward: we distributed catalog request forms at reggae shows and other Caribbean events throughout the U.S. Northeast. Recipients could return the completed forms on-site or mail them back to us. My assumption that a real niche awaited proved correct—requests for catalogs began arriving in steady numbers.

Around January 1997, we published the first sixteen-page volume, offering seventy-six albums on CD and a handful on cassette. We included free shipping and handling for U.S. customers, along with a bulk-buying incentive: "Buy six, get one free" or "Buy ten, get two free." At the center was a pull-out order page, and we added a free-album incentive for customers who referred friends who made a qualifying purchase. On the inside front cover, I included the following editor's message:

> *Welcome to the world's preeminent reggae catalog, "Reggae—Rule the World." This is the first of its kind, bringing you an impressive listing of reggae artists on CDs and cassettes. Our mission is to bring you the best available reggae works at the best prices, in one neat package. With your mail order, you become a permanent*

> *member of our reggae family and will receive all catalog updates with new releases. Nuff Respect!!*

Our marketing and promotion strategy proved effective, as orders grew steadily and customers began requesting more selections. Roughly six months later, we published the second volume—now expanded to twenty-four pages and offering 207 albums, an increase of nearly 300 percent. My updated editor's message was as follows:

> *Welcome to the second edition of the world's preeminent reggae catalog, "Reggae—Rule the World." The response to the first volume was overwhelming, with customers even taking the time to write letters expressing their excitement and appreciation. From the largest to the smallest, orders were shipped within one to two business days of receipt.*
>
> *To further satisfy your reggae needs, we have added tons of selections to this volume. Even more exciting, we can now take orders by telephone. You can now also order CDs that are not listed in this catalog. Yes! Tell us the CDs you need, and we will attempt to locate them for you through our many suppliers. Ejaness Reggae Comprehensive remains dedicated to satisfying your reggae music needs and looks forward to your continued support. Nuff Respect!!*

As our base of new and repeat customers grew, so did the demand for more frequent catalog updates and a broader selection of titles. To sustain and accelerate the business's growth, I needed to hasten our transition from mail order to an online store.

Fortunately, while promoting at an event in Brooklyn, I was approached by a Jamaican web developer, and we quickly struck a deal. First, however, I had to register an Internet domain for the website—a decision I deliberated over for a few days. I wanted a self-explanatory website address that would instantly resonate with my target audience. After careful thought, I chose *ReggaeCD.com*, registered it, and then directed the site's graphic design, content, layout, and intended functionality.

We launched the website in November 1997 and met with immediate success—orders rose sharply and steadily over the subsequent months. We promoted it locally by distributing thousands of *ReggaeCD.com* bumper stickers at events throughout the U.S. Northeast and including one in every order we shipped. I felt genuine elation whenever I spotted those stickers on cars around New York City or received orders prompted by them—even from customers outside the United States.

During stretches of summer weekends in 1998 and 1999, we also rented a flea-market booth in Queens, New York, primarily to promote the company and connect directly with reggae and dancehall fans.

Worldwide, *ReggaeCD.com* found fertile ground among a reggae fan base that had long awaited a reliable, dedicated source for music merchandise. We held a virtual monopoly in that niche until late 1999, when competition began to emerge. By then, we already had customers in more than fifty countries, a number that grew in the years that followed.

We received numerous emails from customers expressing excitement and gratitude for ending their lack of reliable access to reggae. Some without credit cards proposed creative payment alternatives—which we did our best to accommodate—often requiring us to visit money-transfer offices to collect funds.

I recall one customer from Ethiopia who insisted on paying via FedEx, sending up to $200 in cash every few months—wrapped in aluminum foil and tucked inside an envelope. Overwhelmed with gratitude, he contacted me personally and insisted on sending a gift of my choosing from Ethiopia. I requested African carvings, which arrived two weeks later and have been proudly displayed in my home ever since.

One customer from Colombia asked that, for every large order, we remove the CDs from their jewel cases before shipping—an accommodation I assumed helped reduce the customs duties he faced. We did our best to honor such unique requests whenever possible.

Despite the success of *ReggaeCD.com*, and in keeping with the "comprehensive" vision I had for the company from the beginning, I began planning for diversification and expansion into other areas of the music industry. The inherent risks and liabilities of such growth made it necessary to transition from a sole proprietorship to a C corporation. In 1999, I incorporated the business as Ejaness Reggae Comprehensive – ReggaeCD.com, Inc., assuming the roles of President and Chief Executive Officer.

From a Spark to a Flame

I decided the next logical step was to establish our own record label to license, manufacture, and distribute music from Jamaica. Knowing nothing about mechanical licensing, I set out to educate myself. I researched and found a comprehensive book on the laws and business of music licensing and publishing. I read it cover to cover and, using the templates it provided, drafted our own licensing and publishing agreements.

Having heard accounts of unfair treatment by other record labels through exploitative, perpetual contracts with producers and artists, I resolved that our label would be different.

My ethical principles demanded the highest standards of trust and integrity. To that end, I would limit all contracts to five years, giving licensors the freedom to renew or walk away without undue burden. I would negotiate fair advance payments—recoupable only from anticipated royalties—and I committed to issuing accurate mechanical royalty statements on time, while maintaining an open line of communication for any questions or concerns.

In January 2000, I officially added the Ejaness Reggae Comprehensive (ERC) record label and music publishing division to the company's portfolio. The label's mission was as follows:

> *To release lyrically positive, uplifting, and revolutionary music of reggae and all its subgenres, in a persistent endeavor to keep reggae's mantle of socio-political and economic commentary alive and at the forefront of world music. We will do so through selective licensing and distribution, as well as production and recording contracts with the best producers and artists in the business.*

Our next step was to make producers and artists in Jamaica aware that we were ready and open for business. This effort was greatly aided by an in-person interview on a popular radio station during one of my visits to the island. As word spread, the phone calls began to pour in, and in February 2000, I signed the company's first licensing deal.

I then secured a graphic designer and a CD manufacturer, and a couple of months later, released our first album, which I titled *Reggae 2000*. It was a compilation featuring fifteen tracks, showcasing established reggae luminaries such as Anthony B, Bushman, Tanya Stephens, Pinchers, Tristan Palmer, and Determine, alongside some promising rising stars like Stevie Face. On the inside sleeve appeared the following ambitious goal:

> *"Reggae 2000" is the first in this prestigious compilation series that will set a trend in high-quality Reggae productions for the new millennium. Lyrically offering a blend of roots, conscious dancehall, lovers' rock, and occasional humor, it will have you uncontrollably singing these catchy tunes and reflecting on the realities of which they speak. With strong rhythms laid by seasoned musicians and topped with the outstanding vocal stylings of some of Reggae's finest artists and upcoming talents, this package shall endure through time and make its mark in Reggae history.*

We gradually ramped up promotion and distribution. Since it was our first release, we were content with its encouraging yet modest sales. Like other record labels at the time, we were affected by illegal copying and duplication. I recall attending the Caribbean Labor Day parade on Eastern Parkway in Brooklyn and seeing many vendors openly selling bootleg copies of *Reggae 2000*.

Within a year, we licensed enough tracks for three more various-artists compilation albums, released under the titles *Millennium Taxi*, *Twelve Disciples*, and *Reggae for Jesus*. Among the growing roster of high-profile artists featured on these releases were Capleton, Luciano, Buju Banton, Beres Hammond, Tony Rebel, Toots and the Maytals, Jimmy Riley, Glen Washington, Richie Stephens, Pliers, Al Campbell, George Nooks, and Ernie Smith, to name a few.

In addition to our online sales, I secured deals with major wholesale distributors—one serving large retail chains across the United States and six others serving independent record stores. We also maintained ad hoc arrangements with a handful of international distributors. To further drive sales, I invested in radio advertising and made occasional promotional appearances, including interviews on several stations in the tri-state area of New York, New Jersey, and Connecticut, and occasionally in Jamaica. Sales improved steadily but remained modest compared with those of more established record labels.

A new record label is like a new artist: both usually struggle to find a breakout hit. So we soldiered on, releasing three more albums under licensing agreements between 2001 and 2002. Between 2003 and 2004, we released six additional albums under exclusive distribution deals, in which the producers covered all production and manufacturing costs, and we earned a modest per-unit margin on those distributed and sold.

In 2002, we designed and built out the large basement of our new home to accommodate the expanding business. It included a reception/lounge area, sufficient office space and workstations to support up to seven employees, a spacious storeroom, and a bathroom.

In tandem with the record label, we continued to refine and expand the content of *ReggaeCD.com*, which remained our primary source of revenue. We added detailed track listings with audio previews for online sampling before purchase, album reviews, artist biographies, news articles, and a booking page for select artists. We broadened the product range by introducing DVDs and Rasta merchandise.

To capitalize on our strong Internet presence and growing customer base, I decided to launch an online store dedicated exclusively to Bob Marley's music and merchandise.

First, I identified and established accounts with companies licensed to manufacture and distribute Bob Marley clothing, footwear, and other merchandise. Next, I registered *ReggaeKing.com*, collaborated with our web developer to build the site, and launched it in early November 2002. To drive traffic, we invested in pay-per-click advertising on the major search engines. The new store proved an instant success, generating revenue that Christmas season comparable to *ReggaeCD.com*.

We later designed and launched two additional niche-focused e-commerce stores: *DVDTrail.com*, dedicated to movie DVDs, and *HealthyLivity.com*, focused on natural herbal products. Eventually, for easier recall and stronger, more compact brand recognition, I shortened the company's name to simply Ejaness, Inc.

The Full Blaze

Inspired by the growing demand for reggae- and Rasta-inspired clothing and accessories, in 2002, I began envisioning our company's own clothing line. I saw fashion as a natural extension of our role as ambassadors for reggae music—a way to carry its spirit beyond sound and into everyday wear. After deliberating on the name for about a week, I settled on "Reggae Rags." In May 2002, I registered the domain *ReggaeRags.com*, commissioned an artist to design the logo, and later secured the trademark. Our publicized mission for the brand was as follows:

> *The Reggae Rags® clothing line, established in 2002, aims to embolden the urban and international presence of Reggae and Dancehall by depicting and emphasizing the colors, themes, and culture of the music. Reggae Rags employs only the finest-quality materials and printing to create an ever-expanding line of durable garments while paying tribute to this great music and its artistic legends.*

I later worked with an artist and a graphic designer to refine our concepts into production-ready designs, then partnered with reputable manufacturing and screen-printing companies. We were fortunate to have many models volunteer for photo shoots at no charge, bringing the line to life with genuine energy.

We launched the Reggae Rags website in late 2003 and followed with a printed color catalog in early 2004, featuring forty-seven unique items: men's and women's T-shirts, caps, hoodies, tracksuits, jackets, bags, wristbands, and headbands. To our delight, the brand's impact surpassed even our most optimistic expectations as its popularity steadily grew.

We promoted the line intensively through sponsorships and participation in fashion shows, stage shows, and other major events across New York City. We also produced and aired television and radio commercials on independent media outlets in targeted niche markets. Our designs began appearing in reggae and dancehall music videos and were worn on stage by leading artists, giving the brand authentic visibility and credibility.

This growing recognition fueled robust sales through both retail and wholesale channels—primarily via *ReggaeRags.com*—with forty-one retail resellers in fifteen countries worldwide at its peak.

We continued expanding the line through early 2005, adding forty more unique items, including our signature jacket—a crowning piece that truly embodied the brand's spirit. That same year, with the approval of Garnett Silk's family and through the Administrator General's Department of Jamaica, we secured exclusive merchandising rights to this legendary reggae artist for a limited term. In April 2005, we launched a line of his T-shirts, hoodies, and posters—a further acknowledgment of the brand's growing impact.[103]

By mid-2005, brand recognition was firmly entrenched and continued growing, and work on the next wave of clothing designs was already underway.

The Dimming Flames

As Reggae Rags grew, and *ReggaeKing.com,* along with our other online stores, held steady, our original revenue engine—*ReggaeCD.com*—had already entered a month-by-month decline that, by late 2004, accelerated sharply. Other noteworthy online reggae music stores that had begun entering the market in late 1999 were steadily eroding our share, but their impact paled in comparison to the new technological challenge.

The rapid rise of music-download services—most notably the iTunes Music Store, launched in 2003—offered instant gratification that began dismantling the CD format and the businesses built around it. From accounting for 100 percent of our revenue at launch, *ReggaeCD.com's* sales fell relentlessly, and by the end of 2004, represented less than 25 percent of the total.

As detailed in the next chapter, the decline of *ReggaeCD.com*, though significant, would pale in comparison to the profound and devastating impact of my separation and divorce, which began unfolding in late 2005. The emotional and financial toll of that dissolution was enormous, reverberating through every aspect of the company and my life. Although the business continued to operate for another eight years, it never recovered the momentum or heights it had achieved in late 2004 through early 2005. The reasons for its final dissolution in 2013 are told in Chapter 20.

My Labor and Reward

At the outset and throughout its operation, my overarching goal for the company was to promote Jamaican music and culture worldwide, and to that end, I labored tirelessly. Outside my professional employment, I devoted almost every available hour during the company's formative years and heyday to strategizing, planning, promoting, and overseeing its daily operations. On average, I worked from around 6 p.m. to midnight each weekday and from 9 a.m. to 10 p.m. on Saturdays and Sundays. It was a labor of love that brought me profound joy.

Since I had a relatively good income from my professional employment—later supplemented by rental income—I chose not to draw a salary from the company. Instead, I reinvested every net dollar of profit to fuel its growth. While I compensated staff for their standard forty-hour workweek, my reward lay not in short-term personal gain but in seeing the company fulfill its primary mission.

During the company's growth, I was sometimes asked if I would leave my professional job to run the venture full-time. I always reckoned that I was already devoting fifty to seventy hours a week to this entrepreneurial pursuit while maintaining my career—and genuinely enjoying both. I believed that scaling the staff as needed would serve the business better than gambling everything on a single path.

I eventually decided that I would leave my profession, run the company full-time, and begin drawing a salary once annual net revenue exceeded $500,000 for two consecutive years. By misfortune—or perhaps destiny—the company's annual revenue peaked in 2004, then declined and never reached the threshold I had set.

Reflections

I reflect on my entrepreneurial journey with immense pride, satisfied that I made a meaningful contribution to the global accessibility of Jamaican music and culture. By capitalizing on the internet's burgeoning era, I launched *ReggaeCD.com* in 1997 and reached tens of thousands worldwide who previously had limited or no access to reggae. Ultimately, we built a substantial mailing list of 29,821 customers and subscribers and shipped reggae music and merchandise to approximately 80 countries.

The knowledge and experience I gained from starting and running my own company for more than sixteen years have proven invaluable. Through research, trial and error, and sheer persistence, I learned—among many other things—how to:

- incorporate a C corporation;
- implement an accounting system;
- build and maintain a small business computer network;
- establish trade credit and payment terms;
- manage payroll, accounts payable, and accounts receivable;
- file tax returns (quarterly sales, payroll tax, and annual corporate);
- meet workers' compensation insurance requirements;
- register and maintain internet domains;
- operate e-commerce stores;
- draft and negotiate mechanical licensing, publishing, and distribution contracts;
- register a trademark;
- navigate offshore manufacturing, importation, and customs clearance;
- plan advertising campaigns;
- deliver excellent customer service.

Before embarking on my entrepreneurial journey, I understood the dedication and commitment success would demand. Yet I soon discovered that such effort was sustainable only when fueled by genuine passion for the mission—a quality I was fortunate to possess. I also learned early on that driving growth required taking calculated financial risks, but those same risks could threaten the company's very survival.

Through experience, I came to understand the inherently risky nature of the record label business, especially for a small independent one. Marginal returns, or losses, on investments in album releases were often the harsh reality. Hard work, talented artists, and high-quality production offered no guarantee of strong sales volumes. In retrospect, I could—and should—have conducted more thorough research before venturing into this side of the company. Illegal copying and technological shifts delivered unavoidable blows, yet I cannot use them as an excuse for my own insufficient due diligence.

Beyond the rigors of entrepreneurship lay memorable celebratory occasions: radio interviews, features on independently produced television shows, mentions in the press, and—most gratifying of all—meeting many of the leading artists in the reggae genre. It was not uncommon to receive calls from prominent artists and producers or to find myself backstage at major shows, conversing with them in an atmosphere of mutual respect and shared passion for the music.

The industry's warm embrace of our company was deeply heartwarming. What surprised me most about the genre's leading figures was their reciprocal delight when we met—they seemed genuinely appreciative of our efforts to advance the reggae we all loved. Many were thrilled to receive and wear Reggae Rags clothing without any compensation. I recall the legendary veteran artist Freddie McGregor, in 2004, happily pulling a Reggae Rags T-shirt over his planned stage outfit and performing his entire set in it at a large outdoor reggae concert in Queens, New York.

I recall with deep gratitude the exuberant reception from so many people in the reggae music industry when the Reggae Rags clothing line was launched. A leading reggae and dancehall video director reached out to me, offering to shoot our TV commercials at no charge. He wrote the scripts, assembled a production team, directed the shoot, and even arranged for artists to wear Reggae Rags in his music videos. I also remember with appreciation the many models who enthusiastically appeared in commercials, posed for photo shoots, and proudly paraded the garments at fashion shows and stage events.

Above all, my mother lived to witness most of my entrepreneurial journey. I recall her post-retirement summer vacations when she spent time with me in the office, asking countless questions about the business and offering thoughtful counsel. At her suggestion, I incorporated a philanthropic element: starting around 2003, we donated 1 percent of gross proceeds to a designated charity—a practice that continued for several years until the company's downturn. I believe she was proud to see the example of entrepreneurship she had instilled in me take root, and for that, I will always be profoundly grateful.

LIFE LESSONS

1. Entrepreneurship is turning a risky idea into value for others through relentless work. The business may fail, but the impact lives on.

2. The true entrepreneur is measured not in calm waters but by how well they sail through storms.

3. In business, technological change is a double-edged sword: a catalyst for the fast, a coffin nail for the slow.

4. Entrepreneurial passion must bow to due diligence. Blind leaps rarely hit their target.

Ejaness, Inc., company logos, and previous online stores.

Ejaness (E.R.C.) Records' Discography

Albums licensed and/or exclusively distributed (2000–2007)

Album Title	Artist	Catalog No.	Year
Reggae 2000	Various	ERC5741.2	2000
Millennium Taxi	Various	ERC0742.2	2000
Twelve Disciples	Various	ERC0743.2	2000
Reggae for Jesus	Various	ERC0744.2	2001
Beres Hammond and Friends	Various	ERC0745.2	2001
Coming at You	Stevie Face	ERC0746.2	2001
The Man Upstairs	Richie Stephens	ERC0747.2	2002
Covers for Lovers	Richie Stephens	POG.ERC3335.2	2003
I Still Love You	Jackie Brown	ERC.JBM3334	2003
Element of Surprise	Mykal Somer	EEI.ERC3336.2	2003
Kingdom Ambassador	Stitchie	ERC.DBM3337	2004
Bob's Bar	Urban Tribe	AAMP054338	2005
Sleng Teng Progress 2K5	Various	EJ.BTE3338	2005

Front cover of the 2004 12-page Reggae Rags catalog.
(models anonymized for privacy)

The legendary Freddie McGregor performing in Reggae Rags at a 2004 concert in Queens, NY.

CHAPTER 19

Uncharted Path, Unavoidable Storm

The consequences of untamed impulse

The Toll of the Tempest

In 2004, my second marriage—now in its sixth year—was still on the roller-coaster trajectory I described in Chapter 15, heading toward an inevitable derailment that exacted a heavy toll on my health. My blood pressure had risen under the unrelenting strain, and my primary-care physician advised that I begin medication for hypertension. The mounting demands of my career and business required calm and stability at home—a tranquility that had become increasingly scarce.

The frequency and intensity of our verbal disputes had become unbearable. In a last-ditch effort to salvage the marriage, I sought the intervention of a family member, who suggested that Marge and I each make a separate list of the behaviors we knew were causing our discord. We would then sit down calmly, discuss each item, and agree on remedial changes or compromises. We set a one-week deadline to prepare our lists.

On the appointed day for our heart-to-heart conversation, I arrived with a list of around fourteen issues to address; she had none. I did not take this as proof that I was blameless, but rather as evidence that she had not given the exercise the seriousness it required. As I presented my list, point by point, we discussed and reached an agreement on every one. Yet her commitment to those changes lasted less than a month, and our discord returned in full force.

In a continued effort to avoid a divorce that seemed increasingly inevitable, I devised a plan that would separate us for a time. We had both been enamored with the idea of eventually moving to Florida and had already purchased a plot of land near Naples. Given the nature of her work, I believed she could easily find comparable employment at a similar company there.

I suggested we sell our other home—then rented—and use the proceeds to buy or build a house in Florida for her to reside in. We would visit each other in the interim while I remained in our current home, giving us space until I was ready to relocate and—hopefully—we had resolved our differences. She initially agreed, and I felt a surge of relief and elation. Sadly, two weeks later, she told me she had changed her mind. All hope seemed lost, and the specter of divorce now loomed more menacingly than ever.

By then, having lost all desire for time alone together, I routinely retreated to my business office and worked late into the night. She sensed my deliberate avoidance, which only added fuel to the already-burning flame. Eventually, I moved out of our shared bedroom and into my son's room.

Amid this ongoing struggle and my growing contemplation of divorce, I never lost sight of my stepdaughter, Simone. She remained the sole beacon of light in a home darkened by her parents' discord. Her love for us both was unconditional; she never took sides, and her character and demeanor were exemplary. Post-divorce, I envisioned an informal visitation arrangement, since she was neither my biological nor formally adopted child.

The Inevitable Separation

Concluding that our differences were irreconcilable, I asked myself, "Is this the way I want to live the rest of my life?"

The answer was a resounding no.

I told Marge we needed to separate, knowing I would later file for divorce. I understood that financial and emotional consequences would follow—what would the legal costs be, how would marital assets be divided, and could I withstand the anger I feared she would unleash? While I expected this divorce to be more difficult than my first, I underestimated the degree of difficulty that lay ahead.

Strangely, Marge remained calm—perhaps convinced the separation would be temporary and that I would buckle under the financial strain of my decision. I told her which pieces of furniture I wanted to take, and she agreed without protest. In fact, on our last night together, she spoke to me in a soft voice until past midnight, her tone reminiscent of the early days of our relationship. She bade me farewell the next morning and left for work before the movers arrived. On November 5, 2005, I moved out of our matrimonial home into a rented apartment on Long Island, New York.

On the morning of November 6, I awoke to my new reality. Approaching my thirty-eighth birthday, I felt deep trepidation and uncertainty. Yet amid those fears, I discovered an inner strength and began the long-awaited process of deep introspection in the loneliness of my solitude. Regardless of how the divorce would unfold, I needed to assess my past and chart a future for both my personal and professional life. This journey of self-examination would continue for the next couple of years.

The calm of Marge's farewell proved as fleeting as the eye of a storm. As the Jamaican saying goes, "Hell an' powda house"* waited just over the horizon. My decision not to share my new address signaled the permanence of our separation—and marked the resumption of turmoil. Her text and voicemail messages grew increasingly unpleasant. Family members and mutual friends told me about her calls to them, which seemed to seek empathy while also trying to sway their opinions. Not surprisingly, their accounts of her statements never reflected the full severity of our longstanding marital problems and irreconcilable differences.

With the company still operating from the basement offices, I had to return periodically to fulfill my responsibilities. The verbal battles that erupted whenever Marge was home made those visits problematic. Before going, I first had to confirm with my employee whether she was present and kept my increasingly rare appearances brief. My growing absence from the business contributed further to its decline.

About a week before Christmas, Marge calmly asked me to visit on Christmas morning for the gift-opening ritual with my stepdaughter, Simone, who was still adjusting to my absence.

---

* Translation: "Hell and powder house," as in gunpowder, which means a situation of mayhem and turmoil.

Anticipating my refusal, she quickly added, "Don't worry, I'm not going to start any quarrels; I promise I will remain upstairs the entire time you are with her."

Hesitant and doubtful, I went against my better judgment and agreed.

Not surprisingly, her promise was not kept, and within an hour, I had to leave strategically without even saying goodbye to Simone. That turned out to be the last Christmas I spent with her.

Navigating a Tumultuous Divorce

In what might have been an act of leverage through financial pressure or simply an honest lack of resources, Marge soon informed me that she would no longer contribute to the mortgage payments—including real estate taxes and insurance—for our recently constructed, three-year-old home. I was not naïve to this possibility and had already assessed my resources and capacity to cover both my rent and the full mortgage for up to a year. Maintaining my creditworthiness and my ability to rebuild after the divorce depended on it. With only this one-year window of financial survivability, I knew I had to act quickly.

Early in 2006, I retained an attorney to handle my divorce. It was my second time through the process, but this time the financial stakes were far higher. The next step was hiring a process server to hand-deliver the summons and complaint to Marge. As I suspected, it took several attempts. I figured I wouldn't need the process server to confirm when she was served—I would hear from Marge the moment it happened.

Upon delivery of the summons, I received a barrage of increasingly heated text and voicemail messages from Marge. Some of these unsettling messages—received throughout much of the divorce process—remain vividly etched in my memory. Thankfully, none of these anger-evoked unkind wishes ever came true. In retrospect, I conclude that she was simply venting her anger and perhaps still clinging to the hope of a marriage that had long since become irreconcilable.

From age eighteen, I had faithfully kept my commitment to avoid alcohol. That ended during this period of turmoil. One day, as I confided my psychological struggles to a friend who had endured a similarly difficult divorce, he said, "Eric, I know you don't drink, but brother, take a drink every now and then to calm your nerves; it will help."

His words, offered in empathy, marked the beginning of an unhealthy return to alcohol consumption.

I now kept a stock of vodka, rum, beer, and other spirits in my apartment, and I frequently indulged at night. One night, I overdid it and was awakened the next morning—nearly 10 a.m.—by a phone call. I was in a daze, my speech slurred and incoherent. I had missed an 8 a.m. appointment. I suspected I had teetered on the edge of alcohol poisoning and, with a chill, realized I could have died in my sleep. It took the rest of that day and the following night to detox.

Eventually, Marge retained her own attorney. I tried to persuade her of the advantages of an amicable settlement over a contested divorce. "Marge," I said, "I've researched this, and in a contested divorce, a couple typically loses 20 to 30 percent of their assets to legal fees." She remained noncommittal, but I went ahead and prepared a settlement proposal and sent it to her.[104]

My proposal identified and divided our assets after deducting the premarital funds I had contributed toward the purchase of our three-year-old home. Those funds came from my retirement savings and my portion of the proceeds from the sale of the co-op apartment I bought with my first wife in 1992. From the outset, I knew I was at a disadvantage: I was the one seeking the divorce, not her. As I assume anyone in her position would do, she capitalized on that advantage.

She rejected my proposal and stated that her keeping the three-year-old house in any final settlement was nonnegotiable. She also refused to deduct my premarital assets from our joint net worth and asked pointedly, "Yu tink freedom cum cheap?"*

I soon reconciled myself to the reality that my freedom was indeed worth whatever reasonable financial compromise it required. What followed was a series of attorney-mediated negotiations, made somewhat easier by this preconditioning.

---

* Translation: "Do you think freedom comes cheaply?"

Luminescent Interruptions

The same month I separated from Marge—figuratively and literally in need of a new outlook—I underwent LASIK surgery. It marked the end of a long history of vision struggles. From ages nine to twelve, I wore glasses for hyperopia (farsightedness); then, in 1993 at age twenty-six, I was diagnosed with myopia (nearsightedness). The procedure ended twelve years of constant reliance on glasses and contact lenses. The morning after, I opened my eyes to a clear world—it felt as though a long-standing burden had finally been lifted.

Around the same time, my employer offered me the opportunity to apply, study, and sit for the Certified Construction Manager (CCM) exam. Amid the turmoil, it felt like a ray of hope—the encouragement I needed that brighter days still lie ahead. In early 2006, I took the exam alongside a handpicked group of twenty-three mostly managerial colleagues; I was one of only five who passed. On February 25, 2006, CCM was officially added to my credentials.[105]

The Final Phase

Following the sale of our older two-family house in August 2006—the one previously rented—the proceeds were placed in escrow. From these funds, the monthly mortgage payments for the other two jointly held properties were covered. For the first time since my separation nine months earlier, I experienced relief from the relentless financial duress. Near the end of 2006, another reprieve arrived: to ease the strain of my long daily commute from Long Island to Manhattan, I relocated to a new apartment in Queens.

Following appraisals of the business, retirement accounts, and our three-year-old home—and after placing the Florida land on the market—the fifteen-month negotiation process finally concluded. On April 23, 2007, we signed a twenty-three-page Stipulation of Settlement, thankfully avoiding a contested divorce in court. On the day of the signing, Marge was cordial and pleasant and seemed genuinely content with the final resolution. The nearly seven-year roller-coaster ride had finally come to a screeching halt.

In the end, as expected, my net worth was drastically reduced. I had spent more than $25,000 in legal fees, incurred ancillary expenses throughout the multi-year process, and surrendered significant equity in the negotiated settlement. The formal Judgment of Divorce was issued by the court on September 14, 2007.

Since then, I have endeavored to release any lingering animosity and to wish Marge genuine happiness and a compatible soulmate—in the spirit of the Jamaican adage "Ebri huo hab dem tik ah bush."*

There is one thing Marge taught me that has served me well ever since: her "never take no for an answer" approach when purchasing goods or services. She firmly believed that the answer from the lowest-tier employee in any business was rarely the final word. To achieve her goal—whether a better purchase price or service package—she would persistently ask to speak to the next level of management, and if necessary, to the owner as a last resort. I marveled at her success rate; she often secured what I had thought impossible. For this lesson, I will forever be grateful.

Reflections

Going through this divorce helped me understand why so many people remain in dysfunctional marriages despite futile hopes of reconciliation. Walking away demands real bravery—a willingness to step onto an uncharted path strewn with thorns and potholes, where the destination is never guaranteed. Yet despite those challenges, I was wise to heed the Jamaican maxim "Wah gaan bad ah mawning, cyaan cum gud ah eveling."†

This chapter of my journey proved the greatest test of my ability to withstand challenges in their rawest form. I had endured years of profound, health-impacting stress, found the strength to walk away, navigated the shark-infested waters of divorce, suffered significant financial losses, and survived to rebuild what was lost. It taught me the pitfalls of impulsive action and fortified me to face future challenges

---

* Translation: "Every hoe has its stick in the bush," which means that, like the farm tool (a hoe) that must be fitted with the right-sized stick, there is someone for everyone.

† Translation: "What went bad in the morning cannot be made good in the evening," meaning that some bad decisions cannot be reversed, even with the passage of time.

with greater ease and resolve. As the Jamaican proverb wisely reminds us: "Yu pred yuh bed haad, yu haffi liddung pan i'haad."*

Who was ultimately to blame for embarking on a union where incompatibilities in personality and values were obvious yet ignored? I take full responsibility. I was a victim of my own impetuous decisions. I took no time after my first marriage to engage in the wise and necessary introspection required before entering another. Marge, never having been married before, could not have learned from an experience she never had.

Do I regret my second marriage? Strangely, I remain ambivalent.

Would I have traveled this road had I known with certainty what lay ahead? No.

Am I a stronger and more resilient man today because of this difficult path? Yes.

No challenge since then has seemed insurmountable. I have come to believe that the universe, in its infinite wisdom, guides us along predestined paths—a rite of passage in this journey called life.

On the morning of April 24, 2007—the day after signing the stipulation—I pushed my introspection into high gear. At thirty-nine, with sufficient time, youthful energy still ahead, and hard-won wisdom, I committed to reconstructing my personal life. I would carry the lessons from my two failed marriages while holding fast to the vision of one day finding my forever soulmate. That blessing arrived in 2018, thirteen years after my 2005 separation—a story I will happily share in the pages ahead.

LIFE LESSONS

1. Before you marry someone, study his or her qualities that you dislike and ask, "Can I live with them for the rest of my life?"

---

* Translation: "If you spread (make) your bed hard, you have to lie on a hard bed," which means that one must take responsibility for their actions and accept and deal with the consequences.

2. Procrastination disguised as patience is just cowardice in slow motion.

3. Financial wealth and health usually trade places. Which do you value more?

4. True strength lies not in avoidance but in the willingness to confront what ails.

5. Using intimacy to settle conflict is the prey kissing the predator; the feared hunt always resumes.

6. A child bathed in constant parental discord carries the scars forever.

7. The universe teaches best through the endless difficulties stitched into being human.

8. Alcohol is no friend in deed or need; just a salesman peddling escape from reality. Avoid it, lest your escape become permanent.

9. Winning the argument often loses the war. Compromise, even when you're right, guarantees victory.

10. Prior independence is the crucial prerequisite for a marriage of healthy co-dependence.

(This page intentionally left blank.)

PART IV

RENEWAL AND ARRIVAL

(This page intentionally left blank.)

- -

CHAPTER 20

Rebuilding from the Inside Out

Taking stock, release, and resurgence

- -

Taking Inventory

At thirty-nine, with my second divorce settlement finalized, I could finally rebuild the broken parts of my life without hindrance. I looked beyond the horizon for new possibilities. I believe I was blessed with certain attributes—common among many of my Generation X peers—that proved instrumental in this self-restorative journey.

I possessed an ingrained independence—not needing validation for my decisions, nor fearing major life changes—and a resourcefulness instilled by my mother. I adapted when circumstances shifted, modifying my plans to meet new realities. I reckoned that if I could survive an arduous marriage and a difficult divorce—bruised but not broken—then my fortitude was unbreakable.

I chronicle the following successes in rebuilding my life not to aggrandize, but as an example of the human capacity to overcome turmoil and setbacks, to pursue deferred dreams, and to discover new possibilities.

My first order of business was to take inventory of everything in my past and present that was causing unnecessary stress, had outlived its purpose, was yielding diminishing returns on investment, or simply no longer brought me joy.

My nearly ten-year journey as a landlord, managing up to four tenants at a time, brought financial benefits, but these were offset by considerable demands on my time and the persistent challenges of property management. With the rental properties now sold, I decided not to pursue this endeavor any longer.

Deciding the future of my company proved far more difficult. The circumstances surrounding my divorce and its fifteen-month duration had been devastating to my ability to manage and grow the business effectively. As a result, gross annual revenue had fallen to less than 50 percent of its pre-divorce level, while indebtedness remained high.

I had to quickly reduce expenses, which meant operating from a much smaller space and moving excess inventory into a storage facility. With only one employee remaining and the distraction of the divorce finally behind me, I allocated sufficient time to the business to stabilize income and keep debt service current. I felt ambivalent about the company's long-term future but resolved to defer any definitive decision until later.

Regarding my professional career, serendipity arrived shortly after the final divorce judgment on September 14, 2007. Days later, I received the promotion that had been pending since I passed the CCM exam earlier that year. I advanced from Construction Administrator to Construction Manager, accompanied by a salary increase. Whether a mere coincidence or destiny, the timing provided the extra boost I needed to break free from the shackles of the past and embrace my new beginning.

Making Deferred Dreams a Reality

My next step was to revive the unfulfilled dreams I had outlined in Chapter 17. At the top of the list was ending the long hiatus from my pursuit of a Master of Public Administration (MPA). After my reentry application was approved, I resumed classes with renewed vigor in the spring 2008 semester. More than any other new or revived aspiration, the MPA became my most powerful tool for healing and empowerment.

Despite the demands of rigorous research, extensive reading, lengthy papers, and night classes, I found the program profoundly enlightening and rewarding. It represented my first foray beyond the scientific disciplines that had defined my earlier academic path.

My dedication and hard work bore fruit in April 2009, when I was initiated into Pi Alpha Alpha, the National Honor Society for Public Affairs and Administration. I graduated the following month with a 3.9 GPA. Fortuitously, the MPA journey concluded just two months before

I assumed full-time custody and single-parent responsibilities for my son.

Another lingering dream I pursued, starting in late 2009, was to become fluent in both the spoken and written forms of a foreign language. This aspiration had been deferred since high school, when a class-schedule conflict prevented me from studying my first choice: French.

In high school, Spanish had been just another class I endured with little interest. Now it had become my language of choice. French felt impractical without frequent opportunities to use it, so I turned to Spanish—the second most widely spoken language in the United States.

The spark that ignited my fervent pursuit of Spanish came one day while channel surfing. I landed on a Spanish-language TV channel, paused, and listened for a few minutes. I realized I understood fragments of the dialogue, and like an epiphany, it struck me: with modern language-learning tools, becoming reasonably proficient should not be overly difficult.

My three years of high school Spanish had emphasized memorization and recall for written exams far more than actual speaking proficiency. Still, I believed that with my rudimentary foundation, smartphone apps, a commercially available audio program, and total immersion, I could achieve self-taught fluency. After researching options, I invested in the Pimsleur program—a thirty-lesson audio course on CDs that employed spaced repetition and active recall, patterned after the natural way children acquire language. I completed it during my daily train commute in just a couple of months.[106]

Since the Pimsleur program focused primarily on words and phrases used in everyday conversation, I sought more advanced tools. I turned to vocabulary-building apps and discovered a free Spanish grammar e-book, which I studied cover to cover. At the same time, I immersed myself fully in the language by listening exclusively to Spanish music, watching Spanish television, reading Spanish news, and switching the language settings on both my car and phone to Spanish. Within months, I was able to write comfortably and hold substantive conversations with native speakers.

With Spanish being a phonetic language, I found its spelling, writing, and pronunciation far more straightforward than English. The irregularities in its rules felt inherently logical to me, shaped by my own thought process. Despite the challenges of its complex system of tenses, verb conjugations, and grammatical gender for nouns, I became completely enamored with the language.

I've often empathized with native Spanish speakers learning English, with its far greater degree of rule irregularities—especially in spelling and pronunciation. I occasionally advise my native Spanish-speaking friends who struggle with English pronunciation to think of it as poetry: a language that demands more memorization for true mastery.

I discovered that studying a foreign language is a never-ending yet deeply rewarding journey—always with room to expand knowledge, vocabulary, and proficiency. It mirrors one's lifelong relationship with one's own native tongue. Spanish opened my once English-limited world to interactions with new nationalities, cultures, and perspectives. As a lifelong music aficionado, I could now listen to and understand numerous Spanish-language genres, effectively doubling the catalog of music I consumed.

I never possessed great athletic ability, but I have always maintained a strong interest in physical activity, regularly participating in non-contact sports and outdoor pursuits. Winter sports, especially skiing, particularly intrigued me, and in 2006, I made my first visit to a ski slope. After a couple of on-site lessons, I took my first solo run down a gentle, beginner-friendly slope—and loved it.

Though my skills never rose to the intermediate level, I continued to ski once or twice each winter season until February 2015. On my third run down a less-than-ideal, hard-packed, icy slope at Gore Mountain in upstate New York, I suffered my first skiing accident and broke a bone near my left ankle. The healing process required wearing an orthopedic walking boot for about six weeks. Despite the ordeal, I had lived and enjoyed a dream with no regrets. As the Jamaican proverb wisely observes, "Cowad man kip soun bone,"* and I have not returned to the slopes since.

I was also fascinated by golf, which I took up in 2006 and played for a few years. At that time, it served as a therapeutic distraction from the intensity of my divorce process and offered the chance to meet and interact with new people on a weekly or monthly basis. My interest

---

* Translation: "A coward man keeps sound bones," meaning that someone who fears and avoids potential danger will remain safe from injury.

eventually waned, but I still remember the sharp crack of my many impressive drives, watching the ball soar hundreds of yards through the air, and the single birdie I ever sank on the green.

Among the many life lessons the sport offers, patience and humility resonated with me most deeply. It takes years of practice for the average person to reach proficiency, and even the most skilled golfers are routinely humbled by their own inconsistency. The game teaches that perfection—even with one's best effort—is often elusive.

This was also a time to catch up on literary works I had long desired to read. I consumed books on philosophy, biographies, and classic literature with fresh enthusiasm. I was particularly struck by the Greek philosopher Socrates in Plato's *Apology*, who argued that true wisdom lies not in what one knows, but in recognizing what one does not know. A person must first acknowledge the limits of their knowledge before seeking to expand it.[107]

Though the idea seemed intuitive, Socrates expressed it deliberately and in an actionable way. From that point on, this principle became the lens through which I viewed and analyzed both my own and others' words and actions—in personal, professional, and political matters alike.

The realization that many of my long-held dreams had come to fruition in just a few years—after overcoming daunting challenges—was a testament to the virtue of patience and the endurance of hope. I believed then that all my remaining dreams were simply awaiting their right time and place.

A Major Relocation

Throughout my divorce and its financial challenges, I diligently maintained my perfect record of repaying creditors. I knew that an impaired credit rating could significantly hinder my ability to acquire real estate in the future. Post-divorce, I was uncertain where to make my next real estate investment. Upon realizing the much lower housing costs in the nearby state of New Jersey, I purchased a condominium and relocated there in October 2009. My commute to work in Manhattan took the same time—or less—than from my last residence in Queens, New York. I also relocated my company operations and changed its state of incorporation to New Jersey.

My move to New Jersey marked a fresh start, filled with excitement and opportunities for exploration and discovery. The physical distance helped heal past wounds and strengthen my resolve. In essence, I now felt more at home than I had throughout my previous twenty years in the United States. It was also a time to focus on being a single parent, empowering my seventeen-year-old son—who had recently joined me to attend college—to complete his education and prepare for adulthood.

Volunteerism and Mentorship

Influenced by my mother's penchant for always going above and beyond, I routinely volunteered for both small and significant opportunities whenever they arose in my professional and academic life. At work, I chaired forums for consecutive years to resolve issues in the management and delivery of capital projects. I also spearheaded or participated in steering committees and task forces that addressed enterprise-level challenges affecting the Agency's ability to operate effectively and serve the public.

In spring 2014, I received my most impactful long-term volunteer opportunity. As a member of a professional society for construction management, I applied, met the qualifications, and satisfactorily completed training to become a Program Evaluator Volunteer (PEV) for ABET (Accreditation Board for Engineering and Technology). ABET is a globally recognized accreditation organization. A PEV is considered an expert from academia, industry, or government. ABET accredits specific academic programs at colleges and universities to ensure they meet the quality standards of the professions for which they prepare graduates.[108]

The accreditation process is triggered each year when colleges and universities submit self-studies and other required documents for initial accreditation or renewal of prior accredited programs. The self-studies are designed to demonstrate that each program meets the general and program-specific criteria established by ABET.

For each assignment, my PEV commitment typically spanned four to six months. The first three months involved initial assessment, virtual meetings with the team chair and other program evaluators, and preparation for a three-day on-site visit to the institution's campus. My initial assessment required reviewing the institution's voluminous self-study of its undergraduate construction management program to determine compliance with ABET's accreditation criteria.

During the three-day campus visits, I conducted facility tours, examined course syllabi and student work, and interviewed faculty, students, administrators, and other relevant stakeholders. I then used this on-site information to validate the details presented in the self-study and further assess the program's quality. My most memorable experiences were the interviews and open question-and-answer sessions I held with students from diverse backgrounds—listening to their unbridled hopes and career ambitions.

The program evaluation team met daily to discuss and update its findings. Before the final day of each visit, I was responsible for drafting a report summarizing the program's strengths and weaknesses and reviewing it with the team chair and any paired PEV. These findings later formed the basis for ABET's decision to grant or deny program accreditation.

On the final day of each visit, I presented my findings at an exit meeting attended by the institution's president or chancellor, provost, dean, and program chairs for each evaluated program, as well as the team chair and other program PEVs. After each visit, my responsibilities included reviewing the institution's written responses, if any, with the team chair and completing our team performance surveys.

I served as a PEV for ten years, until 2024, working weekends and nights to complete document reviews and evaluations, and taking vacation time from my job to conduct campus visits. During my tenure, I traveled to multiple colleges and universities across the United States. I was even offered the opportunity to evaluate a program related to my specialty at an institution in Jamaica, which I sadly had to decline due to a conflict of interest.

At the conclusion of each assignment, team chairs consistently gave high ratings for my PEV performance and often recommended that I consider serving as a team chair in the future. While appreciative of the recognition, I never pursued the role because of the additional time, commitment, and coordination it would require.

Despite never seeking a leadership role beyond my volunteer PEV duties, in 2022, my professional society informed me of their intent to nominate me as an alternate commissioner and team chair for ABET.

The vastly increased leadership responsibilities in my full-time career left little room or energy for the added demands of that position. Consequently, I declined the nomination and resigned from my PEV role in 2024. Nevertheless, the profound honor of having served institutions of higher learning in this capacity remains invaluable.

Alongside my responsibilities as a PEV, I registered with my professional society to serve as a mentor for individuals pursuing careers in construction management. I shared my knowledge and provided what I hope was invaluable guidance to a few mentees who went on to build successful careers.

The End of Past Relics

Despite all my self-restorative efforts, two remnants of my past life lingered and weighed on me: the jointly owned land in Florida, which remained on the market at the time of my second divorce, and the continued operation of my company—albeit at a mere fraction of its former size.

As part of the Stipulation of Settlement signed on April 23, 2007, some money was placed in a joint account to cover the monthly mortgage payments on the Florida land until it was sold. If the funds were exhausted before the sale, my ex-wife and I would each bear half the ongoing costs from our personal resources. Unfortunately, the Florida real estate market was in a severe downturn, severely limiting the land's salability, and the escrowed funds were eventually depleted.

My ex-wife honored the agreement by paying her 50 percent share of the mortgage for a few months before informing me that she no longer had the resources to continue. I then bore the full cost for another two-plus years. With no upswing in the real estate market on the horizon and the land valued at less than the remaining mortgage balance, covering 100 percent of the monthly payments became untenable. Even in the event of a sale, recouping any meaningful portion of my investment seemed doubtful. Consequently, in 2011, I made the difficult decision to walk away from the land, losing everything I had invested. That final post-divorce shackle was at last broken.

Two years later, in 2013, I had lost all interest in making further investments in the company I had built, even in its potentially lucrative segments. Instead, I focused on salvaging what I could before orchestrating a graceful shutdown. I sold off the remaining inventory at a steep discount, along with some of the company's intellectual property. I also shut down the websites and let the domain registrations for *ReggaeCD.com*, *HealthyLivity.com*, and *DVDTrail.com* expire, returning them to the public domain.

Even so, the proceeds fell short of paying off the remaining business debt for which I had signed personal guarantees, leaving me personally responsible for repayment. It was a bittersweet end to my brainchild—an entrepreneurial enterprise that had operated for sixteen years. On June 19, 2013, the company was formally dissolved with a state-issued certificate of dissolution.

Navigating New Relationships

Following my separation in November 2005, I needed a long hiatus from marriage or any relationship that implied or demanded marital promises. Marriage and the deep emotional commitments it required were no longer a priority, and I made a personal pledge never to repeat the marital mistakes of my past. This hiatus lasted nearly fourteen years.

During this period, I dated women with the aim—admittedly often unsuccessfully—of sustaining long-term, exclusive relationships. I never wanted to convey to my son, by example, that being a so-called player was an admirable trait to emulate. When a relationship was short-lived, it usually ended because of my aversion to any perceived personality traits reminiscent of the past. I recall—not proudly—saying on a few occasions, unsympathetically and dismissively, "I paid a lot of money to end my last marriage, and it will cost me nothing to end this relationship."

In November 2007, I met an amazing and beautiful woman named Jackie. She was an accounting manager who worked in a different division of the Agency. Our paths fortuitously crossed at work under platonic circumstances, and over time, I gradually learned more about her.

She was Colombian by birth, ten years my junior, brilliant, and brimming with warm, radiant energy. Her fair, unblemished skin framed a genuine, enchanting smile. Her long, straight, shiny black hair cascaded to her waist like Rapunzel's. She exuded femininity in her calm composure, graceful walk, and pleasant voice.

Following one of our encounters, I invited her to lunch with a casual "We should go to lunch sometime," to which she replied politely, "Sure."

I had a sixth sense that if we became friends, it could lead to something more serious than I was ready or willing to entertain. Consequently, I delayed following up on the open lunch invitation. That changed when we coincidentally crossed paths months later, in August 2008.

After exchanging a few pleasantries, I said, "Remember, we have a pending lunch. Let me know which day is good for you." We later confirmed the date and time, and I suggested a Thai restaurant a few blocks away.

We spent the lunch hour completely engrossed in conversation, and at the end—undeterred by my sixth-sense trepidation—I asked for her cell phone number. Soon after, we began dating and were frequently spending weekends together.

Over time, I discovered her unquestionable transparency, honesty, and sincerity, as well as her insecurities. She looked at me with a countenance of respect and admiration and was usually joyful in an adorable, childlike way. I nicknamed her in Spanish "Mi paquete de alegría," which translates to "my bundle of joy."

Her requests were always reasonable and simple—more of my time in person or by phone—never inquiring about the long-term trajectory of our relationship. Although I was enthralled by her desirable qualities and felt the depth of her affection, I was neither willing nor able to provide the level of emotional support, presence, and time she deserved. A few months after we began dating, I received permanent custody of my son, which placed its own demands on my time and presence.

While Jackie never raised the prospect of marriage, I viewed the deep emotional commitment she wanted and deserved as essentially equivalent. After about a year into our relationship, I told her I was convinced she possessed the qualities of an ideal wife. However, my self-imposed hiatus from marriage was still far from complete. Consequently, I hardened my emotional unavailability, stifled my admiration, and deliberately avoided falling deeply in love with her. This left me feeling guilty, and I worried that my emotional walls were inflicting a torment on her that she did not deserve.

I gave her reason—through my increasing lack of devotion and growing absence—to end our relationship. Yet it became clear that she had left the final decision to me. In June 2010, under duress, I ended our nearly two-year relationship. The task proved more painful than I had imagined—one that would haunt me for the next seven years.

The end of my relationship with Jackie gave way to another—a five-year relationship with an Italian-born woman named Sofia. Conveniently for me, she was less demanding of my time. We were both divorced single parents, each with a teenage child who needed our attention and guidance. Our time together was reserved for weekends when she wasn't working, and her daughter was with family.

Sofia was genuine, honest, transparent, and deeply affectionate, yet she also possessed combative traits reminiscent of the past, which prompted caution on my part. She occasionally asked about my long-term intentions, subtly hinting at marriage, but I always deflected. I relied on the honest but convenient excuse that we needed to focus on our parental responsibilities and leave thoughts of marriage for the future.

Despite my noncommittal stance, Sofia consistently demonstrated her love and care. One night, after an exercise-induced health issue landed me in the emergency room, she rushed to my aid—sixty miles from her home on Long Island—although she had to work the next morning. On another occasion, when I needed hernia surgery, she was there before, during, and after, caring for me in her home until I recovered sufficiently to travel back to New Jersey. For these acts of love and more, I will forever be grateful.

Around the fourth year of our relationship, Sofia grew more impatient, pressing me with sustained questions about my marital intentions. In September 2016, my deflection tactics no longer sufficed, and she demanded a definitive answer. I gave her the painful but truthful response: no, I could not promise her marriage. She cried, yet she respected my honesty, thanked me for the opportunity to experience what it was like to truly love someone, and even suggested we maintain a platonic friendship.

She later told me that when she shared the news with her parents, her father had a surprising observation. He said that while he had always seen her deep affection for me, he never sensed a matching passion on my part. I reckoned he was right.

Throughout my five-year relationship with Sofia and the few short-lived ones that followed, Jackie never left my mind. The absence of her resonant inner beauty, selfless passion, and feminine grace created a longing that lived in my conscious thoughts and my quietest subconscious moments.

I clung to the unfounded hope that Jackie would still be single when I was finally ready for full commitment. So I tried to maintain a connection over the years, mostly through text messages, but my outreach went largely unanswered. The few responses I received were brief and disengaged.

Whenever our paths crossed by chance, she either pretended not to see me or—worse—met my gaze with total dissociation, avoiding any form of engagement. I realized then that I had broken her heart, but not her pride. She defied the Jamaican saying that "Hul fyah tick easy fi ketch."*

Were all hopes dashed? Should I have forgotten about her? Hope and destiny would be my guides as my redemptive love story unfolds in the next chapter.

LIFE LESSONS

1. Beyond the cold, dark caverns of despair, a light waits, ready to flood you with warmth. Keep walking.

2. After every failure, take inventory and rebuild, never reincorporating what's broken into your new foundation.

3. Resilience is the necessary steel that keeps our columns of resistance from buckling under life's gravitas.

4. Ambitious dreams are mental heartbeats, nurturing our minds and giving meaning to life.

---

* Translation: "Old fire sticks are easy to catch," meaning it is easy to rekindle a past romantic relationship.

5. When planning a self-restorative journey, let education be your passport.

6. Learning a foreign language is an investment with exponential returns.

7. Perfection is as elusive as a desert mirage, but if you stop chasing it, improvement ends.

8. Volunteerism is one of life's greatest symbioses—you usually get back more than you give.

9. When a relic of your past becomes an obstacle to your future—let it go.

10. Short-term losses usually buy long-term wins; don't sweat them.

11. When the vase of your life lies shattered, melt the pieces and remold them into something far more beautiful.

(This page intentionally left blank.)

CHAPTER 21

The Love That Chose Me Back

The moment I became whole

My life experiences up to this point had taught me the power of positive thinking and its magnetic force in attracting blessings into my life. This time, the blessing I sought was a second chance—to regain Jackie's friendship and, hopefully, her love.

Our Beautiful Collision

For over a year, I had neither crossed paths with Jackie nor even glimpsed her from a distance, despite our working on different floors of the same building. In fact, I concluded that she must have relocated and even asked her via text, but—as usual—there was no response.

In August 2017—seven years after our separation—those magnetic forces brought about the most beautiful and unexpected collision of my life. I had just reentered our office building and, perhaps distracted by my phone, was not looking ahead. As I approached the entry turnstiles and was about to pass through, an inner voice said, "Look up." When I did, our eyes locked; she had been similarly distracted and had no time to summon her usual countenance of dissociation. My heart pounded as I smiled and said, "Hi."

She smiled back, returned the greeting, and—without a pause—continued on her way.

I was elated and walked away wondering what her pleasant demeanor meant. Was it merely an unplanned reaction that didn't reflect her true emotions? Had time finally healed the wounds of our painful separation? There was only one way to find out—I needed to initiate a follow-up.

I hurried to my office, thought through various messaging options, but resolved to keep it simple. I sent her this text: "It was really nice seeing you."

I waited in nervous anticipation for a response, which soon arrived: "It was nice seeing you, too."

My heart skipped a beat as renewed hope dispelled my trepidation. What would be my next move?

Without hesitation, I texted, "Would you come to lunch with me one day next week?"

I waited, but no reply came. Had I pushed too hard—too quickly?

Despite no immediate response, I remained overjoyed for the rest of the day and night. Renewed hope stirred that the empty void and guilt I had carried since our separation might finally mend. I resolved that her past countenance of dissociation and her silence on my text messages could have been part of her healing process. Perhaps the distance she maintained was not rooted in lasting animosity—or, if it once was, those feelings had now diminished.

Finally, the next day, I received an affirmative response to my lunch invitation. She chose the restaurant, which I took as a sign that she would dictate the terms of our re-engagement. With butterflies in my stomach, on August 27, 2017, I met her and walked with her to lunch.

As we talked, I realized this was no longer the insecure Jackie of the past; she was confident and fully in command of her emotions. She summarized her dissatisfaction with the way I had ended our relationship and scolded me for my lack of empathy. I apologized profusely and explained the mental torment our separation had caused me during the seven years of our estrangement.

I had pledged to myself that if Jackie gave me the opportunity for renewed friendship, I would never do anything to jeopardize what I had waited seven years to regain. Part of that commitment was to avoid misleading her in any way. Since I was dating someone at the time, I made this known to Jackie, who seemed entirely unperturbed. I took this as a sign that she had no interest in rekindling romance. To the contrary—and perhaps selfishly—I could barely contain my euphoria upon learning she was single. I wondered: Would she remain single until I was truly ready to commit?

We spent the entire lunch in deep, meaningful conversation. I walked away with a profound sense of relief: Jackie harbored no lasting animosity toward me, and perhaps the door stood open for genuine friendship.

Soon after, I sent her this text: "Thank you so much for coming to lunch with me; it truly meant a lot. It will help heal the hole left in my heart. Have a wonderful weekend."

Within moments, she responded: "That's beautiful. In that case, I'm happy we met for lunch."

Our cathartic, platonic lunch dates continued once or twice a month for nearly a year, never crossing the boundaries Jackie had set. On occasion, I shared the challenges of my intimate relationship at the time and the signs that foretold its eventual end. Jackie listened as a friend but showed no particular interest in the outcome.

Initially, I feared that Jackie's newfound confidence and emotional fortitude had diminished her softer, feminine charm, but I soon discovered the opposite. Eventually, on one of our lunch dates, I told her that if we ever rekindled a romantic relationship, it would be premised on my readiness to make her my third and final wife. She listened without speaking, but her body language suggested she remained content with our platonic connection. Still, the most important question lingered unanswered: When would I be truly ready for that deep emotional commitment?

My Path to True Happiness

As the intimate relationship I was in came to its expected end early in the summer of 2018, I faced two options: inform Jackie and woo her into rekindling our romance, or continue noncommittal dating. Since I still had not made the mental and emotional leap that a renewed romance with Jackie required—and felt assured that she preferred to keep our friendship platonic—I chose the second option.

We went on one of our usual lunch dates in early August, after nearly a month had passed since the last. At some point, I casually mentioned that I had ended my previous relationship—which came as no surprise to her—and that I was seeing someone new.

Her reaction was unexpected. She paused for a long moment, confusion clouding her face. Then she erupted: "This will be our last time going to lunch! You haven't changed. Here I was thinking that when your relationship ended, it would mean another chance for us."

I was dumbfounded. My heart sank as the possibility of losing her a second time loomed.

I stammered nervously, "But…but I really didn't know how you felt. You gave me no indication."

She remained solemn, her face etched with deep disappointment.

"No, Jackie, I can't lose you again," I begged. "Please give me some time to resolve this."

My mind raced as I contemplated my next move.

On our walk back from lunch, the energy between us felt as cold as a snowy winter day, though it was the middle of summer. When we parted ways, I shuddered at the thought that this might have been the end of our rekindled friendship.

My thirteen-year hiatus from deep emotional commitment had taught me the virtues of patience and discretion. I now knew unequivocally what I desired in a future relationship. The hiatus had served its purpose and now had to end if I was to recapture Jackie's heart. Coincidentally, my son had moved out a few months earlier that year, finally becoming independent. This meant I could now give Jackie my undivided attention.

I searched my soul for any lingering remnants of commitment phobia, envisioning a path forward with Jackie—if she would grant me the opportunity. A couple of days later, I called her, uncertain whether she would answer but prepared to take whatever measures necessary to regain her trust and her heart.

I breathed a sigh of relief when she answered in a normal tone of voice.

I bared my soul: "I'm scared of losing you and also scared of our next step, but please bear with me through my emotional weakness as I regain the strength to give you the emotional commitment you deserve."

I also promised to end the relationship I had recently started. She listened but offered no promises beyond her willingness to continue our conversations—for which I was eternally grateful.

Our phone conversations became daily, yet I needed to see and speak with her in person. Eventually, I gathered the courage to invite her to my home. On the last Sunday of August 2018, I watched through the window as she walked toward my house—her signature graceful gait and long, flowing black hair on full display. When she entered, and I held her in my embrace, I felt the purity and warmth of her affection that I had unwisely lost but now had the opportunity to regain. This marked the beginning of the most enduring happiness of my entire life.

The Deep Emotional Commitment

Following Jackie's first visit, we spent very little time apart. Her presence in my life once again gave me a new perspective on the redemptive power of love. I no longer hid behind vague platitudes out of fear of revealing my feelings; instead, with ease and frequency, I now declared, "I love you."

I reminded her of the commitment I had made during one of our lunch dates months earlier: if we rekindled our romance, it would mean I was ready to make her my third and final wife.

In mid-September 2018, I asked her to come live with me.

"When exactly are you proposing that I move in?" she asked.

"As soon as possible," I answered.

Shocked by my response, she said she needed time to think about it but suggested November would be a more realistic target.

To my delight, her deliberations lasted only a few hours. Later that day, she gave me the answer I had been eagerly anticipating: "Yes, tell me when. I've not been sleeping well except when I'm with you, so there is no need to continue depriving myself of sleep."

I moved her in on September 29, 2018, and, in keeping with my commitment, proposed to her soon after.

On October 10, 2018, during dinner at a restaurant, I knelt before her, declared my readiness for the deep emotional bond I had avoided for so many years, and formally asked her to marry me. Without hesitation, she accepted—making me the luckiest man in the world.

Living with Jackie was unlike anything I had experienced before. My house—where I had lived for three years—finally felt like a true home, our home. Her warmth was like constant sunshine, undimmed by day or night. The soft pitter-patter of her footsteps as she moved through the house was like gentle rain falling on parched earth, bringing life to what had been a dry desert. I felt enveloped in the protective bubble of our love, cherishing what I had so fortuitously regained. We were inseparable—commuting together by bus to and from Manhattan each day and sharing every lunch hour.

After just a couple of months, our bliss was interrupted by news that Jackie needed to undergo a common medical procedure. Though described as minimally invasive, it required general anesthesia. I believe I hid my fear well, but inside I was stricken. What if something went wrong? The thought of losing her again was unfathomable. I waited with bated breath from the moment she was wheeled into the operating room until I was told she was in recovery—an hour and a half later.

As I entered the recovery room, I could not contain my emotions—tears of joy rolled down my cheeks. Still groggy from the anesthesia and unaware of my tears, her first words were, "Is my blood pressure okay?"

Glancing at the monitor, I smiled and said, "Yes, honey, your blood pressure is fine."

Later that day, I drove her home, overwhelmed by how lucky and privileged I felt to have the opportunity to care for her—for the rest of my life.

The Promise of an Everlasting, Unbreakable Bond

We chose June 14, 2019, as our wedding date. Since this would be Jackie's first marriage, I wanted the size and venue to be entirely of her choosing. After thinking it over for a few days, she decided on a small, intimate midday ceremony with only close family and friends. It would be a simple civil service conducted by a marriage officiant. She selected the venue—the catering room of a New Jersey restaurant on the banks of the Hudson River—with the Manhattan skyline as our backdrop.

I arrived at the beautifully decorated venue around 11 a.m. and greeted our thirty guests as they arrived. In keeping with tradition, I did not see Jackie in her wedding dress until she appeared. When the car pulled up, and she stepped out, I was awestruck by her radiant beauty and elegantly coiffed hair—she was poised and graceful, her smile radiating boundless joy. I rushed forward and embraced her, my heart pounding with adoration.

For the first time, rather than repeating traditional marital vows handed down through generations, I wanted to express the depth of my love and my lifetime commitment in my own words. For the benefit of all our guests, I delivered the following vows in both Spanish and English:

> *Jackie, I know I am the luckiest man in the world because in you I have found my soulmate, my best friend, my bundle of joy, my place of true peace—and today, my precious wife.*
>
> *Honey, you complete me. Before you, life seemed a journey of labor interspersed by moments of happiness, but you have turned that paradigm around, and now each moment with you brings a deep, profound joy.*
>
> *How truly blessed I am to get to share the rest of my life with you, to wake up each morning to your warm embrace, loving eyes, and sweet kisses, and your ever-so-adorable mannerisms and idiosyncrasies.*
>
> *Jackie darling, thanks for giving me this opportunity to love you forever, which I promise to do with all my heart and soul.*
>
> *Darling, you make loving you so easy; even when you're upset, on the rarest of occasions, you are just as adorable, and every day I find myself loving you even more.*
>
> *You're like a diamond that shines brighter with care and grows in value with each passing day.*
>
> *I promise to protect you, cherish you, care for you, and support you in your endeavors. I will be there for you as we pass through life's ups and downs, through the good times and the bad.*
>
> *We will always be grateful for the many blessings life has afforded us, the most important of which will be our everlasting love. I love you so much, my darling.*

Jackie also wrote and declared the following vows in both Spanish and English:

> *Eric, you are my equal, my soulmate. I recognize you as we share the same level of integrity and discipline. The same sense of responsibility, humor, and playfulness. And an unwavering commitment to a life filled with peace and happiness.*
>
> *I love you for giving me back a home—my earthly sanctuary. I love you for your courage, for choosing love over fear, for otherwise, we wouldn't be here—manifesting one of our most cherished dreams.*
>
> *I love you for giving me the experience of a newfound joy—the joy of loving you. I love you for giving me the love, the care, and the security I didn't know I needed to experience my inner child.*
>
> *I love you for giving me the space and leading the way on how to become and experience wholeheartedly the physical side of myself and the world.*
>
> *And above all, I love you and thank you for always clearly seeing who I really am and loving and honoring my authentic self.*
>
> *For these reasons and many more, I am grateful and utterly in love with you.*
>
> *So, today, surrounded by the people we love, I, Jackie, welcome you, Eric, as my beloved husband and life partner.*
>
> *I promise to love you unconditionally, and to respect and honor who you are and who you are yet to become.*

I promise to continue to be a source of peace and joy in your life and to always add value and purpose to our life together.

I promise to continue to grow and learn from and with you. To always speak and listen with my heart, and to always hold your hand and show you how deeply I care for you, no matter the challenges that may come our way. To remember that all things between us are rooted in love.

With these vows and all the love that I am and that I can give, I marry you and join my life and heart to yours.

After our wedding, we spent a perfect honeymoon on the island of Grenada and returned home to continue what has been a never-ending honeymoon.

Living with My Soulmate

Finding my soulmate had always been an ideal I hoped for: a woman with whom I would share a profound, innate connection; communicate effortlessly and deeply; hold similar values and beliefs; and always feel completely at home in her presence. It is that quiet, unconscious bond that persists even as we live out our conscious, tangible, and shared experiences together.

The nearly seven years of my marriage to Jackie have restored my belief in the sanctity and redeeming value of marriage. In her, I have found the long-sought soulmate and best friend I always hoped for. I have experienced deep tranquility and come to understand what it means to be happy, regardless of where I am or the circumstances surrounding me, when I am in her company. Together, we have found joy equally in the simplicities of life and in the more opulent moments.

We have dialogued with profound mutual respect and love, always mindful of each other's idiosyncrasies and sensibilities. I have benefited from my wife's preemptive warnings about her rare hormonal mood swings, rather than being left confused as I was with past partners. We have lovingly resolved the increasingly rare divergent views between us—never embarking on a roller-coaster ride of emotions and estrangement.

We have witnessed with gratitude and humility the many nonphysical and tangible blessings that always seem to come our way, rejoicing in each other's successes as our own.

I have been blessed to be married to a spiritually and highly evolved wife, who always seems enveloped in a glow of positive energy. I have grown to appreciate the good fortune of our shared ethereal beliefs—something that eluded me in past marriages and relationships. We have even experienced the inexplicable coincidence of having the same dream while sleeping just a foot or two apart.

Together, we have learned how to avoid unhealthy externalities—letting go of those we cannot control—and never allowing the unavoidable maladies to invade our inner sanctum. Together, we have navigated the ideological divide of our changing U.S. sociopolitical environment—often frightened when the pendulum swings to one extreme—but believing that justice and equality will, in the end, prevail.

We have vacationed in luxurious places, but they always felt secondary to the mutual joy we feel regardless of where we are together. Each new or planned discovery means nothing unless it is jointly aspired to and shared.

She has taught me the life-changing impact of confronting and addressing past trauma—and its power to improve one's psychological and emotional well-being. I remain in awe of her emotional intelligence: she always looks beyond what the eye can see and seems perpetually connected to a higher level of consciousness.

Jackie occasionally asks, usually before sleep, the rhetorical question, "Why do you love me so much?" My short answer has always been the same: "It's because loving you is easy." It is a powerful statement of an ease dictated by her essence—never having to search for reasons to overlook acerbic traits, because in her I have found none.

In 2018, the reggae group Third World released a song, *Loving You Is Easy*, that became the soundtrack to my answer. In the summer of 2024, we had the improbable fortune of speaking with their lead singer, AJ, at an outdoor concert in New Jersey before they went on stage. I shared the story of what the song meant to us—especially to me.[109]

Later, before they performed, he beckoned to me from the backstage fence and asked, "What is your wife's name again?" Onstage, I heard him announce, "This next song is dedicated to Jackie," before delivering my soundtrack.

Weathering the Tides

Life invariably brings unforeseen challenges, and having a spouse for mutual support in those uncertain times is invaluable. Our own challenges awaited us just beyond the horizon. Less than a year into our marriage, we were confronted with two significant tests.

In February 2020, media reports intensified about the rapidly spreading—and often lethal—COVID-19 coronavirus disease. On March 11, 2020, the World Health Organization (WHO) declared the outbreak a global pandemic. Soon after, nearly all New York City workers who could work remotely were sent home. This marked the beginning of our working full-time from home for approximately one year.

Like most people, we felt great anxiety over the severity of the pandemic and the societal response to it. In my lifetime, the only other pandemic comparable in its rate of fatalities was HIV/AIDS. Yet as the COVID-19 death toll continued to climb, it became clear that it would rapidly approach—and eventually surpass—the cumulative toll of HIV/AIDS, which had peaked in the United States in 1995.[110]

There was the constant fear of contracting the disease whenever we ventured out for necessities—diligently donning face masks and gloves, using hand sanitizer, and sanitizing items bought or delivered. We stopped dining out, avoided air travel, and interacted with family only virtually as we anxiously awaited vaccine availability.

We listened to, watched, and read news reports and anecdotal accounts of the quarantine's negative impact on marital and familial relationships, caused by constant togetherness. There were complaints about a lack of personal space and time, emotional fatigue, stagnating relationships, and conflict arising from the magnification of small differences. Others spoke of a loss of intimacy, the erosion of individual hobbies and pursuits, feeling suffocated, and relationships devolving into mere roommate arrangements. We empathized deeply and felt profound gratitude that none of these maladies manifested in our own relationship.

Instead, with each passing day, our bond, mutual trust, and affection grew even stronger. We found our constant togetherness not only a blessing but an opportunity to reclaim the time lost during our eight-year premarital separation. Beyond longer work hours—albeit from home—we indulged in daily long walks, weekend bike rides, and hikes, and deep, meaningful conversations. I exercised my culinary skills, cooking for her all the famous Jamaican dishes whose ingredients I could find, while she reciprocated with a few Colombian dishes of her own.

Amid the complexities inflicted by the pandemic, in late July 2020, I began experiencing abdominal pain that gradually intensified. Knowing hospitals were overrun with COVID-19 patients—and that seeking care there increased the risk of exposure to the virus—I delayed what became inevitable. On the morning of August 3, 2020, painkillers no longer provided relief, and my fever reached 103 degrees Fahrenheit.

My wife drove me to the emergency room, where I was diagnosed with an infected gallbladder requiring surgical removal—a cholecystectomy. I was admitted and placed on antibiotics, with surgery scheduled for the next day. That night, a thunderstorm knocked out power to the hospital. Although it continued to operate on backup generators, my surgery was delayed until August 5.

My greatest torture leading up to surgery was neither the pain I endured nor the fear of the procedure itself, but the possibility that I could be permanently taken from Jackie. I agonized: How could I lose the privilege I had only recently regained—of loving, caring for, and protecting her? How could I be deprived of the honor of continuing to make her happy for the rest of my life?

Jackie ensured my optimal care in her committed, loving, and vigilant way. She thoroughly interrogated every attending nurse and doctor. I sensed her profound worry but saw only her strength. She never showed weakness—only compassion and optimism. On the morning of the surgery, she accompanied me as far as she was allowed—to the door of the operating room. In that moment, I remained optimistic, convinced that our journey together was a blessing and that this was merely a test, with more good fortune awaiting us beyond.

I awakened after a three-and-a-half-hour surgery to the sweet, soft, soothing sound of Jackie's voice. Her eyes reflected the countenance of a heavy burden lifted, now filled with renewed zeal and quiet joy. Later, when I was moved from recovery back to my room, Jackie shared with me the complicated nature of my laparoscopic surgery, as the surgeon had explained it to her.

The surgery proved complicated due to the widespread nature of the infection, which extended the operative time. In fact, the surgeon had previously informed me that if complications arose beyond his ability to manage them laparoscopically, he would have to convert, mid-operation, to open surgery.

Later that evening, while I was recuperating in my hospital room, the surgeon expressed astonishment at the seriousness of the infection and the near-fatal nature of my condition. He also explained that my recovery could take weeks.

As I lay in bed surveying the aftermath, I saw my swollen abdomen, four bandaged surgical incisions, and from one of them a tube draining bloody fluid into a collection bottle at my side—but I was overcome with gratitude. Those pre-surgery possibilities over which I had agonized were not to be. My life had been prolonged, and with it the privilege of continuing to love and care for Jackie.

For the next two days, I remained in the hospital with Jackie by my side. I was discharged on the afternoon of August 7—still COVID-19 free—and with the comforting knowledge that my challenging road to full recovery lay in the hands of my caring and compassionate wife. This test only served to further cement my confidence that we would overcome all challenges, great or small, that our shared life journey would undoubtedly unfold with the passage of time. Subsequent trials have justified that confidence.

On December 14, 2020, the first COVID-19 vaccine was administered in the United States. I beamed with pride when I heard the announcement that the volunteer recipient was Sandra Lindsay, a Jamaican-born critical care nurse at a hospital in Queens, New York. This televised event, broadcast nationwide, marked the beginning of the largest vaccination campaign in U.S. history. Here was a fellow Jamaican immigrant stepping forward to lead by example—even amid rampant conspiracy theories about the vaccine's potential harmful effects.[111]

Reflections

In my quiet moments, I have often reflected comparatively on my previous two marriages. Why did they fail in various respects, while this, my third, has thrived by every metric I can conceive? Is the success of this marriage due solely to my accumulated experience and increased maturity, or are there other significant factors at play? Could those factors be innate compatibility, shared values, and aligned beliefs? Does this exemplify the commonly held notion that success is often achieved on the third attempt?

It would be to my detriment if I failed to grow wiser from the experience gained during my prior failed marriages. After those failures, I did the necessary introspective work: I recognized my errors, realigned my values, decisions, and actions, remained patient, and was blessed with a second chance at friendship and love with my forever soulmate. Perhaps success on the third attempt reflects a conscious—or unconscious—recognition that life is short, so one must seize the opportunity for lasting love before it slips away.

I have reflected on how falling in love for the first time at age eighteen—with my first wife, Lisa—awakened my capacity to give and receive love, to recognize what it feels like and what it means, and not to miss the signs when they next appear. What I lacked at eighteen, however, was emotional maturity and the relationship lessons that can only be learned through one's own experiences. From those hard-won lessons, I have concluded that the profundity of my love for Jackie is inextricably tied to our deep-rooted compatibility, effective communication, and the mutuality of our values, beliefs, trust, respect, support, and sense of humor.

Thanks to the increased wisdom that has come with time, I have brought the best version of myself to our relationship. As for my wife and soulmate, there is nothing about her I would want to change. For me, "adorable" is now synonymous with Jackie—her essence elevates my well-being every day.

Whenever I look at her, I am entranced by her nonverbal capacity to elicit in me a profound feeling of peace. That fierce emotional independence I maintained before Jackie has gladly given way to mutual reliance—there is now no me without her. She has restored my full faith in the power of marriage to create long-lasting and meaningful happiness.

LIFE LESSONS

1. Positive thinking is a magnet. The stronger it gets, the more blessings stick.

2. No one can steal your hope. It lies inside you and costs nothing to keep alive.

3. They say time heals all wounds, but emotional hurts also need space and distance.

4. The strength of an apology lies not in the words, but in the follow-through that makes things right.

5. Life's crossroads flash vivid signs. Read them carefully. One wrong turn can cost your last shot at happiness.

6. Declaring "I love you" must mean I will do everything in my power—emotionally and materially—to make our lives better.

7. Watch your partner when you're sick. Their actions will show whether "I love you" was ever real.

8. No grand gesture, done out of obligation or vanity, will ever match the magnitude of small things shared in love.

9. Your marital vows are not primarily to your spouse; they are oaths to never betray yourself.

10. Define what a soulmate means to you. If you're lucky enough to find one—hang on for dear life.

11. Marital harmony is guarded by ruthless discernment: swiftly spot anything outside the core two of you and keep it at bay.

12. Like storms that eventually reach shore, life’s trials will test every marriage. Only the deeply anchored ones stand when the waves recede.

Jackie and I on our wedding day, June 14, 2019.

(This page intentionally left blank.)

CHAPTER 22

The Arc of My Professional Life

Reflections on career, letting go, and legacy

Recapping My Career Path

My professional journey began in September 1989 and spanned thirty-five years, concluding in January 2025. In Chapters 11 and 12, I discussed the private sector portion of my career, which lasted almost five years and ended with my transition to the public sector in 1994. That move marked the beginning of a thirty-one-year career with a public service entity I have previously referred to as the Agency—a moniker I will continue to use. My most career-defining step came in 1999, when I seized an opportunity to become a manager in the department responsible for designing and constructing capital projects.

This move marked the beginning of a twenty-six-year upward trajectory in management and leadership, with steadily increasing responsibility and success in capital program planning and execution. These capital programs encompassed long-term plans for building new infrastructure and upgrading existing facilities Agency-wide.

I began as a Project Administrator and advanced steadily through the ranks: Construction Administrator, Construction Manager, Program Manager, Program Officer, and Vice President and Deputy Leader of a capital program division in 2022.

My trajectory reached its apex in mid-2024, when I was delegated the responsibilities of Senior Vice President and Division Leader. In this capacity, I led a capital program division, providing strategic leadership and fostering continuous improvement. The division's portfolio encompassed approximately 180 projects, with a total budget of about $4 billion and a staff of roughly 160 permanent and temporary employees. The projects' varied scopes encompassed state-of-good-repair, upgrades, replacements, and expansions of mission-critical systems and related infrastructure—all essential to the Agency's safe, reliable operations and public service delivery.

Throughout my career, I coordinated and liaised with intra- and extra-departmental executive leaders of the Agency, principals of consulting and contracting firms, state and federal regulators, community boards, and elected public officials. I worked with stakeholders to create shared visions, set goals, and acted jointly to accomplish them.

Other salient career highlights included negotiating consent agreements with government regulators; spearheading top-priority Agency initiatives; leading agency-wide capital feasibility studies; authoring documents for and presenting to the Agency's board; leading or participating in numerous agency-wide steering committees and task forces; and helping to improve the Agency's capital program coordination and constructability review procedures.

In my first Agency-provided managerial class in 2000, I learned about a survey of top U.S. executives. They were asked, "What was the most salient attribute responsible for your ascendancy to the position you currently occupy?" In order of increasing importance, the results were as follows: 10 percent cited knowledge, 30 percent said presentation, and 60 percent said who they knew. This statistic—for which I admittedly never found the exact source—remained a salient reminder on which I reflected at each point I advanced in my career.

Throughout my own professional ascendancy, I found all three attributes to be impactful building blocks. Being knowledgeable provided opportunities for me to be heard, and sharing that knowledge well—in writing or verbal discourse—brought me recognition by and familiarity with Agency leaders. My innate inclination to always present myself well, in dress and comportment, also conveyed to senior leaders my sense of seriousness and purpose.

Principles of Labor and Leadership

I built my long career on several salient core principles. Primary among them were attentiveness to duty, a passion for meeting goals and deadlines, an eagerness to increase my knowledge, and a willingness to expand the scope of my responsibilities. At times, when faced with seemingly insurmountable challenges, I coined and endeavored to live by one of my favorite mantras: "Problems are potential opportunities for growth disguised by anxiety." I always strived to never drop the ball on an issue until a decision or resolution was reached—never easily taking no for an answer.

Early in my career, I experienced the downsides of being a self-described perfectionist—undue stress and anxiety stemming from an all-or-nothing mindset, often fixating on minor details and issues beyond my control. Over time, I came to understand that imposing unrealistic expectations on myself and judging others by my own self-imposed standards were unproductive and strained relationships.

Fortunately, I learned early of Parkinson's Law of Triviality, which observes that groups tend to devote disproportionate time and energy to minor issues rather than more consequential ones. I also embraced the 80/20 rule, or Pareto Principle, which holds that roughly 80 percent of results come from 20 percent of efforts. This allowed me to maximize efficiency by focusing on the few most impactful issues.[112]

I instructed employees never to show me more respect than the respect I showed them, and therefore treated them the way I wanted to be treated. I endeavored to provide staff with the level of responsiveness and guidance I would desire from my own senior managers or leaders. I supported them by stepping in when necessary to resolve challenges beyond their control and by developing procedures that made their jobs less difficult.

I encouraged and motivated staff by including them in the decision-making process and highlighting their strengths before addressing areas for improvement. I explained how their assigned tasks would contribute to their experience, skills, overall development, and career advancement. By encouraging them to think through, derive, and present possible solutions to seemingly insurmountable problems, they were empowered.

I endeavored to treat each project as a team effort and conveyed this to team members through my conduct, my willingness to share responsibilities, and my trust in capable individuals. I encouraged the free expression of ideas and refrained from imposing my own as the only optimal solution—duly weighing the merits of all others.

I recognized the need for—and embraced—a flexible leadership style, adapting it to the circumstances or issues at hand. At times, I adopted visionary, transformational, democratic, autocratic, or laissez-faire approaches.

I endeavored to be visionary at the outset of any initiative, communicating and reinforcing a clear purpose and direction to the team—inspiring them to execute the vision. I aimed to be transformational when organizational changes necessitated guiding staff to adapt to new realities. I employed a democratic approach when the team's creativity, experience, and collaboration were essential to solving problems through brainstorming and consensus.

I used a laissez-faire approach with highly capable team members who demonstrated they could execute their responsibilities and complete assignments without constant reminders or micromanagement. In crises or urgent situations requiring decisive control, I adopted an autocratic style—with a clear "what I say must get done" approach.

I strove to heed the caution of the Jamaican adage "Rakstone a rivva battam nuh kno sun hat"* and always maintained an open-door policy. I listened to the struggles and challenges of staff—whether in their work or personal lives—and endeavored to offer solutions whenever possible.

In 2008, during Barack Obama's unprecedented rise to become the Democratic Party's presidential nominee, I read an article analyzing how his leadership style and unflappable personality were pivotal to his success. The piece described him as embodying five essential qualities of an outstanding leader, referred to as the "five Cs": confidence, consistency, command, care, and calm.

Naturally, as an aspiring leader myself, I decided to conduct an honest, deep introspective analysis of my strengths and weaknesses across all five attributes. Being as objective as I could, I determined that I was confident, consistent, commanding, and caring, but fell short in maintaining calm under stressful circumstances. This realization made that deficiency my salient focus for improvement throughout the rest of my leadership career and in my personal life.

---

* Translation: "A rock at the bottom of the river doesn't feel the heat of the sun," which means that individuals in positions of privilege are often not cognizant of the challenges experienced by others.

I learned through experience that to perform at my optimal level, I needed a vigilant and purposeful work-life balance. Consequently, I endeavored to stay healthy—both physically and mentally—with a mostly consistent daily exercise routine. Especially in the last decade, I have sustained my hobbies of playing tennis, biking, and hiking, and vacationed around three times per year.

Although these key principles of labor and leadership contributed significantly to what I believe was a meaningful and successful career, they represent only a small part of the broader range of possibilities. Still, I hope this synopsis offers some useful wisdom to those who aspire to leadership.

My Final Act and Letting Go

In 2022, when I became Vice President and Deputy Leader, I shared leadership responsibilities for the division with the Senior Vice President and assumed full charge during his absences. Consequently, when he retired in May 2024, I was delegated the responsibilities of Senior Vice President—pending completion of a formal recruitment process. Despite receiving no additional financial compensation, I accepted the delegation—effectively leading the division and continuing to improve its already meritorious key performance indicators.

I was told from the very beginning—indefensibly, in my opinion—of the Agency's intent to find an external candidate to fill the position. Nevertheless, I believed I could change the Agency's resolve through exemplary leadership. I also explored my options and decided that the delegated—or eventually bestowed—position of Senior Vice President would represent the apex and the last chapter of my career with the Agency, having reached retirement eligibility almost two years earlier.

As the newly delegated leader of the division, I quickly set about establishing and implementing what I believed was a necessary and improved vision—one more aligned with my leadership style. Since the division lacked a written mission statement, I solicited input from senior staff and drafted one. To foster greater cross-sectional alignment and cohesion, I scheduled recurring sectional meetings with senior and mid-level managers, as well as skip-level meetings with lower-tier staff.

I rallied the teams to focus more sharply on achieving goals and resolving roadblocks while ensuring compliance with emergent Agency policies and mandates. I leveraged the division's engineering proficiency to find innovative solutions to longstanding challenges and to initiate research and planning for anticipated technological advancements—for integration into our short- and long-term capital plans.

Within a couple of months of accepting the delegated position, the formal job vacancy notice was posted. I applied and was soon granted an interview. I did not take my incumbency for granted and prepared thoroughly for the process. Having sat on both sides of the table—interviewer and interviewee—numerous times throughout my career, I judged, in my perhaps biased opinion, that I aced the interview.

Throughout my career, I was a straight shooter, unwilling to "play ball" or step outside certain boundaries. My integrity and principles were inflexible. Where political considerations—rightly or wrongly—appeared to hold equal or greater weight than pragmatism and common sense, I often found it impossible to stay silent. I was never afraid to speak truth to power. If this meant I had reached my ceiling, then I was ready to walk away, content that I had given my all in accordance with my principles of labor and leadership.

I heeded the wisdom of the Jamaican maxim, "Nuh wait til drum beat before yuh grine yuh axe."* Therefore, from the moment I accepted the delegated position, I began the formal steps necessary to prepare for retirement. With those steps now complete, in November 2024—after six months of leading the division without additional compensation—I inquired about the status of the Agency's decision.

Not surprisingly, I was told that they had selected an external candidate who would start in January 2025.

Smiling, I asked, "Why was I overlooked?"

The response was that I had not been overlooked and that I was expected to continue leading in most respects as Deputy Leader. I was told the new individual was being brought in primarily to build relationships.

---

* Translation: "Don't wait until the drum beats before you grind your axe," which means that one should prepare for all possibilities before it is too late.

I deduced that since no merit-based reason was provided for denying me the position, there was none.

My interpretation—whether right or wrong—was that I would be expected to continue holding the bulk of the division's leadership and programmatic responsibilities while someone else would be paid to simply build relationships.

As for relationship-building, over the years, I had established strong, synergistic relationships with key stakeholders essential to the division's success. In 2015, I initiated monthly partnering sessions with major Agency stakeholders—sessions that continued successfully, enabling us to overcome challenges on capital projects and jointly improve processes and procedures. I had also built solid relationships with the contracting and consulting firms with whom we conducted business.

A few days after being informed of the Agency's decision, I submitted my retirement notice on December 2, 2024, which read as follows:

> *After almost thirty-one years of service to the Agency, I am hereby providing notice of my planned retirement, with my last day of work scheduled for January 10, 2025. Should any unforeseen issues necessitate a change of date, I will advise you. Over my remaining few weeks, I will meet with each of my current nine direct reports, in their various capacities, to provide any necessary knowledge transfer and thereby facilitate the continued optimal functioning of the division.*

It seemed this outcome was unanticipated. I was asked multiple times to reconsider my decision and was told of my enormous value to the Agency. Sign-off on my retirement paperwork was temporarily delayed in the hope that I would change my mind. After a final meeting and last attempt to persuade me to stay, I wrote the following email:

> *I appreciate our conversation yesterday and your expressed desire that I change my retirement plans and continue my employment with the Agency. As you may imagine, my decision was not taken lightly; it was well*

> *thought through and determined to be the best for my family and me at this time. Accordingly, my retirement plans remain as scheduled, with my last day of work being January 10, 2025. I am thankful for having been entrusted with the responsibility of leading the division over the last six-plus months and anticipate nothing but continued excellence from this division. Thanks again.*

In that moment, I reflected on my nearly thirty-one years with the Agency and felt enormous gratitude. The Agency had provided me a path to realize my American dream, recognized my worth, and consistently afforded me opportunities for advancement throughout my tenure. In return, I gave the Agency my dedication and commitment—always striving to improve the performance of everything within my control while influencing those areas that were not. Words cannot express my everlasting gratitude.

Retirement

After announcing my planned retirement to the division's staff, many visited my office in what seemed like a constant stream, or called to express their disappointment. I heard and felt their overwhelming sadness and regret, yet they also understood my reasons for leaving. They soon rallied and organized a retirement celebration for me at a nearby restaurant.

On the evening of my retirement party, I was overwhelmed by the outpouring of love and appreciation for my years of service from coworkers and retired former employees. The attendees included staff of all ranks, as well as current and former executives from various departments across the Agency. I had given the Agency my best, and the Agency had reciprocated, but I never fully realized how profoundly my contribution was appreciated until that moment. Around ten colleagues delivered scripted or unscripted speeches that touched me emotionally; I quote excerpts from five of them here:

> *"When I think of Eric, two words come to mind. The first is integrity, which I see in both his internal and external interactions; people trust him, and it helps us a lot when*

we are doing our jobs. The second word is support, and Eric has supported everyone before and since he took over as Senior VP—supporting an even larger group—and everybody has felt his support. This is why everybody is going to miss you now that you're leaving."

"As Eric embarks on his retirement, we want to express our deepest gratitude for his unwavering support, invaluable wisdom, and passion that have shaped our professional journey. Thank you, Eric, for your leadership as Vice President and interim Senior Vice President, and as a personal mentor and friend to me. It has been a true honor to work for you. Wishing you all the success and happiness in this new chapter of your life."

"Eric is such a professional. I've never seen anybody answer emails so quickly as a boss; it's like half a minute later, he doesn't even break. No matter what you write, he reads every email and answers back. It's been great, high caliber—you're the guy, all the best in everything you do. Wish we had more like you."

"Over the period of time I've known him, Eric has been the consummate professional. Not only has he been the best-dressed person, but he is the person that personally, myself, and I think many other people, went to when they had a problem, went to for guidance, and went to for advice. Eric came up with solutions to problems that people didn't even know existed and then followed through to make sure that the implementation was really carried out correctly.

All the projects that Eric has worked on are a living legacy to his professionalism, talent, and his dedication to delivering not only for the Agency but for the people of New York. Eric, it has been a pleasure working with you. You've really taught me a lot over my career, and I thank you for everything that you've done for myself and for everybody here, so congratulations, all the best."

"Eric brought an uncanny ability to think adaptively and logically about technical challenges, translating that into effective management strategies. He excelled in navigating the complexities of project delivery, managing diverse stakeholders, and leading his teams and the divisions he worked with—especially ours—to greater success.

His meticulous attention to detail, unwavering support, and reserved yet impactful presence have set a high standard for us all. Despite his quiet and private nature, Eric's kindness, willingness to tackle problems, and openness to helping others have fostered strong relationships within our team and the organization. It has left us in a truly commanding and high-profile position moving forward."

"No one in the room has known Eric as long as I have. All I have been hearing from you guys in terms of his gifts, his ability, his fairness, his integrity, his love for what he does, his excellence—we saw it first. You've been a wonderful example to all of us. I'm grateful to have known you, I'm grateful that you worked with us, and that you've done your best. You left your mark, and so, that's all we can expect and that we can all strive for, to do as good as you have done."

Overwhelmed with emotion, I delivered the following farewell speech:

First, let me express my heartfelt thanks to (name redacted) for organizing this event. I had planned to retire quietly, but soon after I informed staff of my planned retirement, and before I could make my wishes for a quiet exit known, he came to my office and informed me that he was planning this event, so I fell in line. I am truly humbled and extremely grateful for the outpouring of appreciation for my years of service that I've received from my colleagues across the Agency, and to all of you here who have taken time out from your busy schedules to join me in celebrating my retirement.

My thirty-five-plus-year career journey—almost thirty-one of which have been with the Agency—has been one marked by seizing every significant opportunity presented to me, being a willing volunteer whenever there was a need, embracing so-called problems as potential opportunities for growth disguised by anxiety, and showing the utmost level of respect to coworkers and stakeholders, regardless of organizational hierarchy.

I then provided a chronological overview of what had been a very eventful and rewarding journey with the Agency, some of which I have already summarized in this and prior chapters. Afterward, I said:

This journey would not have been as successful and rewarding were it not for the many colleagues with whom I've worked along the way, including my supervisors, my direct reports, our capital clients or end-users/maintainers, contractors, consultants, and other stakeholders. The names of all these individuals are too numerous to mention, but I would be remiss if I didn't name a few.

I followed up with a personal thank-you by name to key individuals who had been pivotal to my career advancement. They spanned both genders, multiple ethnicities, and multiple countries of birth. I then closed with the following:

To all my staff, past and present, I'm eternally thankful for your support and truly hope that I was able to provide you with the best guidance and leadership that I could. To my partners across various departments of the Agency and elsewhere, thank you for always taking my calls, responding to my emails, and working with me to resolve tough issues in fair and equitable ways.

And to my dear and precious wife, Jackie, thank you for your love and support; through the good and the stressful times—you have been my oxygen.

As I embark on the next chapter of my life, I don't know fully what lies over the horizon, but I'm sure that the experience, knowledge, and relationships built during my tenure here at the Agency will serve me exceedingly well. Again, thank you all from the bottom of my heart.

Definition of Success and the Concept of Legacy

For me, success has never meant a vast accumulation of financial or material wealth, but rather the achievement of my personal goals in academia, profession, entrepreneurship, volunteerism, and mentorship. While tangible wealth may be a by-product of success, I have never considered it a true measure. True wealth lies in the intangibles—those things money cannot buy. Wherever my goals have intersected with the higher purpose of touching and improving the lives of others, their achievement has amplified my sense of fulfillment and success.

Throughout my thirty-one-year career with the Agency, I was privileged to manage and lead numerous public capital improvement projects that touched the lives of millions. Through my own company, I have helped spread the rhythms of Jamaican music and culture globally, bringing entertainment and joy to tens of thousands.

Above all, without the love of family and friends, professional success and any resulting material wealth can feel meaningless. For this reason, I feel successful and blessed by the abundance of love that now permeates my life.

Although I am still in the throes of embracing my new sunrise—and the final chapter of my life hopefully lies beyond a distant horizon—I feel compelled to answer the question of legacy. I seek none, but if I could be remembered for only one thing, it would be this: I was given a second chance at true love and seized it. That decision changed the trajectory of my life to one of inner peace and abundant happiness.

LIFE LESSONS

1. Problems are potential opportunities for growth disguised by anxiety.

2. Do not waste your energy worrying about things over which you have no influence or control. Concentrate instead on those things within your power.

3. Respect is like a boomerang; show it, and it comes right back to you. The same goes for disrespect, so choose wisely.

4. The degree of a challenge is directly related to one's capacity to overcome it. The universe, in its infinite wisdom, molds challenges to match one's capability.

5. Finding common purpose requires recognition, appreciation, and respect for others' vision and goals.

6. Show up not only with the right qualifications, experience, and work ethic, but also dress well for the part, as you are usually seen before you're heard.

7. Let integrity, principle, and true merit be the foundation of your recognition and opportunities—advantage gained based on anything less is like building on shifting sands.

8. Never drop a challenge to which you've been entrusted until it's resolved; it's like dropping a tennis ball when it's in your court—you lose points.

9. Choose "good enough" over "perfect" when time is of the essence.

10. To say "what you put in is what you get out" is a fallacy of proportions; a small but wisely chosen input can generate an output many times its size or value.

11. Failing to consider others' knowledge and ideas while relying only on your own is the same as failing to use both hands to break a fall. Herein lies the wisdom of teamwork.

12. Inflexibility in one's style of management is like a car with faulty brakes; it's destined to crash.

13. Calmness in a crisis is a skill achieved only through deliberate practice.

14. On the scale of life, career pursuits and personal life precariously hang in the balance; be vigilant so as not to tip the scale.

15. Like a pilot or driver ferrying passengers, you may never know how much you are appreciated until the very end of a journey, so do your best as you travel your chosen path.

16. Let the positive impact you've had on the lives of others and the abundance of love in your life be the measures of your success.

CHAPTER 23

The Journey Ahead

Hope, wisdom, and what still matters most

My retirement at age fifty-seven was not merely the sunset of a professional career; it was the dawn of a new beginning filled with boundless possibilities. It represented an acknowledgment that beyond the rewards of a single career's achievements lay other worthy and meaningful aspirations. I decided that sacrificing health and leisure for more material wealth would not be my path. It was a promotion to being the CEO of "me"—free from the rigors and stress of employment. It would be a dynamic journey, not a static condition, without the limitation of a fixed destination.

To make the most of the youth of my senior years, I would endeavor to craft meaningful and memorable moments. To accomplish this, I would need to remain mentally sharp, physically fit, and aspirational. Realizing deferred dreams and embracing new aspirations would be my ongoing measures of success.

Concurrently, I would need to navigate an increasingly volatile sociopolitical and geopolitical environment, amid the existential risks posed by climate change and—for better or worse—the growing impact of artificial intelligence on the fabric of society.

These core precepts would serve as my guardrails and guide as I embarked on this phase of my life's journey.

Staying Sharp

Shortly after retirement, I received a few overtures from potential private-sector employers, but I ultimately reaffirmed that this would not be my path. I had observed that self-worth—often unconsciously tied to corporate relevance—denies many people long and fulfilling retirement years. I decided to avoid that trap.

Instead of returning to stressful full-time employment, my primary focus would be my mental and physical health—hopefully prolonging both my healthspan and lifespan. The 2021 data showing an average U.S. male healthspan of 62.8 years reinforced my resolve. Not knowing or being guaranteed the longevity of my own health meant that I would endeavor to optimize each day—challenging myself physically and intellectually—while striving to maintain a beginner's mind and keep the faucet of my creativity wide open.[113]

Exercise—biking, hiking, and tennis—had always been part of my lifestyle, and retirement gave me the freedom to indulge more often and sustain my physical vitality. A few months after retiring, I completed my long-anticipated hike to the summit of New Jersey's tallest mountain, Mount Tammany—up its most difficult trail.

Above all, staying sharp would be a dynamic exercise—replete with the necessary periodic assessments and adjustments.

The Sociopolitical Climate of My New Sunrise

While my post-retirement life and decisions were under my control, I would not be insulated from the effects of ongoing sociopolitical and geopolitical developments. This realization prompted me to reflect on the dynamics—both in Jamaica and the United States—that shaped my formative years in the late 1960s and 1970s (discussed in Chapter 2), as well as those that influenced my adulthood here in the U.S. I wondered whether the current sociopolitical climate and its trajectory would bode well for the retirement I hoped to enjoy.

The Cold War dynamics that shaped the internal politics and international relations of most democratic countries arguably ended with the dissolution of the Soviet Union on December 26, 1991. In Jamaica, this arguably contributed, over time, to a gradual weakening of the ideological divide between the two major political parties. In the United States, however, an ideological divide between its two parties has remained deep and perhaps even more entrenched. The debates of the 1960s on social injustice, inequality, and civil rights continue to feel strikingly relevant.

Since the end of the Cold War, the U.S. Democratic Party—generally favoring greater government involvement, progressive taxation, and social programs to address inequality—has held the presidency for nineteen years. In contrast, the Republican Party—broadly advocating smaller government, deregulation, reduced social programs, and lower taxes—has held it for fifteen years.

Each party has maintained a deep-rooted ideological base of voters, with self-identified independents largely responsible for the swing of the pendulum in every presidential election. For me, these periodic shifts have been the U.S. electorate's way of correcting course—never letting the country drift too far toward either extreme. Yet the sociopolitical climate at the time of my retirement felt noticeably different.

It has felt as though the rules of the game are being rewritten in ways that alter reality and may diminish the electorate's power to make informed voting decisions. The advances secured by the Civil Rights and Voting Rights Acts of the 1960s—once seeming sacred and untouchable—now appear vulnerable. Pathways from poverty to economic security for the historically disadvantaged seem increasingly limited. Though as a retiree, I am not personally impacted, these developments continue to weigh heavily on my mind.

A United States that once welcomed legal immigration—with the Immigration and Nationality Act of 1965 and the Immigration Reform and Control Act of 1986—now seems less welcoming. As an immigrant who gained so much from America's generous immigration policies, and in turn contributed positively to the U.S. economy, I grieve the possible denial of such opportunities to others.

The geopolitics and global impact of two rival superpowers that defined the Cold War era now seem to be resurging amidst the growing divide between the United States and a rising China. Jamaica once again finds itself caught between two global giants, performing a delicate balancing act: welcoming necessary Chinese aid and investment while addressing U.S. concerns over Beijing's increasing regional influence. Jamaica's ability to successfully manage these two relationships concerns me greatly.[114]

While wars among European nations have been a common occurrence—one of the regions with the highest number of recorded wars in history—the ongoing twelve-year conflict between Ukraine and

Russia is particularly troubling. Russia's repeated threats to use nuclear weapons, combined with the reality that a few leaders still hold the power of human annihilation, create an undercurrent of perpetual unease. Yet I remain optimistic that within my lifetime, humanity will one day eliminate this existential threat by dismantling every nuclear weapon.[115]

On February 28, 2026, massive U.S.-Israeli strikes targeted Iranian military infrastructure and leadership, triggering an ongoing war, regional instability, and global economic impacts. It was a fresh reminder of the seemingly inevitable cycle of human warfare—an existential threat to others today, but will it one day come to my doorstep, our doorsteps?

Climate Change

The impact of mankind's abuse of our beautiful planet Earth—and Mother Nature's response—has concerned me since my early twenties and remains a preeminent and mounting concern. In early 1997, I expressed my concern in the lyrics of my third unreleased studio-recorded song, titled *Civilization*.

I sang that the advance of civilization was coming at Earth's expense, cataloging the many ills inflicted by humans in three densely packed verses: the destruction of the rainforests and wetlands, overpopulation, overfishing, ocean dumping, loss of biodiversity, poaching and hunting, global warming, and nuclear proliferation. I then dared to ask that we take responsibility.

Over the past decade, Earth has experienced rising land and ocean temperatures, resulting in accelerated glacier melt, rising sea levels, and more extreme weather events. While every country is affected by climate change, the impacts are highly unequal. Lower-income countries in tropical and subtropical latitudes—such as Jamaica—are among the most vulnerable: they face more severe consequences and have the fewest resources for adaptation and recovery.[116]

The United States has not been immune, experiencing an increasing number of severe storms, hurricanes, flooding, and wildfires. I experienced the wrath of Superstorm Sandy when it made landfall in New Jersey on October 29, 2012, and witnessed its devastating impact on homeowners—particularly along the coastlines of New Jersey and New York. Despite the vast resources of the United States, electricity was not restored in my neighborhood until nine days later.

Jamaica, nestled in the Caribbean Sea and squarely within the Atlantic hurricane belt, remains particularly vulnerable to direct and glancing blows from increasingly frequent and intense storms.

I witnessed the devastating aftermath of a direct hit by Category 4 Hurricane Gilbert in 1988. I reflected on the irony when Sandy struck Jamaica directly as a Category 1 hurricane on October 24, 2012—just five days before I felt its much stronger impact in New Jersey. Since Gilbert, I have watched and sighed in relief as Jamaica escaped direct hits from nine other hurricanes that passed close by—each causing some damage but sparing the island the worst.

Just ten months into my retirement, on October 21, 2025, I heard that a tropical wave—having earlier formed over the Caribbean Sea—had strengthened and was now named Tropical Storm Melissa. I anxiously watched and hoped that, like the nine others since Gilbert, Jamaica would escape a direct hit from Melissa.

Sadly, seven days later, on October 28, Melissa slammed into Jamaica as a Category 5 hurricane with sustained winds of 185 miles per hour. This was the strongest hurricane to strike the island since record-keeping began in the mid-1800s. Melissa broke records with the strongest wind gusts ever recorded in a hurricane—reaching 252 miles per hour.

I saw the news reports and endless social media videos of Melissa's devastation: whole towns destroyed, hundreds of thousands of lives upended, and agricultural and forest vegetation razed. The power grid was largely destroyed, and damage sustained mainly across the island's western regions was estimated at billions of U.S. dollars.[117]

I agonized with concern and empathy for my relatives and fellow Jamaicans residing on the island. While my close relatives and friends were fortuitously spared from any severe impact, the fate of hundreds of thousands lay in the balance. I donated to relief efforts and encouraged others to do the same, but I recognized that the road to recovery would be long and painful—requiring years of sustained assistance from the Jamaican diaspora and global citizenry.

This catastrophe was a stark reminder of the existential risk posed by unabated climate change. Admittedly, the inevitability of more severe events occurring in the United States, Jamaica, and across the globe weighs heavily in my decisions about where to spend my retirement years. While I can never outrun the impacts of climate change, I recognize that the resilience I feel in the youth of my senior years will inevitably wane with age.

Riding the Technological Wave

The electronic computer emerged around the mid-twentieth century, not long before my birth in 1967. Since then, the pace of scientific and technological discoveries has accelerated along an exponential trajectory. Most new advancements have built on those that came before, creating a snowball effect that continues to gain momentum.[118]

Among the many technological breakthroughs in my lifetime, the following stand out to me: the moon landing in 1969; the invention of the microprocessor in 1971, which enabled the later mass production of personal computers; the first space shuttle flight in 1981; the birth of the modern internet in 1983; the invention of the World Wide Web in 1989; the launch of the Hubble Space Telescope in 1990; the introduction of the iPhone in 2007; the debut of the Tesla Roadster electric car in 2008; and the 2022 launch of ChatGPT, the first widely accessible large language model (LLM) conversational AI.[119]

On the technology adoption curve, I see myself as part of the early majority—coming just behind the innovators and early adopters and usually willing to embrace new technology only after seeing clear evidence of its value and durability.[120]

I now invariably use AI LLMs for research and editing, and I regularly rely on an AI-powered supervised Full Self-Driving feature while driving. Although I recognize AI's increasingly positive and revolutionary impact in almost every field of human endeavor—such as faster medical diagnoses and drug discovery—I, like many others, worry about its potential negative consequences.

I no longer seek employment, but I often wonder what will happen to the social fabric when AI-powered robotics and automation render most occupations obsolete. Will governments provide timely safety nets to maintain living standards for displaced workers? Will people who lose their careers find new sources of meaning and purpose? And when AI capabilities inevitably surpass human cognition, becoming artificial superintelligence (ASI), will it pose an existential threat to humanity? No one can answer these questions with certainty today, but I believe the answers will emerge within the next decade—hopefully within my lifetime.

As I prefer the path of optimism, my hope is that humanity will collectively ensure AI and ASI remain tools for good: eradicating poverty and disease while accelerating innovation to reduce the existential risk of climate change. In the meantime, I will continue riding the unavoidable wave of technological progress into the hopefully distant sunset of my life.

Deferred Dreams and New Experiences

Part of making every moment of my retirement years meaningful meant reviving what remained of my deferred dreams (shared in Chapter 17). It also meant stepping outside my comfort zone to embrace new experiences and challenges.

During the COVID-19 pandemic and the forced lockdown in 2020, I was playing tennis one day with a neighbor—who happened to be a music teacher—when the conversation turned to playing instruments. I told him about my long-held dream of learning to play the guitar, admitting that I had never pursued it because I doubted I could ever master playing by ear. He shared that he was a trumpeter who had played from sheet music for many years—rarely, if ever, by ear—and had been a member of several bands. That turned out to be exactly what I needed to hear.

I immediately bought an acoustic guitar, and later an electric one. I researched and found a highly recommended book on guitar lessons, then started practicing. In less than a month, I was playing *Amazing Grace* with relatively smooth chord changes. Since then, I have practiced playing over sixty songs and have sung along while recording more than forty of them on my iPhone. I have shared many of these videos with family and friends—perhaps to their occasional annoyance, but hopefully they have been entertained.

As the pace of my practice slowed and became inconsistent after the COVID-19 lockdown lifted, I looked forward to retirement as the chance to resume ardent practice and finally reach my "holy grail" of playing by ear. For a few months after retiring, I stuck to that plan, but it was soon interrupted by my long-dormant dream of authorship when the seeds of this memoir began to germinate.

My dream of becoming a published author was first realized in 1994 when I, as the lead author with my professor as the secondary, summarized my Master of Science thesis in a paper titled "Risk Assessment of Lead Exposure to Lead-Contaminated Particulates in the Area Around the Williamsburg Bridge, Brooklyn, N.Y." I presented this paper at the Twenty-Sixth Mid-Atlantic Industrial Waste Conference, and it was later published in the conference proceedings.[121]

Perhaps inspired by my first publication in 1994, the seeds of this memoir were planted in 1997—a rough idea and outline captured in three pages of handwritten notes that lay dormant for decades.

As the roadmap, meaning, and value of this book gradually unfolded and I began writing, I felt truly alive and purpose-driven. My dream was finally no longer dormant, awakened by the possibility of a long post-retirement journey as an author. This memoir has unlocked a creative, untapped energy within me, fueling thoughts and ideas for future books I hope to write in the coming years.

By the time of my retirement, I had visited only fourteen countries, including a U.S. territory. Since then, that number has grown to eighteen. Like the stereotypical retiree, I envisioned visiting new places—both within the United States and abroad—and having experiences long postponed due to other priorities.

My most anticipated post-retirement overseas adventure—driven by my passion for geology—became a reality on September 2, 2025, when my wife and I had the extraordinarily good fortune to witness an eruption of Kīlauea volcano on Hawai‘i's Big Island. By destiny or pure luck, a round of eruptions began the very morning we arrived and ended later that night.

We stood at a safe distance—just a few hundred yards away—along the crater's edge. We heard the thunderous roar, smelled the sulfurous air, and felt the radiant heat as thousands of gallons of glowing red lava spewed hundreds of feet skyward, while the earth trembled beneath our feet. It was truly one of the most remarkable experiences of my life—feeling the raw power of our living, breathing Mother Earth.

Not as intense but equally intriguing was my venture deep underground into the ancient, inactive Hana Lava Tube on the island of Maui. Formed when the outer layer of a molten lava flow cooled and hardened into a solid crust while the hotter interior lava drained away, these natural tunnels can stretch for miles and remain remarkably stable for centuries—offering a cool, silent contrast to the living fire of Kīlauea.[122]

It is my hope to continue this journey of international discovery—seeking places unseen and experiences unlived—unveiling to my five senses the many wonders and beauty of this, the most beautiful planet we know.

With the musical bug still crawling within me, I continue to hope that one day I will record and release the album I put on hold in 1997—and perhaps even perform my own songs on a real stage. By this, I mean no disrespect to karaoke, which remains my outlet for those unrealized artistic ambitions.

The shining example of philanthropy set by my mother—which I know I may never fully emulate—continues to push me toward a greater purpose. Although I have made charitable financial contributions to deserving causes for years, I hope to invest more of my time and knowledge directly in meaningful endeavors.

Did I Achieve My American Dream?

When I arrived in the United States almost thirty-nine years ago, I hoped to find greater educational and economic opportunities—a brighter future for myself and my family. I envisioned a more straightforward path to a successful career, financial security, and a higher standard of living. Driven by a Jamaican immigrant's optimism and resilience, along with a strong work ethic, I was resolute in pursuing my vision of the American dream.

In my view—and I believe this holds true for most Jamaican immigrants in the diaspora—we did not leave Jamaica out of a lack of patriotism. To the contrary, we were driven by economic, educational, and other ambitions, and in doing so became flagbearers for the island we all love. The Jamaican conviction that anything is possible still flows through our veins.

The Jamaican diaspora, while pursuing the American dream, constitutes a significant source of both tangible and intangible wealth for the nation. We can be relied upon to provide support during periods of adversity—such as hurricane damage—and to serve as ardent and vociferous cheerleaders in celebrating Jamaica's triumphs.

A vivid example of the Jamaican diaspora's economic impact is the scale of their cash remittances. Jamaica consistently ranks among the top remittance-receiving countries worldwide, with these funds accounting for 16 to 22 percent of the country's GDP in recent years. These inflows play a critical role in supporting families, stimulating local businesses, and strengthening national resilience beyond what domestic resources alone could achieve.[123]

As I reflect today on my American journey, I am filled with gratitude. The opportunities I envisioned and the goals for which I aspired and worked hard have largely been realized. Despite its sociopolitical challenges, the United States provided me with the means to accomplish what may have eluded me elsewhere. In return, I invested my labor and leadership, and I believe these contributions to the U.S. economy throughout my long career have been significant and meaningful.

Currently, pathways to legal immigration appear more restricted, and I fear the opportunities I was afforded could be denied to fellow Jamaicans and other immigrants. Yet I remain convinced that America's greatness was built on the ambitions and hard work of immigrants, and I hold hope that the doors—though narrowed—will never be fully closed. Shutting them would be a loss to both nations.

I was overwhelmed with pride when I read in the 2025 Global Gender Gap Report that Jamaica ranked first in the world in educational attainment—achieving near-perfect parity between the sexes across primary, secondary, and tertiary levels. This remarkable standing reflects Jamaica's long-standing commitment to equitable access to learning, especially for girls. The report was only one of many statistics showing that, despite vast disparities in economic prosperity, both Jamaica and the United States have considerable opportunities for mutual exchange and learning.[124]

On January 30, 2026, I watched with pride as another Jamaican from the diaspora ascended the ladder of American leadership. Lorna M. Mahlock—born in Kingston, Jamaica—made history as the first Black woman promoted to lieutenant general (a three-star rank) in the United States Marine Corps. This promotion capped a remarkable career that began when she enlisted at age seventeen, shortly after immigrating to Brooklyn, New York.[125]

These landmark events—along with countless other celebrated and unsung achievements—stand as enduring testaments to the ongoing contributions, commitment, and positive influence of the Jamaican diaspora on U.S. political life, national security, military leadership, and society at large.

My Brilliant Ray of Sunshine

Embarking on a long and meaningful post-retirement journey—realizing long-deferred dreams and living new experiences—could only reach its zenith if shared with the love of my life. My wife, Jackie, is that brilliant ray of sunshine that dispels the shadows and brightens my mornings. She is my anchor when the winds of life's inevitable challenges disturb my sea of tranquility. She is the oxygen that fuels my drive.

As I reflect on my past journey, it's easy to spot missteps along the way and wonder: What if I had made different choices? Yet such thoughts fade quickly when I realize that a different path might have robbed me of Jackie—and the profound love and happiness she has brought into my life.

As I write these final sentences, I picture myself on my deathbed, asking and answering three questions:

- Have I accomplished my dreams and aspirations—or at least tried?
  Yes, I have accomplished many, but more awaits.
- Has my life been purposeful and, in some way, improved the lives of others?
  Yes, but there is much more to do.
- Have I experienced true, enduring love?
  Yes, yes, yes—thanks to Jackie.

Behind me lies a life free of deep regrets; ahead lie only aspirations I still hunger to fulfill before I breathe my last breath.

Until we meet again. As we say in Jamaica, "waak gud."

LIFE LESSONS

1. Knowing when to let go of one achieved purpose and embrace the next is critical to living fully.

2. In the book of life, leave old chapters closed, as your dreams await in the pages that follow.

3. As a candle wick needs wax to sustain its flame, one's lifespan needs a long healthspan to fuel its purpose.

4. AI is here, and it is the future. The only question is whether you'll use it to multiply your potential or let it multiply someone else's.

5. Age delivers experience, and experience delivers wisdom, so be grateful for each delivery.

6. War and unrest rise and fall like tides; don't let the high water drown your peace.

7. Living the American dream is chasing your potential all the way to the top while keeping the door open for everyone still climbing.

Embracing my brilliant ray of sunshine (Jackie) as I look beyond the Pitons of St. Lucia to the journey ahead (December 2025)

Compendium of Life Lessons

Part I: Foundations

1. A family tree should not be an unbending dictate for one's belief system, principles, and actions, but as the roots of a tree meander deep into the ground in search of nourishment, so too can we find strength from the spirit and knowledge rooted in our ancestors.

2. The human race is a quilt where patches of ethnicity are sewn together to make the whole, each contributing to its beauty, form, and function.

3. The stupidity of human division, by race, color, or caste, is inevitably exposed by the shared weight of inescapable catastrophes.

4. No geographic and man-made political boundaries will ever separate us, as we are forever bonded by the shared pulse of human desire and experience.

5. Honor your heritage without apology. What feels ordinary to you today may one day be treasured by humanity.

6. Hardships in childhood quietly and unconsciously plant the seeds of lifelong resilience and ingenuity.

7. The extended family is often a child's earliest classroom, teaching the quiet arts of connection, belonging, and interdependence.

8. Folklore and fables carry morals in one hand, heritage in the other, and in the space between, they quietly unlock a child's imagination and creativity.

9. A child or adolescent without adequate supervision will invariably explore adult vices; only a stroke of luck will save them from life-changing consequences.

10. For a child to thrive amid pervasive maladies, at least one parent must guide wisely and well.

11. A child learns from both spoken words and unverbalized actions.

12. A parent's absence makes a child's heart grow harder, not fonder.

13. Poor life choices and bad financial decisions are symbiotically linked; avoid one, and the other will almost always improve.

14. A promise is like money—if it cannot be traded for something of value, it's worthless.

15. A gun in a home is a dark current running beneath every ordinary day, with fear, accident, and tragedy waiting for its moment.

16. A gun's core purpose is to wound or kill, human or animal; it makes no distinction.

17. To say a gun is for protection from another gun is a gun-perpetuating tragedy.

18. To forgive is not to forget, lest you become a repeat victim of bad memory.

19. If divine redemption is an ever-present promise to spare one the consequences of their deliberate, harmful actions, then what is their deterrent?

20. Turn every negative childhood experience into wisdom: unspoken lessons of what never to emulate or become.

21. A mother's love is the steel of a child's foundation, without which they topple beneath the tremors of adversity and the gale-force winds of life's storms.

22. In the river of parenthood, seed the current with resourcefulness and entrepreneurship; then your children will never thirst.

23. Few virtues are as scarce as self-sacrifice. If you are its beneficiary, you are blessed beyond measure.

24. Philanthropy is the acknowledgment that we are all one connected consciousness: as you do unto another, you do unto yourself.

25. Activism begins with recognizing that leadership is not equally bestowed. If you are among the gifted, step forward when humanity calls.

26. Role models are society's roots; without them, the whole tree weakens.

Part II: Finding My Way

27. Find your lifelong mantra. Let it anchor you, honor every small win, and keep you aimed at becoming your best.

28. Some failures are blessings in disguise. They redirect us toward paths far richer than any success could have carved. In the throes of despair, trust that the universe knows best.

29. Never waste a second chance to reach your zenith; a third is not guaranteed.

30. Disasters are inevitable and often unpredictable. Survival hangs on the thin line where preparation meets luck. Prepare well, then discharge the rest to the universe.

31. True love cannot manifest without the willingness to be open and vulnerable to unreciprocated desire. Still, the immeasurable reward outweighs any disappointment.

32. Respect any religious belief or practice, provided it uplifts the spirit, improves well-being, and makes society more humane. Anything less simply hasn't earned your reverence.

33. Arguably, no one—religious, atheist, or agnostic—has enough evidence to defend their deepest convictions by logic alone. In the final step, everyone places faith in uncertainty.

34. Stay stubbornly open to the universe's ethereal possibilities and never stop searching for truth.

35. Trust the universe in all its grandeur. It is infinitely intelligent and will guide humanity to its ultimate destiny.

36. Let initial rejection stir resolve, not despair, for far greater opportunities always lie ahead.

37. Never be seduced by extravagant promises of grandeur in places, people, or things. Believe only what your own experience confirms.

38. If opportunity is the door, determination, grit, and hard work are the only keys that ever fit the lock.

39. Never let success or contentment lull you into complacency. What follows can undo everything.

40. Sleep can kill you quicker than speed, the moment it finds you at the wheel.

41. Let 'Why?' be your litmus test for cheap or expensive alike. The low price may betray you tomorrow; the high price may betray you today.

42. Be fiercely proud of where you began. Those struggles, lessons, and triumphs forged the resilient achiever—you.

43. The path to success is rarely the one planned. Detour signs of great opportunity will appear; the wise recognize them, and the brave change course.

44. Acting on anecdotes and intuition is reckless when the facts are within reach.

45. A well-timed confession of your struggles could be the one key that unlocks true compassion and forgiveness.

46. Dead-end road? U-turn. Dead-end job? Same rule.

Part III: Trials and Transformation

47. African slavery came in three forms—chains on the body, chains on the mind, chains on the wallet—only the first was broken.

48. Conscious and unconscious racism are two sides of the same coin, wielding the same power and inflicting the same pain.

49. Civil rights should be like the air—free, limitless, and owed to every lung that draws breath.

50. Critics decry affirmative action while pretending merit is color-blind—it never was and may never be.

51. A rainbow shows, in every color at once, that the storm has ended. We are the human rainbow; united, we can end the hurricane of division.

52. Standing up for your rights is never just for you; it catalyzes change that benefits many.

53. Like an undammed river, hope without buildup generates no power.

54. Unity, however elusive, is the engine of every great success. Division is the broken wheel that derails everything else.

55. When core values collide, a marriage survives only through self-sacrifice. Someone must love more than they need to win.

56. When the bond between two hearts breaks, do not reach for another's heart until you have studied the pieces of your own.

57. Adults rarely recast their mold. Incompatible values and habits don't vanish because we wish them to; they simply wait in the dark.

58. On life's journey, ignore a warning sign only if you are ready to live with the wreckage.

59. Transparency is the warmth that keeps love alive. Without it, everything freezes.

60. If someone cannot hold your gaze, believe the eyes, not their words.

61. When a relationship turns into a roller coaster, get off before the coming derailment.

62. Children need two parents the way an airliner needs two pilots. One might land the plane, but is it worth the risk?

63. Love has many dialects—most are gentle. Tough love is the one that sounds like anger but delivers rescue.

64. Your children learn parenting from you. So, what kind of parents are you teaching them to be?

65. A child is a sponge with eyes and ears. They see and reenact your actions, hear and remember your words.

66. To a child, separation and divorce feel like an unconscious rejection of half of who they are.

67. An absent parent is the missing piece of a child's life puzzle. The picture will never be complete.

68. Blessings often come in small packages. So does the child you accept who is not your blood but becomes yours by choice.

69. A child's unbridled honesty is a mirror you cannot dodge—look, listen, learn.

70. Stand tall against injustice today, so your children never have to stoop tomorrow.

71. Celebrate your children's successes but teach them to mine strength from every failure.

72. A parent's last great gift is emancipation. Holding on only impedes the flight you taught them to take.

73. Aspirations are the fuel of a meaningful life. When the tank runs dry, so does the soul.

74. A dream is a lush green valley you envision but cannot reach, until you've climbed every mountain that stands in the way.

75. When a dream starts feeling like a nightmare, wake up. There are other aspirations that let you sleep.

76. On my deathbed, let it be that I pursued every worthy dream, won some, lost some, but regretted none.

77. Entrepreneurship is turning a risky idea into value for others through relentless work. The business may fail, but the impact lives on.

78. The true entrepreneur is measured not in calm waters but by how well they sail through storms.

79. In business, technological change is a double-edged sword: a catalyst for the fast, a coffin nail for the slow.

80. Entrepreneurial passion must bow to due diligence. Blind leaps rarely hit their target.

81. Before you marry someone, study his or her qualities that you dislike and ask, "Can I live with them for the rest of my life?"

82. Procrastination disguised as patience is just cowardice in slow motion.

83. Financial wealth and health usually trade places. Which do you value more?

84. True strength lies not in avoidance but in the willingness to confront what ails.

85. Using intimacy to settle conflict is the prey kissing the predator; the feared hunt always resumes.

86. A child bathed in constant parental discord carries the scars forever.

87. The universe teaches best through the endless difficulties stitched into being human.

88. Alcohol is no friend in deed or need; just a salesman peddling escape from reality. Avoid it, lest your escape become permanent.

89. Winning the argument often loses the war. Compromise, even when you're right, guarantees victory.

90. Prior independence is the crucial prerequisite for a marriage of healthy co-dependence.

Part IV: Renewal and Arrival

91. Beyond the cold, dark caverns of despair, a light waits, a light ready to flood you with warmth. Keep walking.

92. After every failure, take inventory and rebuild, never reincorporating what's broken into your new foundation.

93. Resilience is the necessary steel that keeps our columns of resistance from buckling under life's gravitas.

94. Ambitious dreams are mental heartbeats, nurturing our minds and giving meaning to life.

95. When planning a self-restorative journey, let education be your passport.

96. Learning a foreign language is an investment with exponential returns.

97. Perfection is as elusive as a desert mirage, but if you stop chasing it, improvement ends.

98. Volunteerism is one of life's greatest symbioses—you usually get back more than you give.

99. When a relic of your past becomes an obstacle to your future—let it go.

100. Short-term losses usually buy long-term wins; don't sweat them.

101. When the vase of your life lies shattered, melt the pieces and remold them into something far more beautiful.

102. Positive thinking is a magnet. The stronger it gets, the more blessings stick.

103. No one can steal your hope. It lies inside you and costs nothing to keep alive.

104. They say time heals all wounds, but emotional hurts also need space and distance.

105. The strength of an apology lies not in the words, but in the follow-through that makes things right.

106. Life's crossroads flash vivid signs. Read them carefully. One wrong turn can cost your last shot at happiness.

107. Declaring "I love you" must mean I will do everything in my power—emotionally and materially—to make our lives better.

108. Watch your partner when you're sick. Their actions will show whether "I love you" was ever real.

109. No grand gesture done from obligation or vanity will ever match the magnitude of small things shared in love.

110. Your marital vows are not primarily to your spouse; they are oaths to never betray yourself.

111. Define what a soulmate means to you. If you're lucky enough to find one—hang on for dear life.

112. Marital harmony is guarded by ruthless discernment: swiftly spot anything outside the core two of you and keep it at bay.

113. Like storms that eventually reach shore, life's trials will test every marriage. Only the deeply anchored ones stand when the waves recede.

114. Problems are potential opportunities for growth disguised by anxiety.

115. Do not waste your energy worrying about things over which you have no influence or control. Concentrate instead on those things within your power.

116. Respect is like a boomerang; show it, and it comes right back to you. The same goes for disrespect, so choose wisely.

117. The degree of a challenge is directly related to one's capacity to overcome it. The universe, in its infinite wisdom, molds challenges to match one's capability.

118. Finding commonality of purpose requires recognition, appreciation, and respect for the vision and goals of others.

119. Show up not only with the right qualifications, experience, and work ethic, but also dress well for the part, as you are usually seen before you're heard.

120. Let integrity, principle, and true merit be the foundation of your recognition and opportunities—advantage gained based on anything less is like building on shifting sands.

121. Never drop a challenge to which you've been entrusted until it's resolved; it's like dropping a tennis ball when it's in your court—you lose points.

122. Choose "good enough" over "perfect" when time is of the essence.

123. To say "what you put in is what you get out" is a fallacy of proportions; a small but wisely chosen input can generate an output many times its size or value.

124. Failing to consider others' knowledge and ideas while relying only on your own is the same as failing to use both hands to break a fall. Herein lies the wisdom of teamwork.

125. Inflexibility in one's style of management is like a car with faulty brakes; it's destined to crash.

126. Calmness in a crisis is a skill achieved only through deliberate practice.

127. On the scale of life, career pursuits and personal life precariously hang in the balance; be vigilant so as not to tip the scale.

128. Like a pilot or driver, you may never know how much you are appreciated until the very end of a journey, so do your best as you travel your chosen path.

129. Let the positive impact you've had on the lives of others and the abundance of love in your life be the measures of your success.

130. Knowing when to let go of one achieved purpose and embrace the next is critical to living fully.

131. In the book of life, leave old chapters closed, as your dreams await in the pages that follow.

132. As a candle wick needs wax to sustain its flame, one's lifespan needs a long healthspan to fuel its purpose.

133. AI is here, and it is the future. The only question is whether you'll use it to multiply your potential or let it multiply someone else's.

134. Age delivers experience, and experience delivers wisdom, so be grateful for each delivery.

135. War and unrest rise and fall like tides; don't let the high water drown your peace.

136. Living the American dream is chasing your potential all the way to the top while keeping the door open for everyone still climbing

Endnotes

[1] Clinton V. Black, *History of Jamaica*, rev. ed. (London: Longman Caribbean, 1988), 9–35, 44. This section covers the history of the Taíno, Columbus's arrival, the Taíno's decimation, and the British conquest.

[2] Kenneth Morgan, *A Concise History of Jamaica* (Cambridge: Cambridge University Press, 2023), 54–57; "Estimates," *Slave Voyages: Trans-Atlantic Slave Trade Database*, https://www.slavevoyages.org/assessment/estimates; Erica Johnson, "Confusing Labels: French 'Emigrants' and 'Prisoners of War' in Jamaica during the Haitian Revolution," *Age of Revolutions* (blog), June 22, 2023, https://ageofrevolutions.com/2023/06/22/confusing-labels-french-emigrants-and-prisoners-of-war-in-jamaica-during-the-haitian-revolution/; Thomas C. Holt, *The Problem of Freedom: Race, Labor, and Politics in Jamaica and Britain, 1832–1938* (Baltimore: Johns Hopkins University Press, 1992), 115–120; Walton Look Lai, *Indentured Labor, Caribbean Sugar: Chinese and Indian Migrants to the British West Indies, 1838–1918* (Baltimore: Johns Hopkins University Press, 1993), 42–45, 102–108, 128–135; Rebecca Tortello, "Pieces of the Past: The Arrival of the Lebanese," *Jamaica Gleaner*, October 6, 2003, accessed February 26, 2026, https://old.jamaica-gleaner.com/pages/history/story0056.htm. Various immigrant groups have arrived since the British conquest. For white British immigrants, see Morgan; for Africans forcibly brought from Africa, see "Estimates"; for French refugees, see Johnson; for indentured laborers, see Holt and Look Lai; for Syrian and Lebanese, see Tortello.

[3] FamilySearch Wiki, "Genealogical Proof Standard – International Institute," https://www.familysearch.org/en/wiki/The_Genealogical_Proof_Standard_-_International_Institute. Professional genealogists adhere to the Genealogical Proof Standard (GPS), which requires information to be based on original records and the critical evaluation of all evidence. Conversely, user-generated family trees on commercial sites often contain unchecked or unsubstantiated data and should be treated as research hints rather than definitive sources, requiring verification through primary archival documents.

[4] Walton Look Lai, *Indentured Labor*, Caribbean Sugar: Chinese and Indian Migrants to the British West Indies, 1838–1918 (Baltimore: Johns Hopkins University Press, 1993), 24–37. The economic drivers for indentured labor

recruitment patterns and emigration from specific regions of India, and the limited role of caste in shielding against colonial-era economic distress, are detailed in this source.

[5] National Archives (UK), "Indian Indentured Labourers," https://www.nationalarchives.gov.uk/help-with-your-research/research-guides/indian-indentured-labourers/. Indian indentured laborers were usually recorded in colonial documents and immigration registers by a single name, as many did not use fixed surnames in their home regions.

[6] Bharatpedia, "Guha (surname)," https://en.bharatpedia.org/wiki/Guha_(surname) (accessed February 26, 2026). The Guha surname is commonly associated with the Bengali Kayastha caste, originating from villages in the Bengal region (now West Bengal and Bangladesh).

[7] Christer Petley, "Reproducing Capital: The Long Family," in *Lucky Valley: The Legacy of the Longs in Jamaica* (Cambridge: Cambridge University Press, 2024). First-cousin marriage was a known strategy in some Jamaican families during the colonial and early post-colonial era to preserve land and wealth within the kinship group, particularly where inheritance customs risked fragmenting family holdings.

[8] Deanna Ashley, Affette McCaw-Binns, and Jean Golding, "Maternal Mortality in Jamaica," *The Lancet* 327, no. 8479 (March 1, 1986): 486–488, https://doi.org/10.1016/S0140-6736(86)92939-9. In Jamaica during the 1930s–1940s, maternal mortality remained high compared to earlier decades, with common causes of death during or shortly after childbirth including puerperal sepsis (infection), hemorrhage, and hypertensive disorders of pregnancy. These risks were exacerbated by limited access to antenatal care, hospital delivery for high-risk cases, and antibiotics (not widely available until after World War II), contributing to premature deaths among women in their late thirties and early forties.

[9] Stanley Mirvis, *The Jews of Eighteenth-Century Jamaica: A Testamentary History of a Diaspora in Transition* (New Haven: Yale University Press, 2020), 11–25. Sephardi and Ashkenazi Jews arrived in the late fifteenth and eighteenth centuries, respectively.

[10] Stanley Mirvis, *The Jews of Eighteenth-Century Jamaica: A Testamentary History of a Diaspora in Transition* (New Haven: Yale University Press, 2020), 20–28; Manchester Parish Development Committee, "Chapter 5: The Cultural and Historical Environment," in *Sustainable Development Plan for Manchester, Jamaica* (Mandeville, Jamaica: Manchester Parish

Development Committee, 2011), https://manchesterpdc.files.wordpress.com/2011/03/09chap-5-history-march-04.pdf. St. Elizabeth, as a major settlement area for European immigrants, including Jewish families, is detailed in Mirvis; the historical boundary change of St. Elizabeth parish to form Manchester parish on December 13, 1814, is documented in Manchester Parish Development Committee.

[11] Diana Thorburn and Dana Marie Morris, *Jamaica's Foreign Policy: Making the Economic Development Link*, working paper R0703 (Kingston, Jamaica: Caribbean Policy Research Institute, June 2007), 11–13, https://www.capricaribbean.org/sites/default/files/documents/r0703jamaicas-foreign-policymaking-economic-development-link200707.pdf. Jamaica's early post-independence economy relied heavily on U.S. trade and investment (especially bauxite and tourism), with a pro-U.S. foreign policy in the 1960s.

[12] Kareen Felicia Williams, "The Evolution of Political Violence in Jamaica 1940–1980" (PhD diss., Columbia University, 2011), 171–174, https://academiccommons.columbia.edu/doi/10.7916/D8WS91D7. The two-party political system, prime ministers of the late 1960s and early 1970s, sharpening political rivalries between the JLP and PNP, socio-economic grievances, increasing violence, squatter community bulldozing (e.g., Back-O-Wall for Tivoli Gardens), and persistent class/color hierarchies from the colonial era.

[13] Diana Thorburn and Dana Marie Morris, *Jamaica's Foreign Policy*, 14–21. The resurgence of the PNP under Michael Manley (1972) and his platform of democratic socialism, and foreign policy.

[14] United States, National Advisory Commission on Civil Disorders, *Report of the National Advisory Commission on Civil Disorders* (Washington, DC: Government Printing Office, 1968), esp. chaps. 1–2, 4–5, 11–12. The escalation of the Vietnam War and its impact on the U.S. economy, the shift of the Civil Rights movement toward economic inequality and Black Power, and the severity of the "long hot summer" urban uprisings in 1967 (which included over 150 riots).

[15] Encyclopædia Britannica, s.v. "Jamaica: Self-government," https://www.britannica.com/place/Jamaica/Self-government; World Bank, *Current Economic Position and Prospects of Jamaica* (Washington, DC: World Bank, December 17, 1968), https://documents1.worldbank.org/curated/en/465181468284365764/pdf/m

ulti0page.pdf; Dovelyn Rannveig Mendoza, "Jamaica: From Diverse Beginning to Diaspora in the Developed World," Migration Policy Institute, June 16, 2010, https://www.migrationpolicy.org/article/jamaica-diverse-beginning-diaspora-developed-world. All sources accessed February 26, 2026. Details and outcomes of the Colonial Development and Welfare Act, Jamaica's First Five-Year Plan, and its achievement, and emigration during this era.

[16] Council of Economic Advisers, *Economic Report of the President 1968* (Washington, DC: U.S. Government Printing Office, 1968), esp. 3–15, 25–40; Muzaffar Chishti and Faye Hipsman, "Fifty Years On, the 1965 Immigration and Nationality Act Continues to Reshape the United States," Migration Policy Institute, October 15, 2015, https://www.migrationpolicy.org/article/fifty-years-1965-immigration-and-nationality-act-continues-reshape-united-states. The impact on the U.S. economy caused by Vietnam War spending, the low general unemployment rate, and the persistence of poverty (over thirty million Americans), and the effect of the Immigration and Nationality Act of 1965.

[17] Stephen Davis, *Reggae Bloodlines: In Search of the Music and Culture of Jamaica* (New York: Da Capo Press, 1992), 80–110; Kevin O'Brien Chang and Wayne Chen, *Reggae Routes: The Story of Jamaican Music* (Kingston: Ian Randle Publishers, 1998), 45–75; Rex Nettleford, *Cultural Action and Social Change: The Case of Jamaica* (Ottawa: International Development Research Centre, 1979), esp. 45–110, https://idl-bnc-idrc.dspacedirect.org/server/api/core/bitstreams/7fa6b4cc-64e0-4381-99fb-9e7104dea850/content. The cultural transition from ska to rocksteady (c. 1967) and then to reggae (c. 1968), including the key artists and the global impact of the genre; the growing influence of the Rastafari movement on music and social commentary and its initial marginalization by the establishment; and the burgeoning literary and theater scene.

[18] "The Sixties," in *The American Yawp: A Massively Collaborative Open U.S. History Textbook*, vol. 2, ed. Joseph L. Locke and Ben Wright (Stanford, CA: Stanford University Press, 2019), http://www.americanyawp.com/text/27-the-sixties/; Encyclopædia Britannica, s.v. "1960s counterculture," https://www.britannica.com/topic/1960s-counterculture. The rise of the U.S. counterculture movement in the late 1960s, with its roots in opposition to the Vietnam War and the Civil Rights Movement, its focus on individualism, alternative lifestyles, and challenging traditional social norms, and its impact on music (rock and roll, folk) and fashion.

[19] "*A Learner's Grammar of Jamaican*," Open Grammar Project, 2018, https://opengrammar.github.io/jam/learners_grammar-jam.pdf; Peter L. Patrick, "JC Jamaican Patwa (Creole English)," Creolica.net, July 31, 2007, https://www.creolica.net/jcpp.pdf. The definition of Jamaican Patwa as a creole language with its own grammar and lexicon, and its linguistic evolution.

[20] Velma Pollard, "Dread Talk – The Speech of the Rastafari in Jamaica," *Caribbean Quarterly* 26, no. 4 (1980): 32–41, https://ufdcimages.uflib.ufl.edu/CA/00/40/00/44/00001/PDF.pdf; "Rastafari," RE:Online, Religious Education Council of England and Wales, 2019, https://www.reonline.org.uk/wp-content/uploads/2019/06/Rastafari.pdf, section on "Expression and Worship." Iyaric's (Dread Talk) development by Rastafari from the mid-20th century onward and its influence on mainstream Jamaican Patois.

[21] Anika Gerfer, "Global Reggae and the Appropriation of Jamaican Creole," *English World-Wide* 39, no. 3 (2018): 257–284, https://www.academia.edu/37252200/Global_reggae_and_the_appropriation_of_Jamaican_Creole; Jérôme K. Dagnini, "The Importance of Reggae Music in the Worldwide Cultural Universe," *Études Caribéennes* 16 (2011), https://journals.openedition.org/etudescaribeennes/4740. The impact of reggae music on Jamaican Patois's global visibility and the increasing affirmation of its legitimacy as a full creole language by linguistic scholars dates to the 1970s.

[22] "Elaine Perkins," PBCJ AV Library, June 13, 2025, https://www.libraryatpbcj.com/post/dennis-howard-2-6. Elaine Perkins's *Dulcimina: Her Life in Town* aired weekdays from 1967 to 1980 and followed the story of a young woman from the country navigating life in Kingston.

[23] Fawzia Dar, "Trauma of Slavery: A Critical Study of *Roots* by Alex Haley," *Journal of Literature, Languages and Linguistics* 58 (2019): 1–7, https://www.iiste.org/Journals/index.php/JLLL/article/download/48311/49911; Elisa Bordin, "Looking for Kunta Kinte: Alex Haley's *Roots* and African American Genealogies," *Iperstoria* 6 (2015): 73–82, https://iperstoria.it/article/download/426/460/1244. Alex Haley's novel *Roots: The Saga of an American Family* (1976) and the subsequent 1977 television miniseries are widely credited with generating widespread public awareness of the brutal conditions of the transatlantic slave trade and the lasting trauma of chattel slavery.

[24] Martha Warren Beckwith, *Black Roadways: A Study of Jamaican Folk Life* (Chapel Hill: University of North Carolina Press, 1929; repr., New York: Negro Universities Press, 1969), 100–120. In Jamaican folklore, a Rolling Calf Duppy is a frightening ghost that appears as a large bull or other animal with fiery red eyes and a chain dragging behind it.

[25] Sarita G., "Legacies that Survive Across Time and Space: A Critical Reading of The 'Trickster' Character Anansi from West African Folklore," *Dialog: A Journal of English Studies* (2023): 1–14, https://dialog.puchd.ac.in/wp-content/uploads/2023/09/12.-Legacies-that-Survive-Dialog-1.edited.pdf. The Anansi folklore tradition originated with the Asante people of Ghana and was brought to Jamaica through the transatlantic slave trade. Anansi is a trickster figure, typically depicted as a spider with human qualities, whose stories teach lessons about resourcefulness, scheming, and the consequences of actions.

[26] International Association of Athletics Federations (World Athletics), "All-Time Medal Table – Olympic Games" and "World Championships," https://worldathletics.org/records/all-time-toplists; "Champs – the Biggest Deal in Jamaica," World Athletics, April 8, 2014, https://worldathletics.org/news/feature/boys-girls-champs-jamaica-zharnel-hughes-issa. Track and field is one of Jamaica's most successful sports, consistently ranking among the top nations in sprint events and producing Olympic and World Championship medalists at a rate far exceeding its population size. The annual ISSA Boys and Girls Championships ("Champs") is a national event where high schools compete, serving as the primary incubator for future Olympic talent.

[27] Sandra W. Meditz and Dennis M. Hanratty, eds., "Jamaica - Health and Welfare," in *Caribbean Islands: A Country Study* (Washington, DC: GPO for the Library of Congress, 1987), https://countrystudies.us/caribbean-islands/23.htm. In the mid-1980s, there was a scarcity of licensed dentists and a prevalence of unlicensed dentists, with slightly more than 100 registered dentists islandwide.

[28] *Towns and Communities Act* (Jamaica, 1843, as amended), § 9(c), https://laws.moj.gov.jm/library/statute/the-towns-and-communities-act/download. The Jamaican law concerning public profanity is officially the Towns and Communities Act (1843, as amended), which includes specific provisions (often referred to colloquially as the "Bad Word Law") against using indecent, profane, or obscene language in any public place, carrying a penalty of arrest or a fine.

[29] "Obeah Histories," Obeah Histories project (led by Diana Paton et al.), https://obeahhistories.org/; *The Obeah Act* (Jamaica, 1898, as amended), §§ 2–3, https://laws.moj.gov.jm/library/statute/the-obeah-act. Obeah is a system of spiritual and healing practices rooted in West African religious traditions, specifically brought to the Caribbean during slavery. It is not an organized religion but a folk magic system often used for protection, healing, or, conversely, for casting curses. While Obeah is widely practiced or believed in, it was (and remains) illegal under the Obeah Act in Jamaica.

[30] "Who Were the Windrush Generation?" BBC News, June 20, 2025, https://www.bbc.com/news/articles/c3w4q1ee1p4o; and *Windrush 75: An E-book* (Canberra: The Conversation, 2023), https://cdn.theconversation.com/static_files/files/2747/Windrush_e-book_final_(2).pdf?1689252059. The Windrush era is the period from 1948 to 1971 when large numbers of people from Caribbean countries (including Jamaica) immigrated to the United Kingdom in search of work after World War II. The name is derived from the ship HMT Empire Windrush, which brought the first large group of Caribbean immigrants to Britain in 1948.

[31] Centers for Medicare & Medicaid Services, "Medicare and Medicaid Programs; Conditions of Participation for Home Health Agencies," *Federal Register* 54, no. 150 (August 14, 1989): 33354–33373 (codified at 42 CFR § 484.36; New York State aligned with these standards for certified agencies). Home Health Aides (HHA) training and supervised practical experience requirements in New York State in the 1980s.

[32] Electoral Commission of Jamaica, "1980 General Election Box by Box Results," https://ecj.com.jm/wp-content/uploads/2017/12/1980GeneralElectionBoxbyBox.pdf; National Library of Jamaica, "Members of Parliament (Election Results from 1944–)," http://www.nlj.gov.jm/Civicspage/members_of_parliament_since_1944.pdf. Data regarding the political tenure of Winston Jones and the JLP's landslide victory in 1980 (fifty-one seats to the PNP's nine), which ended Michael Manley's democratic-socialist era and ushered in Edward Seaga's pro-market policies.

[33] "Caring and Learning Together: A Case Study of Jamaica," UNESCO Early Childhood and Family Policy Series (Paris: UNESCO/OAS, n.d.), https://www.oas.org/cotep/GetAttach.aspx?aid=144&cId=75&lang=en. Details on Jamaica's early childhood education during the 1970s and on 1975 salary subsidies and basic school operations.

[34] Sandhya Handa, "A Brief Background on Jamaica" (Blacksburg: Virginia Polytechnic Institute and State University, 1996), 11, https://vtechworks.lib.vt.edu/bitstreams/20f16ea1-fc9f-40f6-b422-44c64b9b4ab0/download. The Jamaican primary and secondary public education during the 1970s and 1980s, including the CEE, high school system, and culminating examinations. Starting in 1958, students in Jamaica took the national Common Entrance Examination (CEE) to enter high school (secondary in the US) as early as age ten.

[35] World Bank, *Jamaica Secondary Education: Improving Quality and Extending Access* (Washington, DC: World Bank, 1999), https://documents.worldbank.org/curated/en/830691468771888579/pdf/multi-page.pdf; Ministry of Education, Youth & Information, *Primary Exit Profile 2019 National Report* (Kingston: MOEYI, 2019), https://pep.moey.gov.jm/wp-content/uploads/2019/08/REVISEDPEP-2019-NATIONAL-REPORT-July-23-2019-formatted-V4.pdf. The ROSE program and the introduction of the GSAT aimed to expand access and subsequent reforms.

[36] Rex Nettleford et al., "Golden Jubilee: UWI at 50," *Caribbean Beat* no. 32 (July/August 1998), https://www.caribbean-beat.com/issue-32/golden-jubilee-uwi-50; and "The UWI Timeline," University of the West Indies, https://uwi.edu/timeline. Discusses the history of UWI, its three-term structure, and the shift from the three-term system to the semester system starting with the 1990/1991 academic year.

[37] "The 'duppies' of JOS/Jolly Joseph still haunt the JUTC," *Jamaica Observer*, August 29, 2014, https://www.jamaicaobserver.com/2014/08/29/the-duppies-of-jos-jolly-joseph-still-haunt-the-jutc. Explains that the private minibus system emerged after the collapse of the government-operated Jamaica Omnibus Service (JOS), which ran the municipal bus service in the Kingston area from 1953 until 1983.

[38] "FST Undergraduate Student Awards," Faculty of Science and Technology, University of the West Indies, Mona, https://www.mona.uwi.edu/fst/fst-undergraduate-student-awards#geo. Discusses the annual undergraduate geology scholarship, provided since 1981, which was one of the highest-value non-government awards at UWI in 1987 and was funded by multiple corporate sponsors within the mining and related industries.

[39] "About UWI," Office of Student Recruitment, University of the West Indies at Mona, https://www.mona.uwi.edu/prospects/about-uwi. Explains that UWI is a regional institution jointly funded and supported by fifteen Caribbean

territories and that its Mona campus hosts a large, diverse cohort of students from across the English-speaking Caribbean.

[40] "About Us," University of Technology, Jamaica, https://www.utech.edu.jm/about-utech. The College of Arts, Science and Technology (CAST) was established in 1958 and was a major technical tertiary institution in Jamaica; it was formally upgraded and renamed the University of Technology, Jamaica (UTech) in 1995.

[41] "A Flashback to Michael Manley's Free Education System," *Jamaica Observer*, February 27, 2022, https://www.jamaicaobserver.com/2022/02/27/a-flashback-to-michael-manleys-free-education-system/. Explains that the imposition of the 10 percent student cess by the JLP administration in February 1986 was a controversial policy shift toward cost-sharing, formally ending the system of free education from primary to tertiary levels that had been implemented by Prime Minister Michael Manley's PNP government in 1973.

[42] Pinchers, "*Hackle Mi Body*," on *The Biggest Ragga Dancehall Anthems 1987*, VP Records/Greensleeves, 1987; reissued on *The Biggest Ragga Dancehall Anthems 1987*, VP Records, 2008. "*Hackle Mi Body*," a popular reggae/dancehall single by Pinchers (Delroy Thompson), was released in 1987 and was a major success, making it a culturally resonant song at the time of its performance.

[43] "About Us," Earthquake Unit, University of the West Indies, Mona, https://www.mona.uwi.edu/earthquake/about. Explains that the Earthquake Unit was established at UWI, Mona, in 1953 and has historically served as the primary center for seismic research and monitoring for Jamaica and the Eastern Caribbean, collaborating closely with government disaster management agencies.

[44] R. D. Koehler et al., "Enriquillo–Plantain Garden Fault Zone in Jamaica: Paleoseismology and Seismic Hazard," *Bulletin of the Seismological Society of America* 103, no. 2A (2013): 971–983, https://pubs.usgs.gov/publication/70073701; and Organization of American States, "Kingston Metropolitan Area Seismic Hazard Assessment: Executive Summary and Conclusions," Caribbean Disaster Mitigation Project, accessed January 2, 2026, https://www.oas.org/cdmp/document/kma/seismic/seis_sum.htm. Discusses the Kingston metropolitan area's seismic vulnerability.

[45] "Introduction: Reconciling Religion and Culture in Jamaica," Catholics and Cultures, January 15, 2014, https://www.catholicsandcultures.org/jamaica/introduction. Catholicism in Jamaica has historically been a small minority, declining from nearly 5 percent in the 1982 census to lower figures later, with Protestant churches dominating the religious landscape.

[46] "Religion in Jamaica," *Encyclopædia Britannica*, https://www.britannica.com/place/Jamaica/Religion; "Faith in Jamaica," *VisitJamaica.com*, https://www.visitjamaica.com/discover-jamaica/music-culture/religion-faith; and "Jamaican Religion," Jamaica Global Online, https://www.jamaicaglobalonline.com/jamaican-religion. The history and dominance of Christianity in Jamaica, the importation and creolization of denominations, and local spiritual movements.

[47] "28 Fundamental Beliefs," General Conference of Seventh-day Adventists, 2020, https://adventist.org/wp-content/uploads/2020/06/ADV-28Beliefs2020.pdf; and "Ellen G. White Biography," Ellen G. White Estate, https://whiteestate.org/about/egwbio/. The doctrine of the Seventh-day Adventist Church, the adherence to Saturday worship, the emphasis on health reform and the imminent Second Coming of Christ, and the co-founding role and prophetic authority of Ellen G. White (1827–1915), are foundational to the denomination's theology.

[48] "Rastafari," RE:Online, 2019, https://www.reonline.org.uk/wp-content/uploads/2019/06/Rastafari.pdf. A detailed documentation of Rastafarian beliefs, teachings, and wisdom.

[49] Charles Darwin, *On the Origin of Species by Means of Natural Selection, or the Preservation of Favoured Races in the Struggle for Life* (London: John Murray, 1859), https://www.gutenberg.org/files/2009/2009-h/2009-h.htm. G. Brent Dalrymple, "Radiometric Dating, Geologic Time, and the Age of the Earth: A Reply to 'Scientific' Creationism," U.S. Geological Survey Open-File Report 86-110 (1986), https://pubs.usgs.gov/of/1986/0110/report.pdf. The theory of evolution by natural selection and the Bible-based and scientifically established age of the earth.

[50] National Commission on Terrorist Attacks Upon the United States, *The 9/11 Commission Report: Final Report of the National Commission on Terrorist Attacks Upon the United States* (New York: W. W. Norton & Company, 2004), 1–50. The attacks on the World Trade Center and the sequence of events.

[51] "Biological consequences of the 2nd law of thermodynamics," ComPADRE Nexus Physics, https://www.compadre.org/nexusph/course/Biological_consequences_of_the_2nd_law_of_thermodynamics, on living systems as open systems and death as equilibrium/disintegration. The Second Law of Thermodynamics states that the total entropy (disorder) of an isolated system can only increase (or remain constant in reversible processes) over time, reflecting the natural tendency of energy to dissipate and become less available for work. Applied to a living organism, this means that at death, the organized thermal, chemical, and electrical energies sustaining life become unstructured and diffuse into the environment.

[52] "S.1200 - Immigration Reform and Control Act of 1986," *Congress.gov*, https://www.congress.gov/bill/99th-congress/senate-bill/1200. The Immigration Reform and Control Act of 1986 (IRCA), signed into law on November 6, 1986, granted amnesty to millions of undocumented immigrants who met certain criteria, allowing them to legalize their status and eventually petition for family members.

[53] U.S. Department of Health and Human Services, Public Health Service, "Medical Examination of Aliens: HIV Infection Added to List of Dangerous Contagious Diseases," Federal Register 52, no. 96 (May 19, 1987): 18566–18567, https://www.govinfo.gov/content/pkg/FR-1987-05-19/pdf/FR-1987-05-19.pdf. The mandatory HIV testing requirement for permanent visa applicants was implemented in 1987.

[54] U.S. Department of Labor, Wage and Hour Division, "History of Federal Minimum Wage Rates Under the Fair Labor Standards Act, 1938–2009," accessed January 5, 2026, https://www.dol.gov/agencies/whd/minimum-wage/history/chart. The federal minimum wage in the United States was $3.35 per hour from January 1, 1981, until March 31, 1990.

[55] New York City Department of City Planning, *The Newest New Yorkers: Characteristics of the City's Foreign-Born Population*, 2013 ed. (New York: NYC Department of City Planning, 2013), 30, 143, https://www.nyc.gov/assets/planning/download/pdf/data-maps/nyc-population/nny2013/nny_2013.pdf; "New York City Immigrants: The 1990s Wave," *Current Issues in Economics and Finance* 11, no. 6 (June 2005), Federal Reserve Bank of New York, https://www.newyorkfed.org/medialibrary/media/research/current_issues/ci11-6.pdf. "Hey Mon," *In Living Color*, season 1, episode 7 (Fox, May 27, 1990), on YouTube. The 1990 estimate of the Jamaican immigrant

population in New York City and the surrounding region (335,716), the high labor-force participation, and the recurring sketch featuring the Hedley family.

[56] Bob Marley and the Wailers, "*Rat Race*," on *Rastaman Vibration*, Tuff Gong/Island Records, 1976. The quoted line, "when you think it's peace and safety, it's sudden destruction," is a direct allusion to 1 Thessalonians 5:3 of the Holy Bible (King James Version), a reference frequently used within Rastafari and Christian theology related to the sudden arrival of the final judgment.

[57] U.S. National Archives and Records Administration, "The Constitution of the United States," https://www.archives.gov/founding-docs/constitution-transcript; Social Security Administration, "Social Security Act of 1935," https://www.ssa.gov/history/35act.html; U.S. Congress, Civil Rights Act of 1964, Pub. L. No. 88-352, 78 Stat. 241 (1964), https://www.archives.gov/milestone-documents/civil-rights-act; U.S. Congress, Voting Rights Act of 1965, Pub. L. No. 89-110, 79 Stat. 437 (1965), https://www.archives.gov/milestone-documents/voting-rights-act; and U.S. Congress, Fair Housing Act of 1968, Pub. L. No. 90-284, 82 Stat. 81 (1968), https://www.justice.gov/crt/fair-housing-act-1. The constitutional amendments ratified since 1789 and other acts.

[58] U.S. Department of State, *Visa Bulletin*, January 1990, vol. VI, no. 30, 1–3; and New York State Board of Law Examiners, "Foreign Legal Education – Rule 520.6." At the time, spouses of legal permanent residents were placed in the Second Preference (2A) category and subject to delayed processing, often exceeding one year. The requirements for foreign-trained lawyers from common-law jurisdictions (like Jamaica) to sit for the New York Bar under Section 520.6 of the Rules of the Court of Appeals.

[59] NYU Tandon School of Engineering, "History," accessed January 6, 2026, https://engineering.nyu.edu/about/history. Polytechnic University, located in Brooklyn, New York, was formally founded in 1854 as the Brooklyn Collegiate and Polytechnic Institute. It was later merged with New York University (NYU) and is now known as the NYU Tandon School of Engineering.

[60] Austin W. Marxe School of Public and International Affairs, Baruch College, "About the School," https://marxe.baruch.cuny.edu/about/. Bernard M. Baruch College, commonly referred to as Baruch College, is a senior college of the City University of New York (CUNY) system. Its Marxe School of Public and International Affairs has offered a Master of Public

Administration (MPA) degree since 1979 and is consistently ranked as one of the leading public administration programs in the New York metropolitan area.

[61] Lauri Fitzpatrick, "African Names and Naming Practices: The Impact Slavery and European Domination had on the African Psyche, Identity and Protest" (Master's thesis, Ohio State University, 2012), 42–46, 58, https://rave.ohiolink.edu/etdc/view?acc_num=osu1338404929. The intentional suppression of African cultural identities included the forced renaming of individuals and the denial of indigenous languages and religious practices. Also, see endnote 23 for more on Alex Haley's *Roots* and its cultural impact.

[62] Thomas C. Holt, *The Problem of Freedom,* 215–220. Following the 1838 emancipation, discriminatory practices persisted, including restrictive labor laws and voting qualifications. Activism to combat these social and racial inequities was led by various groups, including local leaders, religious figures, and political advocates both on the island and through pressure exerted on the British Parliament.

[63] Olive Senior, *Encyclopedia of Jamaican Heritage* (St. Andrew, Jamaica: Twin Guinep Publishers, 2003), 447–448. The "Free Villages" started mostly after 1838.

[64] Clinton V. Black, *History of Jamaica*, 187–250. Details on the Morant Bay Rebellion and the British government's response, and the struggles following universal suffrage in 1944 to independence in 1962.

[65] Errol Miller, "Education Reform in Independent Jamaica," 217–218, accessed March 2, 2026, https://errolmiller.com/wp-content/uploads/2018/01/Education-Reform-in-Independent-Jamaica.pdf. The 70/30 policy was part of broader post-independence efforts to use education as a tool for social equity and mobility.

[66] Carl Stone, *Class, Race and Political Behaviour in Urban Jamaica*, 18–24. Black leadership grew post-independence in political and professional fields, while control over the key economic sectors remained with minority groups and foreign corporations.

[67] "13th Amendment to the U.S. Constitution: Abolition of Slavery," National Archives, https://www.archives.gov/milestone-documents/13th-amendment. "Civil War Casualties," American Battlefield Trust, https://www.battlefields.org/learn/articles/civil-war-casualties. The

ratification process of the Thirteenth Amendment and its immediate impact on the legal status of the enslaved, and the Civil War death toll.

[68] "Jim Crow Law," Encyclopædia Britannica, https://www.britannica.com/event/Jim-Crow-law. State-level Jim Crow statutes disenfranchised the Black population by creating a "racial caste system" that enforced segregation, suppressed voting, and institutionalized economic disadvantage.

[69] *Brown v. Board of Education of Topeka*, 347 U.S. 483, 492–495 (1954). The Supreme Court held that "separate educational facilities are inherently unequal," overturning the *Plessy v. Ferguson doctrine* of "separate but equal."

[70] U.S. Bureau of the Census, *1990 Census of Population and Housing: Summary Social, Economic, and Housing Characteristics: United States* (Washington, DC: U.S. Government Printing Office, 1992), 1–3, Table 1, https://www.census.gov/content/dam/Census/library/publications/1990/dec/cph-r-2.pdf. The 1990 Black population was recorded at approximately 29.9 million, representing 12.1 percent of the total U.S. population.

[71] U.S. Department of Health and Human Services, Office of the Assistant Secretary for Planning and Evaluation, "Indicators of Welfare Dependence: Annual Report to Congress, 1998," September 30, 1998, https://aspe.hhs.gov/reports/indicators-welfare-dependence-annual-report-congress-1998-1. The 1990s AFDC (Aid to Families with Dependent Children) dependency demographics.

[72] Ron Haskins, "Welfare Reform, Success or Failure? It Worked," Brookings Institution, February 15, 2006, https://www.brookings.edu/articles/welfare-reform-success-or-failure-it-worked/. The welfare reform shifted from AFDC, established by the Social Security Act of 1935, to Temporary Assistance for Needy Families (TANF), with resulting impacts on work incentives.

[73] Suzanne Model, "Caribbean Immigrants: A Black Success Story?" *International Migration Review* 25, no. 2 (Summer 1991): 248–272, https://people.umass.edu/smodel/IMR_25.pdf. Black immigrants often utilize different social networks and cultural capital to navigate the U.S. labor market compared to native-born African Americans.

[74] Reuel Rogers, "Black Like Who? Afro-Caribbean Immigrants, African Americans, and the Politics of Group Identity," *Journal of American Ethnic History* 20,

no. 4 (Summer 2001): 166–169. William Julius Wilson, *The Truly Disadvantaged: The Inner City, the Underclass, and Public Policy* (Chicago: University of Chicago Press, 1987), 56–62. Sociologists have observed the differences in exposure to role models and sense of possibilities between Black immigrants from majority-Black Caribbean countries and native-born African Americans, and how the exodus of the Black middle class from inner cities left a "social isolation" that deprived remaining residents of local role models and job networks.

[75] "Affirmative Action," *Encyclopædia Britannica*, https://www.britannica.com/topic/affirmative-action. This entry tracks the conservative shift against race-conscious policies and the rise of the "reverse discrimination" argument in the 1980s and 1990s.

[76] Frank Dobbin and Alexandra Kalev, "Why Diversity Programs Fail," *Harvard Business Review*, July–August 2016, 54. This article discusses the "meritocracy myth"—how Black professionals often receive higher performance ratings but lower compensation and promotion rates than their White counterparts.

[77] National Science Foundation, *Women, Minorities, and Persons with Disabilities in Science and Engineering: 1994* (Arlington, VA: National Science Foundation, 1994), tables 5-11 and 5-12. This report addresses the "glass ceiling" in STEM and professional services like geology and how Black scientists were significantly less likely than white scientists with equal tenure to hold management positions during the early 1990s.

[78] Laura Benditt, "Race, Gender, and Public-Sector Work," working paper, Stanford University Department of Sociology, 2015, 73–75, https://sociology.stanford.edu/sites/sociology/files/benditt_2015.pdf. Eric Grodsky and Devah Pager, "The Structure of Disadvantage: Individual and Occupational Determinants of the Black-White Wage Gap," *American Sociological Review* 66, no. 4 (2001): 542–67, esp. 13, 20–21, 25–27, https://cde.wisc.edu/wp-content/uploads/sites/839/2019/01/cde-working-paper-1999-28.pdf. Celine McNicholas, Margaret Poydock, and Lynn Rhinehart, "Unions Promote Racial Equity," Washington, DC: Economic Policy Institute, July 31, 2023, https://www.epi.org/publication/unions-promote-racial-equity/. Black workers often seek the public sector for protection against discrimination in the private labor market (see Benditt); Black workers receive greater pay and managerial equity in the public sector (see Grodsky); and unions play a role in narrowing the racial wage gap and providing grievance procedures for Black workers (see McNicholas).

[79] Pamela Braboy Jackson, Peggy A. Thoits, and Howard F. Taylor, "Composition of the Workplace and Psychological Well-Being: The Effects of Tokenism on America's Black Elite," *Social Forces* 74, no. 2 (1995): 543–57, esp. 543–46, 550–55, https://academic.oup.com/sf/article-pdf/74/2/543/6517509/74-2-543.pdf. This article discusses the "resilience" required by Black professionals in the private sector and the psychological toll of "tokenism."

[80] Joseph Sciorra, "Italians Against Racism: The Bensonhurst Case," n.d., 193-209. The 1989 murder of Yusuf Hawkins resulted in subsequent protest marches led by Al Sharpton and racial polarization that transformed New York City politics.

[81] Independent Commission on the Los Angeles Police Department, *Report of the Independent Commission on the Los Angeles Police Department* (Los Angeles: The Commission, 1991), 3–15. Discusses the Rodney King beating incident and the systemic issues within the LAPD.

[82] Richard H. Girgenti, *A Report to the Governor on the Disturbances in Crown Heights*, vol. 1 (Albany: New York State Division of Criminal Justice Services, 1993), chap. 3. Discusses the investigation into the NYPD response and the underlying tensions between the Black and Hasidic communities during the Crown Heights riot.

[83] Hiroshi Fukurai, Richard Krooth, and Edgar W. Butler, "The Rodney King Beating Verdicts," n.d., chap. 4, https://people.ucsc.edu/~hfukurai/documents/RodneyKing.pdf. James Queally and Matt Pearce, "When LA Erupted In Anger: A Look Back At The Rodney King Riots," NPR, April 26, 2017, https://www.npr.org/2017/04/26/524744989/when-la-erupted-in-anger-a-look-back-at-the-rodney-king-riots. Discusses how the jury composition and change of venue to Simi Valley (a predominantly white suburban area) arguably influenced the acquittal, resulting in riots with over fifty deaths and $1 billion in property damage, and provides photographic documentation.

[84] Gwendolyn Y. Purifoye and Derrick R. Brooms, "Without Risk Reduction: How Black Men's Well-being and Humanity Are Compromised in Mobile Public Spaces," Sociology of Race and Ethnicity (2025), https://journals.sagepub.com/doi/10.1177/23326492241287164. An ethnographic examination of public transportation where Black men endure hyper-surveillance, threats of harm, institutional neglect of safety, and compromised dignity and well-being.

[85] Joyce King, *Hate Crime: The Story of a Dragging in Jasper, Texas* (New York: Pantheon Books, 2002). A comprehensive account of James Byrd Jr.'s murder and the trial of his assailants.

[86] Jemima Pierre, "Black Immigrants in the United States and the 'Cultural Narratives' of Ethnicity," *Identities: Global Studies in Culture and Power* 11, no. 2 (2004): 141–70, esp. 141–45, 155–57, https://repositories.lib.utexas.edu/bitstreams/15b4042a-102b-49d7-b2aa-c497785ab008/download. Discusses the Diallo shooting as evidence that race trumps class advancement, education, or cultural narratives in exposing Black people to profiling and violence.

[87] David Card, Alexandre Mas, and Jesse Rothstein, "Tipping and the Dynamics of Segregation," *Quarterly Journal of Economics* 123, no. 1 (2008): 177–218, esp. 177–85, 200–205, https://davidcard.berkeley.edu/papers/segr-nbhood.pdf. An analysis of the "tipping point" theory and how middle-class minority entry to city neighborhoods often triggered rapid white departures (white flight).

[88] New York City Department of City Planning, *Population Growth and Race/Hispanic Composition* (New York: DCP, 2004). Furman Center for Real Estate and Urban Policy, *State of New York City's Housing and Neighborhoods 2004* (New York: NYU Wagner, 2005), 68–87. Discusses white flight to Staten Island and Census data showing Staten Island's 17.1 percent growth (1990–2000), largely white-majority, and the myth of declining property values in Brooklyn after our 1997 purchase (see Furman Center).

[89] Pew Research Center, "Dissecting the 2008 Electorate: Most Diverse in U.S. History" (Washington, DC: Pew Research Center, April 30, 2009), 1–5, https://www.pewresearch.org/politics/2009/04/30/dissecting-the-2008-electorate-most-diverse-in-us-history/. The final exit poll data confirmed Obama won 43 percent of the white vote, 95 percent of the Black vote, and 67 percent of the Hispanic vote.

[90] Democratic Policy and Communications Committee, *Fact Sheet: Ending Gridlock in the Senate* (Washington, DC: DPCC, 2013), 1–3; Keeanga-Yamahtta Taylor, *From #BlackLivesMatter to Black Liberation* (Chicago: Haymarket Books, 2016), 75–80. Discusses the unprecedented use of the filibuster and Senate Minority Leader Mitch McConnell's stated strategy to make Barack Obama a "one-term president," and the analysis of "symbolic inclusion"

versus structural change and the limits of presidential power in addressing systemic racism.

[91] Taylor, *From #BlackLivesMatter to Black Liberation*, 153-176, 188–212. A chronological overview and analysis of most of the high-profile police shootings and deaths of unarmed Black individuals, including the circumstances of each case (e.g., Tamir Rice, age twelve, shot while playing with a toy gun), and the birth of the BLM movement.

[92] Gabriel R. Sanchez, "Americans Continue to Protest for Racial Justice 60 Years After the March on Washington," *Brookings Institution*, August 25, 2023, https://www.brookings.edu/articles/americans-continue-to-protest-for-racial-justice-60-years-after-the-march-on-washington/. Notes a noticeable demographic shift in the multiracial composition of protesters by 2020.

[93] U.S. Department of Justice, Civil Rights Division, "Search Cases and Matters," https://www.justice.gov/crt/search-cases-and-matters; "Special Litigation Section Case Summaries," https://www.justice.gov/crt/special-litigation-section-case-summaries. Includes individual case summaries and closing memoranda regarding federal civil rights investigations, and systemic "pattern or practice" findings related to other jurisdictions.

[94] Mary C. Waters, Philip Kasinitz, and Asad L. Asad, "Immigrants and African Americans," *Annual Review of Sociology* 40 (2014): 369–90, esp. 373–78, https://cooperative-individualism.org/waters-mary_immigrants-and-african-americans-2014.pdf. Discusses the "immigrant trap"—the psychological distance some Black immigrants place between themselves and African American civil rights struggles, and often initially rely on a "meritocratic" view of the U.S. that shifts after experiencing systemic racism firsthand.

[95] Marcus Garvey, *Philosophy and Opinions of Marcus Garvey*, ed. Amy Jacques Garvey (The Journal of Pan African Studies eBook edition, 2009 [original 1923–1925]), vol. 1: 4.

[96] Kirsten N. Morehouse and Mahzarin R. Banaji, "The Science of Implicit Race Bias: Evidence from the Implicit Association Test," *Daedalus* 153, no. 1 (2024): 21–50, https://direct.mit.edu/daed/article-pdf/153/1/21/2303739/daed_a_02047.pdf. Discusses the distinction between "implicit" (unconscious) and "explicit" (deliberate) bias, and why the outcome for the victim remains the same regardless of the perpetrator's intent.

[97] Nelson Mandela, *Long Walk to Freedom: The Autobiography of Nelson Mandela* (Boston: Little, Brown and Company, 1994), 622.

[98] U.S. Immigration and Naturalization Service, Statistical Yearbook of the Immigration and Naturalization Service, 1996 (Washington, DC: U.S. Government Printing Office, 1997), table 47, 153. Notes that the citizenship swearing-in ceremonies at the U.S. District Court for the Eastern District of New York (Brooklyn) are historic events; during the mid-1990s, the court naturalized thousands of new citizens monthly, reflecting the peak of the post-1965 immigration wave.

[99] National Human Genome Research Institute, "Human Genomic Variation," Genome.gov, accessed January 13, 2026, https://www.genome.gov/about-genomics/educational-resources/fact-sheets/human-genomic-variation. States that any two humans are approximately 99.6 percent genetically identical at the genome level when accounting for all types of variants (though often cited as 99.9 percent when considering only single-nucleotide differences). This profound similarity holds across individuals from every ethnic group and nationality.

[100] Naomi A. Schapiro, "Separation and Reunification: The Experiences of Adolescents Living in Transnational Families," Journal of Adolescent Health 52, no. 6 (2013): 48–68, esp. 56, https://hia.berkeley.edu/wp-content/uploads/2016/08/shapiro-article_separation-and-reunification-2013.pdf. On the prevalence of "split-household" arrangements among West Indian immigrants and the sociological term "transnational motherhood/fatherhood."

[101] "Gov't Gets $6b for NCB," *Jamaica Observer*, January 11, 2002, https://www.jamaicaobserver.com/2002/01/11/govt-gets-6b-for-ncb; and "Michael Lee-Chin," Forbes profile, accessed February 16, 2026, https://www.forbes.com/profile/michael-lee-chin/. Michael Lee-Chin, born in Port Antonio, Jamaica, became a billionaire investor in Canada. In 2002, through his company AIC Limited, he acquired a controlling interest (75 percent) in National Commercial Bank Jamaica Limited (NCB). This landmark purchase was widely reported and celebrated in Jamaica as an example of diaspora success.

[102] New York State Department of State, Division of Corporations, "Types of Businesses Operating in New York State," https://dos.ny.gov/types-businesses-operating-new-york-state. A sole proprietorship is an unincorporated business owned and run by one individual. In New York,

this structure offers simplicity but leaves the owner personally liable for all business debts and legal obligations.

[103] Kesi Asher, "Silk Sells on Cotton Shirts," *Jamaica Gleaner*, September 26, 2005, http://jamaica-gleaner.com/gleaner/20020926/ent/ent5.html. (URL taken from printed copy; link may no longer be active.)

[104] Marsha Kline Pruett and Tamara D. Jackson, "The Economics of High-Conflict Divorce: Costs and Consequences," *Family Law Quarterly* 33, no. 1 (1999): 72–75. This 20 to 30 percent represents a common benchmark used by legal experts in the early 2000s to illustrate the "litigation tax" in high-conflict cases, where cumulative legal fees, expert testimony, and court costs often consumed this much of a couple's total net worth.

[105] Construction Management Association of America, "CCM Certification," https://cmaanet.org/certification/ccm. The Certified Construction Manager (CCM) is a professional credential accredited by the American National Standards Institute (ANSI), with standards of practice and eligibility requirements.

[106] "The Pimsleur Method," Pimsleur (Simon & Schuster), accessed January 24, 2026, https://www.pimsleur.com/the-pimsleur-method. The Pimsleur Method, developed by Dr. Paul Pimsleur, uses graduated interval recall (spaced repetition for long-term retention) and active recall (prompting the learner to speak before hearing the answer), combined with core vocabulary and structures in thirty-minute audio lessons. It draws inspiration from how children naturally learn language through listening, imitation, and repetition, with no heavy reliance on reading or grammar drills.

[107] Plato, *Apology*, trans. Benjamin Jowett (Project Gutenberg, 2008), https://www.gutenberg.org/files/1656/1656-h/1656-h.htm. The Socratic paradox: "I know that I know nothing."

[108] "About ABET," https://www.abet.org/about-abet/, and "Program Evaluators," ABET, https://www.abet.org/accreditation/program-evaluators/.

[109] Third World, "*Loving You Is Easy*," track 6 on *More Work to Be Done*, Ghetto Youths International, 2019, streaming audio. The album was nominated for a Grammy Award for Best Reggae Album in 2020, reflecting the group's enduring influence on Jamaican music.

[110] "A Timeline of HIV and AIDS," HIV.gov, last updated January 2025, https://www.hiv.gov/hiv-basics/overview/history/hiv-and-aids-timeline. In

the United States, AIDS-related deaths peaked in 1995 before the introduction of highly active antiretroviral therapy in 1996–1997, which led to a sharp decline; cumulative U.S. deaths from HIV/AIDS since 1981 are estimated at 700,000–800,000, a toll surpassed by COVID-19 deaths (over 1.23 million as of 2025–2026).

[111] "'I Trust Science,' Says Nurse Who Is First to Get Vaccine in U.S.," *The New York Times*, December 14, 2020 (updated December 17, 2020), https://www.nytimes.com/2020/12/14/nyregion/us-covid-vaccine-first-sandra-lindsay.html. The first COVID-19 vaccine dose in the United States was administered on December 14, 2020, to Sandra Lindsay, following FDA emergency use authorization for the Pfizer-BioNTech vaccine on December 11, 2020, and initiated the national rollout, prioritizing healthcare workers and long-term care residents.

[112] C. Northcote Parkinson, Parkinson's Law, and Other Studies in Administration (Boston: Houghton Mifflin, 1957), 24–27; Richard Koch, The 80/20 Principle: The Secret to Achieving More with Less (New York: Currency/Doubleday, 1998), 12–15.

[113] World Health Organization, "Healthy life expectancy (HALE) at birth – United States of America," WHO Global Health Observatory, data for 2021 (latest available), https://www.who.int/data/gho/data/indicators/indicator-details/GHO/hale-healthy-life-expectancy-at-birth. Healthy life expectancy at birth for males in the United States was 62.8 years in 2021 (down from 64.2 years in 2000), reflecting years expected in full health. This contrasts with a total life expectancy of 73.7 years for men in the same year, creating a healthspan-lifespan gap of about 11 years, driven by chronic noncommunicable diseases.

[114] U.S. Department of State, "Jamaica," accessed January 29, 2026, https://www.state.gov/countries-areas/jamaica/ (outlines strong U.S.-Jamaica bilateral partnership); Council on Foreign Relations, "China's Growing Influence in Latin America," updated June 6, 2025, https://www.cfr.org/backgrounder/china-influence-latin-america-argentina-brazil-venezuela-security-energy-bri. Since the early 2000s, Jamaica has deepened economic ties with China (e.g., through Belt and Road Initiative investments in infrastructure, bauxite, and tourism) while maintaining close historical and security ties with the United States.

[115] Meredith Reid Sarkees and Frank Wayman, Resort to War: 1816–2007 (Washington, DC: CQ Press, 2010), 69–71; Council on Foreign Relations, "Conflict in Ukraine," Global Conflict Tracker, last updated December 16,

2025, https://www.cfr.org/global-conflict-tracker/conflict/conflict-ukraine; Claire Mills, "Russia's Use of Nuclear Threats During the Ukraine Conflict," House of Commons Library Briefing Paper CBP 9825, December 20, 2024, https://commonslibrary.parliament.uk/research-briefings/cbp-9825. Europe has one of the highest totals of recorded wars in history (around 40 interstate wars from 1816–2007 per the Correlates of War Project), and the Russo-Ukrainian conflict began in 2014 (Crimea annexation, Donbas) and escalated to full-scale war in 2022 (see Sarkees), and Russia has repeatedly threatened nuclear use since 2022 (see Mills).

[116] Intergovernmental Panel on Climate Change (IPCC), Climate Change 2021: The Physical Science Basis (Cambridge: Cambridge University Press, 2021), Summary for Policymakers, pp. 4–12, and Technical Summary, pp. 33–40, https://www.ipcc.ch/report/ar6/wg1/downloads/report/IPCC_AR6_WGI_FullReport.pdf; and IPCC, Climate Change 2022: Impacts, Adaptation and Vulnerability (Cambridge: Cambridge University Press, 2022), Summary for Policymakers, pp. 8–15, 67–73, 103–110, https://www.ipcc.ch/report/ar6/wg2/downloads/report/IPCC_AR6_WGII_FullReport.pdf. The past decade (2011–2020) was the warmest on record, with accelerated glacier melt, ~20 cm global sea-level rise since 1900, and increased intensity of many extreme weather events. Lower-income tropical/subtropical countries like Jamaica face disproportionate impacts due to higher exposure, greater sensitivity, and limited adaptive capacity.

[117] Caribbean Disaster Emergency Management Agency (CDEMA), "Situation Report No. 19 (Final): Hurricane Melissa," Bridgetown, Barbados: CDEMA, December 19, 2025, https://www.cdema.org/images/2025/sr19-hurricane-melissa20251219_final.pdf. Hurricane Melissa (October 2025) remains a landmark event in Caribbean meteorological history, surpassing the intensity of Hurricane Gilbert (1988), and had a significant impact on the Jamaican economy and infrastructure.

[118] Ray Kurzweil, *The Singularity Is Near: When Humans Transcend Biology* (New York: Viking, 2005), 10–25, 68–72. Discusses the concept of exponential technological growth in the modern era.

[119] Paul E. Ceruzzi, *A History of Modern Computing*, 2nd ed. (Cambridge, MA: MIT Press, 2003), 222–226. OpenAI, "Introducing ChatGPT," OpenAI Blog, November 30, 2022, https://openai.com/blog/chatgpt. Discusses the impact on personal computing by the Intel 4004 microprocessor, released in 1971, and notes that ChatGPT marks a significant milestone in public access to generative artificial intelligence.

[120] Everett M. Rogers, *Diffusion of Innovations*, 5th ed. (New York: Free Press, 2003), 280–285. The "early majority" is a key category in the diffusion of innovations theory, representing the first large group of a population to adopt a new technology after the innovators and early adopters.

[121] Eric G. Jones and S. K. Ong, "Risk Assessment of Lead Exposure to Lead-Contaminated Particulates in the Area Around the Williamsburg Bridge, Brooklyn, N.Y.," in *Proceedings of the Twenty-Sixth Mid-Atlantic Industrial Waste Conference,* ed. C.P. Huang (Lancaster, PA: Technomic Publishing, 1994), 678–690.

[122] U.S. Geological Survey, "Lava Tubes," Hawaiian Volcano Observatory, accessed February 19, 2026, https://www.usgs.gov/volcanoes/hawaii/lava-tubes. Many of the lava tubes on Maui, such as those in the Hana Lava Tube, are millions of years old and remain stable for exploration.

[123] World Bank, "Personal remittances, received (percent of GDP) – Jamaica," accessed March 2026, https://data.worldbank.org/indicator/BX.TRF.PWKR.DT.GD.ZS?locations=JM. Jamaica's remittances as a percentage of GDP and high global ranking reflect its diaspora's substantial economic contribution.

[124] World Economic Forum, *Global Gender Gap Report 2025* (Geneva: World Economic Forum, 2025), 15–18, 45–47, https://reports.weforum.org/docs/WEF_GGGR_2025.pdf. Jamaica's ranking in the 2025 Global Gender Gap Report.

[125] "Lorna M. Mahlock Promoted to Lieutenant General," U.S. Marine Corps Press Release, January 30, 2026.

Bibliography

"A Flashback to Michael Manley's Free Education System." *Jamaica Observer*, February 27, 2022. https://www.jamaicaobserver.com/2022/02/27/a-flashback-to-michael-manleys-free-education-system/.

"About ABET." ABET. https://www.abet.org/about-abet/.

"About Us." Earthquake Unit, University of the West Indies, Mona. https://www.mona.uwi.edu/earthquake/about.

"About Us." University of Technology, Jamaica. https://www.utech.edu.jm/about-utech.

"About UWI." Office of Student Recruitment, University of the West Indies at Mona. https://www.mona.uwi.edu/prospects/about-uwi.

"Affirmative Action." *Encyclopædia Britannica*. https://www.britannica.com/topic/affirmative-action.

A Learner's Grammar of Jamaican. Open Grammar Project, 2018. https://opengrammar.github.io/jam/learners_grammar-jam.pdf.

"A Timeline of HIV and AIDS." HIV.gov. Last updated January 2025. https://www.hiv.gov/hiv-basics/overview/history/hiv-and-aids-timeline.

Asher, Kesi. "Silk Sells on Cotton Shirts." *Jamaica Gleaner*, September 16, 2005. http://jamaica-gleaner.com/gleaner/20020916/ent/ent5.html. (URL taken from printed copy; link may no longer be active)

Ashley, Deanna, Affette McCaw-Binns, and Jean Golding. "Maternal Mortality in Jamaica." *The Lancet* 327, no. 8479 (March 1,

1986): 486–88. https://doi.org/10.1016/S0140-6736(86)92939-9.

Austin W. Marxe School of Public and International Affairs, Baruch College. "About the School." https://marxe.baruch.cuny.edu/about/.

Barreto, Matt. "Early Primaries, Viability and Changing Preferences for Presidential Candidates." *Presidential Studies Quarterly* 40, no. 2 (June 2010): 271–91. http://mattbarreto.com/papers/psq_primary.pdf.

Beckwith, Martha Warren. *Black Roadways: A Study of Jamaican Folk Life*. Chapel Hill: University of North Carolina Press, 1929. Reprint, New York: Negro Universities Press, 1969.

Benditt, Laura. "Race, Gender, and Public-Sector Work." Working paper, Stanford University Department of Sociology, 2015. https://sociology.stanford.edu/sites/sociology/files/benditt_2015.pdf.

"Biological Consequences of the 2nd Law of Thermodynamics." ComPADRE Nexus Physics. https://www.compadre.org/nexusph/course/Biological_consequences_of_the_2nd_law_of_thermodynamics.

Black, Clinton V. *History of Jamaica*. Rev. ed. London: Longman Caribbean, 1988.

Bob Marley and the Wailers. "*Rat Race*." On *Rastaman Vibration*. Tuff Gong / Island Records, 1976.

Bordin, Elisa. "Looking for Kunta Kinte: Alex Haley's Roots and African American Genealogies." *Iperstoria* 6 (2015): 73–82. https://iperstoria.it/article/download/426/460/1244.

Brown v. Board of Education of Topeka, 347 U.S. 483 (1954).

Card, David, Alexandre Mas, and Jesse Rothstein. "Tipping and the Dynamics of Segregation." *Quarterly Journal of Economics* 123, no. 1 (2008): 177–218. https://davidcard.berkeley.edu/papers/segr-nbhood.pdf.

Caribbean Disaster Emergency Management Agency (CDEMA). "Situation Report No. 19 (Final): Hurricane Melissa." Bridgetown, Barbados: CDEMA, December 19, 2025. https://www.cdema.org/images/2025/sr19-hurricane-melissa20251219_final.pdf.

"Caring and Learning Together: A Case Study of Jamaica." UNESCO Early Childhood and Family Policy Series. Paris: UNESCO/OAS, n.d. https://www.oas.org/cotep/GetAttach.aspx?aid=144&cId=75&lang=en.

Centers for Medicare & Medicaid Services. "Medicare and Medicaid Programs; Conditions of Participation for Home Health Agencies." *Federal Register* 54, no. 150 (August 14, 1989): 33354–73. Codified at 42 CFR § 484.36.

Ceruzzi, Paul E. *A History of Modern Computing*. 2nd ed. Cambridge, MA: MIT Press, 2003.

"Champs – The Biggest Deal in Jamaica." World Athletics, April 8, 2014. https://worldathletics.org/news/feature/boys-girls-champs-jamaica-zharnel-hughes-issa.

Chang, Kevin O'Brien, and Wayne Chen. *Reggae Routes: The Story of Jamaican Music*. Kingston: Ian Randle Publishers, 1998.

Chishti, Muzaffar, and Faye Hipsman. "Fifty Years On, the 1965 Immigration and Nationality Act Continues to Reshape the United States." Migration Policy Institute, October 15, 2015.

https://www.migrationpolicy.org/article/fifty-years-1965-immigration-and-nationality-act-continues-reshape-united-states.

"Civil War Casualties." American Battlefield Trust. https://www.battlefields.org/learn/articles/civil-war-casualties.

Construction Management Association of America. "CCM Certification." https://cmaanet.org/certification/ccm.

Council of Economic Advisers. *Economic Report of the President 1968*. Washington, DC: U.S. Government Printing Office, 1968.

Council on Foreign Relations. "China's Growing Influence in Latin America." New York: CFR, updated June 6, 2025. https://www.cfr.org/backgrounder/china-influence-latin-america-argentina-brazil-venezuela-security-energy-bri.

Council on Foreign Relations. "Conflict in Ukraine." Global Conflict Tracker. Last updated December 16, 2025. https://www.cfr.org/global-conflict-tracker/conflict/conflict-ukraine.

Dagnini, Jérôme K. "The Importance of Reggae Music in the Worldwide Cultural Universe." *Études Caribéennes* 16 (2011). https://journals.openedition.org/etudescaribeennes/4740.

Dalrymple, G. Brent. "Radiometric Dating, Geologic Time, and the Age of the Earth: A Reply to 'Scientific' Creationism." U.S. Geological Survey Open-File Report 86-110, 1986. https://pubs.usgs.gov/of/1986/0110/report.pdf.

Dar. "Trauma of Slavery: A Critical Study of the Roots by Alex Haley." *Journal of Literature, Languages and Linguistics* 58 (2019): 1–7.

https://www.iiste.org/Journals/index.php/JLLL/article/download/48311/49911.

Darwin, Charles. *On the Origin of Species by Means of Natural Selection*. London: John Murray, 1859.

Davis, Stephen. *Reggae Bloodlines: In Search of the Music and Culture of Jamaica*. New York: Da Capo Press, 1992.

Democratic Policy and Communications Committee. *Fact Sheet: Ending Gridlock in the Senate*. Washington, DC: DPCC, 2013.

Dobbin, Frank, and Alexandra Kalev. "Why Diversity Programs Fail." *Harvard Business Review*, July–August 2016.

"Elaine Perkins." PBCJ AV Library, June 13, 2025. https://www.libraryatpbcj.com/post/dennis-howard-2-6.

Electoral Commission of Jamaica. "1980 General Election Box by Box Results." https://ecj.com.jm/wp-content/uploads/2017/12/1980GeneralElectionBoxbyBox.pdf.

"Ellen G. White Biography." Ellen G. White Estate. https://whiteestate.org/about/egwbio/.

Encyclopædia Britannica. "Jamaica: Self-government." https://www.britannica.com/place/Jamaica/Self-government.

"Faith in Jamaica." VisitJamaica.com. https://www.visitjamaica.com/discover-jamaica/music-culture/religion-faith.

FamilySearch Wiki. "Genealogical Proof Standard." https://www.familysearch.org/en/wiki/The_Genealogical_Proof_Standard_-_International_Institute.

Fitzpatrick, Lauri. "African Names and Naming Practices: The Impact Slavery and European Domination had on the African Psyche,

Identity and Protest." Master's thesis, Ohio State University, 2012. https://rave.ohiolink.edu/etdc/view?acc_num=osu1338404929

"FST Undergraduate Student Awards." Faculty of Science and Technology, University of the West Indies, Mona. https://www.mona.uwi.edu/fst/fst-undergraduate-student-awards.

Fukurai, Hiroshi, Richard Krooth, and Edgar W. Butler. "The Rodney King Beating Verdicts." n.d. https://people.ucsc.edu/~hfukurai/documents/RodneyKing.pdf

Furman Center for Real Estate and Urban Policy. *State of New York City's Housing and Neighborhoods 2004*. New York: New York University, 2005.

Garvey, Marcus. *Philosophy and Opinions of Marcus Garvey*. Edited by Amy Jacques Garvey. 2 vols. in 1. Dover, MA: Majority Press, 1986. First published 1923–1925.

Gerfer, Anika. "Global Reggae and the Appropriation of Jamaican Creole." *English World-Wide* 39, no. 3 (2018): 257–84. https://www.academia.edu/37252200/Global_reggae_and_the_appropriation_of_Jamaican_Creole.

Girgenti, Richard H. *Report to the Governor on the Disturbances in Crown Heights*. Vol. 1. Albany: New York State Division of Criminal Justice Services, 1993.

"Gov't Gets $6b for NCB." *Jamaica Observer*, January 11, 2002. https://www.jamaicaobserver.com/2002/01/11/govt-gets-6b-for-ncb.

Grodsky, Eric, and Devah Pager. "The Structure of Disadvantage: Individual and Occupational Determinants of the Black-White Wage Gap." *American Sociological Review* 66, no. 4 (2001):

542–67. https://cde.wisc.edu/wp-content/uploads/sites/839/2019/01/cde-working-paper-1999-28.pdf.

G, Sarita. "Legacies that Survive Across Time and Space: A Critical Reading of The 'Trickster' Character Anansi from West African Folklore." *Dialog: A Journal of English Studies* (2023): 1–14. https://dialog.puchd.ac.in/wp-content/uploads/2023/09/12.-Legacies-that-Survive-Dialog-1.edited.pdf.

"Guha (surname)." Bharatpedia. https://en.bharatpedia.org/wiki/Guha_(surname.

Handa, Sandhya. "A Brief Background on Jamaica." Blacksburg: Virginia Polytechnic Institute and State University, 1996. https://vtechworks.lib.vt.edu/bitstreams/20f16ea1-fc9f-40f6-b422-44c64b9b4ab0/download.

Haskins, Ron. "Welfare Reform, Success or Failure? It Worked." Brookings Institution, February 15, 2006. https://www.brookings.edu/articles/welfare-reform-success-or-failure-it-worked/.

Holt, Thomas C. *The Problem of Freedom: Race, Labor, and Politics in Jamaica and Britain, 1832–1938*. Baltimore: Johns Hopkins University Press, 1992.

Holy Bible: King James Version. Standard ed. New York: Oxford University Press, 2008.

In Living Color. Season 1, episode 7, "Hey Mon." Aired May 27, 1990, on Fox.

Independent Commission on the Los Angeles Police Department. *Report of the Independent Commission on the Los Angeles Police Department*. Los Angeles: The Commission, 1991.

Intergovernmental Panel on Climate Change. *Climate Change 2021: The Physical Science Basis*. Edited by V. Masson-Delmotte et al. Cambridge: Cambridge University Press, 2021. https://www.ipcc.ch/report/ar6/wg1/downloads/report/IPCC_AR6_WGI_FullReport.pdf.

Intergovernmental Panel on Climate Change. *Climate Change 2022: Impacts, Adaptation and Vulnerability*. Edited by H.-O. Pörtner et al. Cambridge: Cambridge University Press, 2022. https://www.ipcc.ch/report/ar6/wg2/downloads/report/IPCC_AR6_WGII_FullReport.pdf.

International Association of Athletics Federations (World Athletics). "All-Time Medal Table – Olympic Games" and "World Championships." https://worldathletics.org/records/all-time-toplists.

"Introduction: Reconciling Religion and Culture in Jamaica." Catholics and Cultures, January 15, 2014. https://www.catholicsandcultures.org/jamaica/introduction.

"'I Trust Science,' Says Nurse Who Is First to Get Vaccine in U.S." *The New York Times*, December 14, 2020 (updated December 17, 2020). https://www.nytimes.com/2020/12/14/nyregion/us-covid-vaccine-first-sandra-lindsay.html.

Jackson, Pamela Braboy, Peggy A. Thoits, and Howard F. Taylor. "Composition of the Workplace and Psychological Well-Being: The Effects of Tokenism on America's Black Elite." *Social Forces* 74, no. 2 (1995): 543–57. https://academic.oup.com/sf/article-pdf/74/2/543/6517509/74-2-543.pdf.

"Jamaica - Health and Welfare." In *Caribbean Islands: A Country Study*, edited by Sandra W. Meditz and Dennis M. Hanratty. Washington, DC: GPO for the Library of Congress, 1987. https://countrystudies.us/caribbean-islands/23.htm.

"Jamaican Religion." Jamaica Global Online. https://www.jamaicaglobalonline.com/jamaican-religion.

Johnson, Erica. "Confusing Labels: French 'Emigrants' and 'Prisoners of War' in Jamaica during the Haitian Revolution." *Age of Revolutions* (blog). June 22, 2023.

"Jim Crow Law." *Encyclopædia Britannica*. https://www.britannica.com/event/Jim-Crow-law.

Jones, Eric G. W., and S. K. Ong. "Risk Assessment of Lead Exposure to Lead-Contaminated Particulates in the Area Around the Williamsburg Bridge, Brooklyn, N.Y." In *Proceedings of the Twenty-Sixth Mid-Atlantic Industrial Waste Conference*, edited by C. P. Huang. Lancaster, PA: Technomic Publishing, 1994.

King, Joyce. *Hate Crime: The Story of a Dragging in Jasper, Texas*. New York: Pantheon Books, 2002.

Koch, Richard. *The 80/20 Principle: The Secret to Achieving More with Less*. New York: Currency/Doubleday, 1998.

Koehler, R. D., P. Mann, C. S. Prentice, L. Brown, B. Benford, and M. Wiggins-Grandison. "Enriquillo–Plantain Garden Fault Zone in Jamaica: Paleoseismology and Seismic Hazard." *Bulletin of the Seismological Society of America* 103, no. 2A (2013): 971–83. https://pubs.usgs.gov/publication/70073701.

Kurzweil, Ray. *The Singularity Is Near: When Humans Transcend Biology*. New York: Viking, 2005.

Look Lai, Walton. *Indentured Labor, Caribbean Sugar: Chinese and Indian Migrants to the British West Indies, 1838–1918.* Baltimore: Johns Hopkins University Press, 1993.

Manchester Parish Development Committee. "Chapter 5: The Cultural and Historical Environment." In the *Sustainable Development Plan for Manchester, Jamaica.* Mandeville, Jamaica: Manchester Parish Development Committee, 2011. https://manchesterpdc.files.wordpress.com/2011/03/09chap-5-history-march-04.pdf.

Mandela, Nelson. *Long Walk to Freedom: The Autobiography of Nelson Mandela.* Boston: Little, Brown and Company, 1994.

Mahlock, Lorna M. "Lorna M. Mahlock Promoted to Lieutenant General." U.S. Marine Corps Press Release, January 30, 2026.

McNicholas, Celine, Margaret Poydock, and Lynn Rhinehart. "Unions Promote Racial Equity." Washington, DC: Economic Policy Institute, July 31, 2023. https://www.epi.org/publication/unions-promote-racial-equity/.

"Members of Parliament (Election Results from 1944-)." National Library of Jamaica. http://www.nlj.gov.jm/Civicspage/members_of_parliament_since_1944.pdf.

Mendoza, Dovelyn Rannveig. "Jamaica: From Diverse Beginning to Diaspora in the Developed World." Migration Policy Institute, June 16, 2010. https://www.migrationpolicy.org/article/jamaica-diverse-beginning-diaspora-developed-world.

"Michael Lee-Chin." *Forbes.* Accessed February 16, 2026. https://www.forbes.com/profile/michael-lee-chin/.

Miller, Errol. "Education Reform in Independent Jamaica." Accessed March 2, 2026. https://errolmiller.com/wp-content/uploads/2018/01/Education-Reform-in-Independent-Jamaica.pdf.

Mills, Claire. "Russia's Use of Nuclear Threats During the Ukraine Conflict." House of Commons Library Briefing Paper CBP 9825, December 20, 2024. https://commonslibrary.parliament.uk/research-briefings/cbp-9825.

Ministry of Education, Youth & Information. *Primary Exit Profile 2019 National Report*. Kingston: MOEYI, 2019. https://pep.moey.gov.jm/wp-content/uploads/2019/08/REVISEDPEP-2019-NATIONAL-REPORT-July-23-2019-formatted-V4.pdf.

Mirvis, Stanley. *The Jews of Eighteenth-Century Jamaica: A Testamentary History of a Diaspora in Transition*. New Haven: Yale University Press, 2020.

Model, Suzanne. "Caribbean Immigrants: A Black Success Story?" *International Migration Review* 25, no. 2 (Summer 1991): 248–76. http://people.umass.edu/smodel/IMR_25.pdf.

Morehouse, Kirsten N., and Mahzarin R. Banaji. "The Science of Implicit Race Bias: Evidence from the Implicit Association Test." *Daedalus* 153, no. 1 (2024): 21–50. https://direct.mit.edu/daed/article-pdf/153/1/21/2303739/daed_a_02047.pdf.

Morgan, Kenneth. *A Concise History of Jamaica*. Cambridge: Cambridge University Press, 2023.

National Archives (UK). "Indian Indentured Labourers." Research Guide. https://www.nationalarchives.gov.uk/help-with-your-research/research-guides/indian-indentured-labourers/.

National Commission on Terrorist Attacks Upon the United States. *The 9/11 Commission Report*. New York: W. W. Norton & Company, 2004.

National Human Genome Research Institute. "Human Genomic Variation." Genome.gov. Accessed January 13, 2026. https://www.genome.gov/about-genomics/educational-resources/fact-sheets/human-genomic-variation.

National Science Foundation. *Women, Minorities, and Persons with Disabilities in Science and Engineering: 1994*. Arlington, VA: National Science Foundation, 1994.

Nettleford, Rex. *Cultural Action and Social Change: The Case of Jamaica*. Ottawa: International Development Research Centre, 1979. https://idl-bnc-idrc.dspacedirect.org/server/api/core/bitstreams/7fa6b4cc-64e0-4381-99fb-9e7104dea850/content.

Nettleford, Rex. "Golden Jubilee: UWI at 50." *Caribbean Beat* no. 32 (July/August 1998). https://www.caribbean-beat.com/issue-32/golden-jubilee-uwi-50.

New York City Department of City Planning. *Population Growth and Race/Hispanic Composition*. New York: DCP, 2004.

New York City Department of City Planning. *The Newest New Yorkers: Characteristics of the City's Foreign-born Population*. New York: DCP, 2004. https://www.nyc.gov/assets/planning/download/pdf/data-maps/nyc-population/nny2000/nny2000.pdf.

"New York City Immigrants: The 1990s Wave." *Current Issues in Economics and Finance* 11, no. 6 (June 2005). Federal Reserve Bank of New York. https://www.newyorkfed.org/medialibrary/media/research/current_issues/ci11-6.pdf.

New York State Board of Law Examiners. "Foreign Legal Education – Rule 520.6." https://www.nybarexam.org/foreign/foreignlegaleducation.htm.

New York State Department of State, Division of Corporations. "Types of Businesses Operating in New York State." https://dos.ny.gov/types-businesses-operating-new-york-state.

"1960s Counterculture." *Encyclopædia Britannica.* https://www.britannica.com/topic/1960s-counterculture.

NYU Tandon School of Engineering. "History." https://engineering.nyu.edu/about/history.

"Obeah Histories." Obeah Histories Project. https://obeahhistories.org/.

The Obeah Act. Jamaica, 1898, as amended. https://laws.moj.gov.jm/library/statute/the-obeah-act.

OpenAI. "Introducing ChatGPT." OpenAI Blog, November 30, 2022. https://openai.com/blog/chatgpt.

Organization of American States. "Kingston Metropolitan Area Seismic Hazard Assessment: Executive Summary and Conclusions." Caribbean Disaster Mitigation Project. https://www.oas.org/cdmp/document/kma/seismic/seis_sum.htm.

Parkinson, C. Northcote. *Parkinson's Law, and Other Studies in Administration*. Boston: Houghton Mifflin, 1957.

Patrick, Peter L. "JC Jamaican Patwa (Creole English)." Creolica.net, July 31, 2007. https://www.creolica.net/jcpp.pdf.

Petley, Christer. "Reproducing Capital: The Long Family." In *Lucky Valley: The Legacy of the Longs in Jamaica*. Cambridge: Cambridge University Press, 2024.

Pew Research Center. "Dissecting the 2008 Electorate: Most Diverse in U.S. History." Washington, DC: Pew Research Center, April 30, 2009. https://www.pewresearch.org/politics/2009/04/30/dissecting-the-2008-electorate-most-diverse-in-us-history/.

Pierre, Jemima. "Black Immigrants in the United States and the 'Cultural Narratives' of Ethnicity." *Identities: Global Studies in Culture and Power* 11, no. 2 (2004): 141–70. https://repositories.lib.utexas.edu/bitstreams/15b4042a-102b-49d7-b2aa-c497785ab008/download.

Pinchers. "*Hackle Mi Body*." Track 6 on *The Biggest Ragga Dancehall Anthems 1987*. VP Records/Greensleeves, 1987.

Plato. *Apology*. Translated by Benjamin Jowett. Project Gutenberg, 2008. https://www.gutenberg.org/files/1656/1656-h/1656-h.htm.

Pollard, Velma. "Dread Talk – The Speech of the Rastafari in Jamaica." *Caribbean Quarterly* 26, no. 4 (1980): 32–41. https://ufdcimages.uflib.ufl.edu/CA/00/40/00/44/00001/PDF.pdf.

"Program Evaluators." ABET. https://www.abet.org/accreditation/program-evaluators/.

Pruett, Marsha Kline, and Tamara D. Jackson. "The Economics of High-Conflict Divorce: Costs and Consequences." *Family Law Quarterly* 33, no. 1 (1999): 69–82.

Purifoye, Gwendolyn Y., and Derrick R. Brooms. "Without Risk Reduction: How Black Men's Well-being and Humanity Are Compromised in Mobile Public Spaces." *Sociology of Race and Ethnicity* (2025). https://journals.sagepub.com/doi/10.1177/23326492241287164

Queally, James, and Matt Pearce. "When LA Erupted In Anger: A Look Back At The Rodney King Riots." NPR, April 26, 2017. https://www.npr.org/2017/04/26/524744989/when-la-erupted-in-anger-a-look-back-at-the-rodney-king-riots.

"Rastafari." RE:Online. Religious Education Council of England and Wales, 2019. https://www.reonline.org.uk/wp-content/uploads/2019/06/Rastafari.pdf.

"Religion in Jamaica." *Encyclopædia Britannica.* https://www.britannica.com/place/Jamaica/Religion.

Rogers, Everett M. *Diffusion of Innovations*. 5th ed. New York: Free Press, 2003.

Rogers, Reuel. "Black Like Who? Afro-Caribbean Immigrants, African Americans, and the Politics of Group Identity." *Journal of American Ethnic History* 20, no. 4 (Summer 2001): 163–92.

"S.1200 - Immigration Reform and Control Act of 1986." Congress.gov. https://www.congress.gov/bill/99th-congress/senate-bill/1200.

Sanchez, Gabriel R. "Americans Continue to Protest for Racial Justice 60 Years After the March on Washington." Brookings Institution, August 25, 2023.

https://www.brookings.edu/articles/americans-continue-to-protest-for-racial-justice-60-years-after-the-march-on-washington/.

Sarkees, Meredith Reid, and Frank Wayman. *Resort to War: 1816–2007*. Washington, DC: CQ Press, 2010.

Schapiro, Naomi A. "Separation and Reunification: The Experiences of Adolescents Living in Transnational Families." *Journal of Adolescent Health* 52, no. 6 (2013): 685–90. https://hia.berkeley.edu/wp-content/uploads/2016/08/shapiro-article_separation-and-reunification-2013.pdf.

Sciorra, Joseph. "Italians Against Racism: The Bensonhurst Case." *In Defense of Tradition: Semiotics of the Italian-American Experience*, n.d., 193–209.

Senior, Olive. *Encyclopedia of Jamaican Heritage*. Kingston: Twin Guinep Publishers, 2003.

Slave Voyages: Trans-Atlantic Slave Trade Database. "Estimates." Accessed March 4, 2026. https://www.slavevoyages.org/assessment/estimates.

Social Security Administration. "Social Security Act of 1935." https://www.ssa.gov/history/35act.html.

Stone, Carl. *Class, Race and Political Behaviour in Urban Jamaica*. Kingston: Institute of Social and Economic Research, 1973.

Taylor, Keeanga-Yamahtta. *From #BlackLivesMatter to Black Liberation*. Chicago: Haymarket Books, 2016.

The American Yawp: A Massively Collaborative Open U.S. History Textbook. Vol. 2. Edited by Joseph L. Locke and Ben Wright.

Stanford, CA: Stanford University Press, 2019. http://www.americanyawp.com/text/27-the-sixties/.

"The 'Duppies' of JOS/Jolly Joseph Still Haunt the JUTC." *Jamaica Observer*, August 29, 2014. https://www.jamaicaobserver.com/2014/08/29/the-duppies-of-jos-jolly-joseph-still-haunt-the-jutc.

"The Pimsleur Method." Pimsleur (Simon & Schuster). https://www.pimsleur.com/the-pimsleur-method.

"The UWI Timeline." University of the West Indies. https://uwi.edu/timeline.

Third World. "*Loving You Is Easy*." Track 6 on *More Work to Be Done*. Ghetto Youths International, 2019. Streaming audio.

Thorburn, Diana, and Dana Marie Morris. "Jamaica's Foreign Policy: Making the Economic Development Link." Caribbean Policy Research Institute, 2007. https://www.capricaribbean.org/sites/default/files/documents/r0703jamaicas-foreign-policymaking-economic-development-link200707.pdf.

Tortello, Rebecca. "Pieces of the Past: The Arrival of the Lebanese." *Jamaica Gleaner*, October 6, 2003. https://old.jamaica-gleaner.com/pages/history/story0056.htm.

The Towns and Communities Act. Jamaica, 1843, as amended. https://laws.moj.gov.jm/library/statute/the-towns-and-communities-act/download.

"13th Amendment to the U.S. Constitution: Abolition of Slavery." National Archives. https://www.archives.gov/milestone-documents/13th-amendment.

"28 Fundamental Beliefs." General Conference of Seventh-day Adventists, 2020. https://adventist.org/wp-content/uploads/2020/06/ADV-28Beliefs2020.pdf.

United States. National Advisory Commission on Civil Disorders. *Report of the National Advisory Commission on Civil Disorders*. Washington, DC: Government Printing Office, 1968.

U.S. Bureau of the Census. *1990 Census of Population and Housing: Summary Social, Economic, and Housing Characteristics: United States*. Washington, DC: Government Printing Office, 1992. https://www.census.gov/content/dam/Census/library/publications/1990/dec/cph-r-2.pdf.

U.S. Congress. Civil Rights Act of 1964. Pub. L. No. 88-352, 78 Stat. 241 (1964). https://www.archives.gov/milestone-documents/civil-rights-act.

U.S. Congress. Fair Housing Act of 1968. Pub. L. No. 90-284, 82 Stat. 81 (1968). https://www.justice.gov/crt/fair-housing-act-1.

U.S. Congress. Voting Rights Act of 1965. Pub. L. No. 89-110, 79 Stat. 437 (1965). https://www.archives.gov/milestone-documents/voting-rights-act.

U.S. Department of Health and Human Services, Public Health Service. "Medical Examination of Aliens: HIV Infection Added to List of Dangerous Contagious Diseases." *Federal Register* 52, no. 96 (May 19, 1987): 18566–67. https://www.govinfo.gov/content/pkg/FR-1987-05-19/pdf/FR-1987-05-19.pdf.

U.S. Department of Health and Human Services. Office of the Assistant Secretary for Planning and Evaluation. "Indicators of Welfare Dependence: Annual Report to Congress, 1998."

September 30, 1998. https://aspe.hhs.gov/reports/indicators-welfare-dependence-annual-report-congress-1998-1.

U.S. Department of Justice. Civil Rights Division. Various investigation reports and case summaries. https://www.justice.gov/crt/search-cases-and-matters.

U.S. Department of Labor, Wage and Hour Division. "History of Federal Minimum Wage Rates Under the Fair Labor Standards Act, 1938–2009." https://www.dol.gov/agencies/whd/minimum-wage/history/chart.

U.S. Department of State. "Jamaica." Washington, DC: U.S. Department of State, accessed January 29, 2026. https://www.state.gov/countries-areas/jamaica/.

U.S. Department of State. *Visa Bulletin*, January 1990, vol. VI, no. 30, 1–3.

U.S. Geological Survey. "Lava Tubes." Hawaiian Volcano Observatory. https://www.usgs.gov/volcanoes/hawaii/lava-tubes.

U.S. Immigration and Naturalization Service. *Statistical Yearbook of the Immigration and Naturalization Service, 1996.* Washington, DC: U.S. Government Printing Office, 1997.

U.S. National Archives and Records Administration. "The Constitution of the United States." https://www.archives.gov/founding-docs/constitution-transcript.

Waters, Mary C., Philip Kasinitz, and Asad L. Asad. "Immigrants and African Americans." *Annual Review of Sociology* 40 (2014):

369–90. https://cooperative-individualism.org/waters-mary_immigrants-and-african-americans-2014.pdf.

Williams, Kareen Felicia. "The Evolution of Political Violence in Jamaica 1940–1980." PhD thesis, Columbia University, 2011. https://academiccommons.columbia.edu/doi/10.7916/D8WS91D7.

Wilson, William Julius. *The Truly Disadvantaged: The Inner City, the Underclass, and Public Policy*. Chicago: University of Chicago Press, 1987.

"Who Were the Windrush Generation?" BBC News, June 20, 2025. https://www.bbc.com/news/articles/c3w4q1ee1p4o.

Windrush 75: An e-book by The Conversation. Canberra: The Conversation, 2023. https://cdn.theconversation.com/static_files/files/2747/Windrush_e-book_final_(2).pdf?1689252059.

World Bank. *Jamaica Secondary Education: Improving Quality and Extending Access*. Washington, DC: World Bank, 1999. https://documents.worldbank.org/curated/en/830691468771888579/pdf/multi-page.pdf.

World Bank. "Personal Remittances, Received (percent of GDP) – Jamaica." Washington, DC: World Bank, accessed March 2026. https://data.worldbank.org/indicator/BX.TRF.PWKR.DT.GD.ZS?locations=JM.

World Economic Forum. *Global Gender Gap Report 2025*. Geneva: World Economic Forum, 2025. https://reports.weforum.org/docs/WEF_GGGR_2025.pdf.

World Health Organization. "Healthy Life Expectancy (HALE) at Birth." Global Health Observatory.

https://www.who.int/data/gho/data/indicators/indicator-details/GHO/hale-healthy-life-expectancy-at-birth.

Thank you for traveling with me as I retraced my Jamaican-American journey. My hope is that in these life lessons you've found echoes of your own experiences, or that they bring you guidance and strength as you chart your own path. The time you've dedicated to my story means the world to me, and I would truly love to hear your thoughts.

Scan the QR code or visit: **ericgwjones.com**

For speaking engagements and all other outreach:
ericjones@ericgwjones.com

www.ingramcontent.com/pod-product-compliance
Lightning Source LLC
LaVergne TN
LVHW020654110826
845149LV00012B/1996